MAN AND NATURE
The Chinese Tradition and the Future

The Council for Research in Values and Philosophy
Cultural Heritage and Contemporary Life
Series III. Asia, Volume 1

Edited by
Tang Yi-Jie
Li Zhen
George F. McLean

Lanham • New York • London

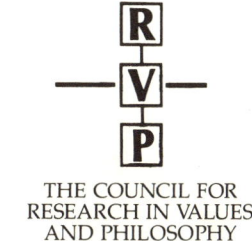

THE COUNCIL FOR
RESEARCH IN VALUES
AND PHILOSOPHY

Copyright © 1989 by

The Council for Research in Values and Philosophy

University Press of America,® Inc.

4720 Boston Way
Lanham, MD 20706

3 Henrietta Street
London WC2E 8LU England

All rights reserved

Printed in the United States of America

British Cataloging in Publication Information Available

Co–published by arrangement with
The Council for Research in Values and Philosophy

Library of Congress Cataloging-in-Publication Data

Man and nature : the Chinese tradition and the future / edited by Tang Yi-Jie, Li Zhen, George F. McLean.
 p. cm — (Cultural heritage and contemporary life. Series III, Asia ; vol. 1)
 Volume derived from the first of a series of joint colloquia sponsored by the Dept. of Philosophy of Peking University, International Society for Metaphysics, and the Council for Research in Values and Philosophy.
 Includes bibliographies and index.
 1. Man—Congresses.   2. Philosophy of nature—Congresses.   3. Philosophy, Chinese—Congresses.   I. T'ang, I-chieh.   II. Li, Chen.   III. McLean, George F.   IV. Pei-ching ta hsüeh. Che hsüeh hsi.   V. International society for Metaphysics.   VI. Council for Research in Values and Philosophy.   VII. Series.
  BD450.M2656   1989
  181'.11—dc19   89-30881 CIP

ISBN 0–8191–7412–2 (alk. paper)
ISBN 0–8191–7413–0 (pbk.: alk. paper)

All University Press of America books are produced on acid-free paper.
The paper used in this publication meets the minimum requirements of American National Standard for Information Sciences—Permanence of Paper for Printed Library Materials, ANSI Z39.48–1984.   ∞

ACKNOWLEDGEMENTS

Grateful acknowledgement is made to the Department of Philosophy of Peking University for the development of the joint-colloquium which this volume represents. The concern of these philosophers for the multiple philosophical traditions of China and the world, past and present, laid the foundation for discussions of great richness and depth. The future orientation of their thought drew the philosophers visiting from many countries into exciting and creative interchange.

In particular, Prof. Prof. Huang Nan-sheng, Chairman of the Department, and Prof. Li Zhen assured that all was well prepared and extended generous care and hospitality to the visiting scholars. With Prof Tang Yi-jie, President of the International Academy of Chinese Culture, they developed the concept and theme of the colloquium and brought together a team of eminent scholars from Peking and other Universities.

Gratitude is extended also to the team of scholars who assembled at considerable personal sacrifice from all parts of the world to take part in the colloquium. They gave warm testimony of the deep and generous councern of all peoples for the great efforts underway in China. Their work on hermeneutic approaches and ethical implications provided an effective complement to the themes of the Chinese philosophers with whom they constituted a true community of scholars at work upon constructing for the future.

In this effort communication and hence translation has been crucial. Hence, special thanks is extended to those who through translating the texts and discussions painstakingly built the bridge of language across which ideas flowed freely and well.

In the preparation of the manuscripts for presentation and for Press many labored with great generosity both in China and here. Among these I can name only Mrs. B. Kennedy, who must stand for her colleagues in many lands, and the James A. McLeans.

PREFACE

This volume contains the results of a joint symposium on "Man and Nature," co-sponsored by the International Society for Metaphysics and the Philosophy Department of Peking University and held in Beijing on July 25-27, 1987. The work is the fruit of the cooperation of philosophers of many nations: Japan, the Philippines, India, Belgium, Canada, the United States and China.

This symposium is the first which the Philosophy Department of Peking University has co-sponsored with scholars from other nations in recent years. The experience of this Symposium has proven that cooperation between philosophers of various countries in an exchange of scholarly concerns, insights and ideals is not only interesting and stimulating, but of great benefit to all participants in thinking creatively on crucial issues of our day.

The historical reality is that of a world becoming smaller and of communication between nations and peoples becoming ever closer. In these circumstances the shared problems which threaten the peace and even the existence of all peoples increase and intensify. Hence, it has become an urgent contemporary task for philosophers to develop a deep awareness of the problems to awaken reason and to think creatively on the toals and means for the protection of the peace and indeed of life. The promotion of peace and friendship between the peoples is then a holy and honorable duty of philosophers and other scholars, whether they be Marxists or liberals or conservatives, existential phenomenologists or analysts, Hindu, Confucian or Neo-thomist. The lofty aim of philosophy--along with other fields of academic work--is to promote the welfare and to deepen and enrich the happiness of mankind.

We would like to express our profound thanks to Professor George F. McLean for his enthusiastic work in developing this joint Symposium. We are very grateful to all the scholars from China and other lands, whose rich contributions and open and enlightened discussion constituted the success of the Symposium. Finally, we express our gratitude as well to the Administration of Peking University and to the State Commission of Education for their sponsorship and support.

Hang Nan-sheng *Philosophy Department*
Tang Yi-jie *Peking University*
Li Zhen *Beijing, PRC*

November, 1988

INTRODUCTION

The contents of the present volume on "Man and Nature" derive from the first of a series of joint colloquia sponsored by the Department of Philosophy of Peking University with The International Society for Metaphysics (ISM) and the Council for Research in Values and Philosophy (RVP).

The times are particularly appropriate for this work. Throughout the world, intensive efforts were made after World War II to develop scientific and technical structures for economic, industrial and political life. More recently attention has turned to the search for ways in which the life of nations might better reflect persons and their creativity. Everywhere, it is hoped that this will contribute, not only to economic development, but to raising the quality of the life of persons and of entire peoples. This appears to be consistent effort of such diverse steps as the liberation movements of the 1950's, the Second Vatican Council in the 1960's, the student and minority movements of the 1970's, and efforts in this decade toward social reconstruction and *perestroika*. This promises to be the point of convergence for human efforts in these years of proximate preparation for the XXI'st Century.

This has placed a special responsibility upon philosophers to seek out the resources available for this work in the cultural traditions of their various nations, to analyze the precise nature of the present challenge, and to elaborate the component insights required for facing the problems and constructing the vision needed by mankind for the future.

To respond to this need the ISM and RVP joint colloquia have had the following characteristics:

(1) They are planned particularly for work with philosophers in areas in which metaphysics in principle has not been a point of recent interest, but who inevitably are concerned with the basic issues in philosophy.

(2) They focus upon a specific theme of common interest, which they treat in terms, not of a dialogue of opposing views, but of a point of mutual concern and cooperative inquiry regarding ideas still in flux.

(3) The number of participants at these colloquia have been kept to 15 or less so that all might join around the same table and all might be actively engaged.

(4) The number of papers presented has generally been held to one or at the most two papers during a three-hour session in order to promote in-depth discussion. Over a period of three days the cumulative effect of these discussions has been deeper joint insight regarding the central issue and complementary

understanding which broadens horizons.

The present colloquium has been particularly successful. It took place in the midst of intensive changes in the life of the people of China. These have challenged philosophers to work intensively and simultaneously on a number of levels. They have had to reach deeply into the heritage of China to discover and articulate anew the deepest inspirations and aspirations of their people; they have had to do the same for Marxism in order to find new potentialities in this philosophies; and they have had to look forward to ways in which these resources could be articulated in truly new ways for new times. Hence, the visiting philosophers joined an on-going, deeply authentic and vibrant philosophical quest.

The theme chosen for the discussions was "Man and Nature" (to be followed by an exchange colloquium on "Man and Society"). The first term stands, of course, for "mankind", but appeared the most appropriate in the language context. The term "nature" included the physical universe, but extended much further, for the term "nature" means also mankind and even heaven. It stands then for the entirety of reality. The topic for discussion then was not merely the physical context or the material implementation of human life, but the much broader issue of the total horizon of that life.

In this light the discussions were rich and complex. They concerned both past and present philosophies, the spiritual as well as the material dimensions of the person, and looked perhaps above all for the horizons which were needed in order to develop a vision adequate for the future.

In this the resources of the participating philosophers proved quite complementary, both in drawing upon the past and for the work that lie ahead. Philosophers rich in a tradition of unity and stability looked with special interest at traditions built on dualism and dynamism; philosophers worried about the effect of an invasive and destructive practice on physical nature had hopes of drawing upon others more steeped in attitudes of harmony and mutual promotion. All sought sufficient understanding of the range of reality from matter to spirit in order to be able to integrate theory, practice and contemplation within their efforts to build the future. All shared richly what they had, and all listened and reflected intently.

More specifically the flow of the discussions is reflected, with slight adjustment, in the disposition of the Parts of this volume. The papers of the Chinese philosophers, discussed in the morning sessions, treated sequentially classical Chinese, Marxist, and modern European philosophy in relation to "Man and Nature"; the afternoon papers by the visiting scholars treated hermeneutics, the sense of the person and ethics. Together they joined in an effort to understand the resources available from the past, the modes of interpreting and applying those in the present and the role of materialism and subjectivity in developing an ethics for the future.

Part I concerns the resources of classical Chinese philosophy. Prof. Zhang Dai-Nian considers the range of theories regarding the relation of man to nature from a theory of original harmony which would be disturbed by any human action or machine to a theory by which mankind is called to assist nature in its changes and to help all things to perfect fulfillment. Here the human person has a central and honored place. Prof. Tang Yi-jie points to the great emphasis placed upon integration and the harmony of heaven and man, of knowledge and practice, and of feeling and scenery; unity and integration mark all three orders of world, ethics and art. Prof. Fang Litian shows a parallel dynamic relation of utilization and conservation, of exploitation and improvement. The Chapter by Prof. K. Schmidt tracing a series of understandings of nature in Western thought includes the formally structured view of ancient Greece and the more dynamic sense of nature in the Christian Middle Ages. Clearly, there is much to draw upon for future development in both East and West.

At the same time, it is noted that some elements of importance for our times are lacking in the classical Chinese thinkers, particularly, the logic required for analytic thought, a systematic structure for understanding, and a strong sense of the dynamic character of nature. A way is needed to draw upon the complementary resources from the classical Western tradition. In turn, this could be reciprocated by the Chinese themes of harmony and integration.

But how is this to be done; how is this wealth of wisdom from the past and even from another culture to be interpreted so as to live in our day? Should one--can one--seek to recreate the mind and life of times past; or must the past be made to live in new and dynamic ways in the present? In Part II the paper of Prof. McLean looks into the origin of a tradition as the expression of the cumulative free choices of a people and as bearing normative weight in making possible the free choices of the present. This concerns also the work of application, for the tradition lives only in those free and creative decisions made in its light, not as static repetitions of the past but as building a future that is ever new. Prof. G. Florival deepens this hermeneutic suggestion by tracing it to the very nature of being, while Prof. Chatterjee illustrates the richness of the resources regarding nature which have been developed in this manner in the Indian tradition.

Part III undertakes the work of constructing a modern approach to understanding the relation of man and nature by focusing upon the materialist approaches of Marxist thought. Profs. Huang Nansheng and Zhao Guangwu acutely analyze the continuities of physical nature, extending even from that which is not known, through nature as affected by man and humanized, to the human body and appropriate human interaction. Prof. Li Zhen approaches the issue in terms of opposition and struggle initiated with a hostile nature in primitive times and continued in terms of master and slave in the institutions of the ancient and medieval periods. A resolution is suggested through understanding all in terms of the one matter in evolution and the achievement by modern man of a mastery which is then converted into friendship.

Part IV directs attention to subjectivity and spirit as an additional dimension of reality. It is pointed out by Profs. Chen Kuide and Zhang Shi-Ying that Western thought has drawn its dynamism particularly from its unresolved dualism of spirit and matter, and subject and object, reflected in the parallel tension of transcendence and immanence. The panoramic paper of Prof. Zhu Desheng follows the restless history of metaphysical work upon this relationship. Earlier, the paper of G. Florival had noted the related rich hermeneutic significance of contemporary efforts in a personalist approach, while that of K. Schmidt pointed to the positive role of religion inspiring medieval culture and the struggles for liberation of the oppressed of our day.

Finally, Part V attempts to unite these elements in an ethical view for the future of mankind. The paper of J. Farrelly develops a notion of nature as guide to human action. Prof. T. Imamichi treats of ways in which our ethics must undergo development in order to be adequate for the new circumstances of our times. Prof. M. Dy extends this to the choice of values, their articulation in the various notions of ideology and their critique. Looking toward the future he echoes a passage of Wang Yang-Min cited by Prof. Tang, namely, "Knowledge is the purpose of practice and practice is the work of knowledge; knowledge is the beginning of practice and practice is the end result of knowledge." In Dy's terms this wedding of knowledge and practice in our day implies a search for institutions "to mediate man and technology, to render nature more humanized and man more . . . at home with his world. Ideology in its original sense of integration may then become a utopia, and man a co-creator with the One."

G. McLean, Sec. *Council for Research in Values and Philosophy*

TABLE OF CONTENTS

Preface

Introduction

PART I. Classical Philosophies on Man and Nature

1. Theories Concerning Man and Nature in Classical Chinese Philosophy
   by *Zhang Dai-Nian*, Peking Univ. — 3-12
2. On the Unity of Man and Heaven
   by *Tang Yi-jie*, Peking Univ. — 13-24
3. Liu Zongyuan's and Liu Yuxi's Theories of Heaven and Man
   by *Fang Li-tian*, People's Univ. of China, Beijing — 25-32
4. Paradigms of Nature in Western Thought
   by *Kenneth L. Schmitz*, King's College, Univ. of Toronto, Canada — 33-54

PART II. Hermeneutics and the Application of Classical Philosophies to Contemporary Life

5. Hermeneutics and Heritage
   by *George F. McLean*, Sec., RVP — 57-70
6. Towards an Hermeneutics of Nature and Culture
   by *Ghislaine Florival*, Université Catholique de Louvain, Louvain-la-Neuve, Belgium — 71-83
7. Man and Nature in the Indian Context
   by *Margaret Chatterjee*, Indian Institute of Advanced Studies, Simla, India — 85-99

PART III. Marxism on Man and Nature

8. On the Relationship Between Man and Nature
   by *Huang Nan-sheng* and *Zhao Guangwu*, Peking Univ. — 103-112
9. Slave - Master - Friend, Philosophical Reflections Upon Man and Nature
   by *Li Zhen*, Peking Univ. — 113-127

PART IV. Person, Subjectivity and Nature

10. Man vs. Nature and Natural Man: One Aspect of the Concept of Nature in China and the West
    by *Chen Kuide*, Fudan Univ., Shanghai — 131-141
11. Western and Chinese Philosophy on Man and Nature
    by *Richard T. De George*, Univ. of Kansas — 143-148
12. The Development of the Principle of Subjectivity in Western Philosophy and of the Theory of Man in Chinese Philosophy
    by *Zhang Shi-Ying*, Peking Univ. — 149-167

xii *Introduction*

    13. The Fate of Metaphysics   169-192
        by *Zhu Desheng*, Peking Univ.

PART V. *Ethics and Nature*

    14. Human Nature Reflected in Moral Experience   195-208
        by *John Farrelly*, De Salles Hall, Washington
    15. The Concept of an Eco-ethics and the
        Development of Moral Thought   209-218
        by *Tomonobu Imamichi*, Emeritus,
        University of Tokyo
    16. On Nature and Values, Ideology and Hope   219-228
        by *Manuel Dy*, Ateneo de Manila Univ.,
        Philippines

Index

PART I

CLASSICAL CHINESE PHILOSOPHIES

on

MAN AND NATURE

CHAPTER I

THEORIES CONCERNING MAN AND NATURE IN CLASSICAL CHINESE PHILOSOPHY

ZHANG DAI-NIAN

RELATION OF HEAVEN AND MAN

The relationship between man and nature is one of the fundamental issues in Chinese philosophy; the ancients called it the "relation of Heaven and man." Ssu-ma Ch'ien, the famous historian of the Han period, *and the author of Shih-chi (Historical Records)*, stated the purpose of his work as follows: "I want hereby to elucidate the relation of Heaven and man, to discern its historical development from Past to Present, and to state my distinctive views." This expresses clearly the academic aim of ancient Chinese thinkers.

Thinkers both before and after Ssu-ma Ch'ien emphasized the relation of Heaven and man. What is called Heaven in ancient China had various implications, but after the middle period of the Warring States most thinkers mean mainly nature by Heaven. When Confucius speaks about "the Mandate of Heaven" in the Spring and Autumn period, and when Mo Tzu talks about the "Will of Heaven" in the early period of the Warring States, what they refer to as Heaven is invariably the Supreme Master of the World. When in the middle period of the Warring States Chuang-tzu speaks about the contrast between Heaven and man, and when in the late period of the Warring States Hsun-tzu stresses the distinction between Heaven and man, they also mean boundless nature. When Tung Chung-shu in the Han Dynasty considers Heaven as "the supreme ruler of hundreds of deities," he is referring to God with a will. Wang Ch'ung thinks of Heaven as the celestial body which includes the sun, the moon and all the stars; Chang Tsai of the Song Dynasty means by Heaven the boundless expanse of the great wild, that is, actually the totality of nature. Cheng Hao and Cheng Yi mean by Heaven the supreme entity of the universe.

In short, what most thinkers refer to as Heaven is the vast objective world, actually, vast nature; while what is referred to as man is mankind or human society. Hence, the relationship between Heaven and man is actually the relationship between man and nature. Around this issue, the various schools of thought begin their disputes.

SEPARATION AND UNITY OF HEAVEN AND MAN

Generally speaking, the doctrines concerning the relationship between Heaven and man in Chinese philosophy can be divided into two types. One type lays comparatively greater stress on the unity of Heaven and man, while the other stresses the separation of the two. The doctrines stressing the unity of Heaven and man are much more influential; nevertheless those stressing the separation of the two, though held only by a minority of thinkers, make a distinctive contribution.

The doctrine stressing "the unity of Heaven and man" comes from Mencius who put forward the proposition that "to know (human) nature is to know Heaven." But how is this so? According to Mencius, human nature is given by Heaven--derived from Heaven--so the two are interconnected. Heaven in Mencius' sense has a double meaning: both the supreme ruler and the supreme law of necessity. Though he gives neither a clear definition of Heaven nor a detailed demonstration of the proposition that to know nature is to know Heaven, yet his view that nature and Heaven are interconnected is quite influential. Tung Chung-shu held that "Heaven and man resemble each other," believing that the structure of the human body and that of the heavenly bodies are similar: in Heaven there are 12 months and more than 360 days in a year, while in man there are 12 major joints and 366 minor joints in the bones; Heaven has 4 seasons while man has 4 limbs; Heaven has sun and moon, while man has ears and eyes. As this view is obviously quite far-fetched, later thinkers seldom accepted it.

In the Song Dynasty, Chang Tsai definitely put forward the proposition of "the coincidence of Heaven and man." By this Chang Tsai means principally the unity of the "heavenly ways" and human nature. What he terms "heavenly ways" refers to the total process of nature as a whole; and what he terms "human nature" refers to the most fundamental attributes of man as an existential being. He believes that the identity of the content of the heavenly ways with those of human nature consists in the changes and variations arising from internal contradictions. He says: "What is meant by nature and heavenly ways is nothing but change." "What is called Way is the Great Harmony which implies the nature of the interaction of floating and sinking, rising and falling, moving and being static." Chang Tsai objects to the separation of Heaven and man, stressing that mankind originates from Heaven and Earth, is able to know heaven, and that this knowledge is actually Heaven's self-knowledge.

The theory of Cheng Yi is somewhat different from that of Chang Tsai. He affirms that heavenly and human ways are the same. What he calls heavenly ways refer to the general laws of nature, while human ways refer to the supreme norms of human life; he believes that the two are identical. The content of heavenly ways are Yuan, Heng, Li and Zhen, i.e., birth, growth, fulfillment and maturity. Later on, this idea is further elaborated by Chu Hsi, who considers Yuan as the origin of all things on earth: "It is spring in season and human-heartedness in man." Heng is the growth and thriving of all things on earth: "It is summer in season and rites in man." Li is the flowering and fructifying: "It is autumn in season and righteousness in man." Zhen is the maturity of fruits: "It is winter in season and wisdom in man." Thus Chu Hsi, drawing a forced analogy between the natural laws of vegetable growth and the moral principles of human life, commits the mistake of far-fetchedness. Yet Cheng and Chu are not altogether without reason in believing that there is a certain relevant relationship between the general laws of nature and the moral principles of mankind.

Concerning the traditional idea of the coincidence of Heaven and man, one problem as in need of explanation. According to scientific research, people in primitive society did not distinguish the human from the external world; primitive people did not possess self-consciousness and perceived no distinction or opposition between man and nature. Only after the dawn of civilization was man distinguished from nature and only then was the distinction and opposition between the two was fully realized. This is called human self-consciousness.

Is it true then that the coincidence of Heaven and man in ancient China is similar to the confusion of man and nature in primitive ways of thinking? This requires an historical and logical investigation, as the idea of the coincidence of Heaven and man was formulated in ancient China in a period when Chinese civilization had long been developed. Is it possible that philosophical idea goes back to the primitive stage of thought? According to historical records, in remote antiquity before the legendary monarchs Yao and Sun, there was indeed a distinction between Heaven and man: that is, a severance of the ties between Earth and Heaven in the traditional Zhuan Xu period. According to tradition, "men and deities were all mixed up before the period of Monarch Zhuan Xu, when every human being could make direct contact with the deities. Then Zhuan Xu separated men from the deities, making it certain that Heaven is Heaven and Earth is Earth, so that people on Earth could not make direct contact with Heaven. This is the so-called "severance of ties between Earth and Heaven."

In my view, this "severance of ties" implies the distinction of man from nature. What is more, as Zi Chan in the Spring and Autumn period had already drawn a clear distinction between heavenly and human ways, it seems unlikely that Mencius in the Warring States period would fail to reach the stage of distinguishing Heaven and man. The so-called coincidence of Heaven and man is then a re-affirmation of the unity of Heaven and man on the basis of an affirmation of the distinction between the two--it is a dialectical or more advanced way of thinking.

Hsun-tzu and Liu Yu-xi of the Tang Dynasty objected to the coincidence of Heaven and man and stressed the distinction between the two. Hsun-tzu declares: "The one who well understands the difference between Heaven and man can be said to be supreme among men." The one who is supreme among men is the loftiest personality, and necessarily knows the difference between Heaven and man. Hsun-tzu puts forward the famous proposition that "the Heavenly ways are constant--it neither exists for the sake of the good emperor Yao nor desists because of the evil king Jie." He believes that nature has its own objective laws of necessity which have nothing to do with order or disorder, fortune or misfortune in human society. Heaven and man each have different functions. "Heaven has its seasons, Earth its treasures and man his order." He believes in the transformation of nature in the sense of "harnessing the Mandate of Heaven in order to use it"--an idea which is often stressed in the history of Chinese philosophy.

Liu Yu-xi put forward the proposition that Heaven and man triumph over each other. He thought that "Heaven is the greatest among shapes," while "man is the best among animals." Thus Heaven and man have distinctive functions: the function of Heaven is to "reproduce," and thus it is able to give birth to all things on earth; while the function of man is to "establish laws," and thus it is able to establish standards for the judgment of right and wrong. In the natural world, the strong are superior and the powerful dominate the weak; in human society, however, a code of behavior is established according to which the worthy are superior and no one can dominate others by means of power. This awareness of the distinction between natural laws and moral criteria is profound.

Chang Tsai, though declaring that Heaven and man coincide, also acknowledges that "Heaven and man have reason to triumph over each other. While stressing the unity of heavenly ways with human nature, he also acknowledges the distinction between Heaven and man. Yet he strongly advocates the coincidence of Heaven and man. This makes it clear that the conception of the coincidence of Heaven with man does not exclude a separation of Heaven from man.

MAN BETWEEN HEAVEN AND EARTH

Although the theories in Chinese philosophy concerning the relationship between Heaven and man can be divided into two types, these types share quite a few basic elements. For example, most thinkers affirm that man is born of Heaven and Earth, and enjoys an outstanding position between Heaven and Earth; that is to say, they all affirm that man is a product of nature and possesses in nature a position superior to all other things.

Mencius says: "Heaven has long given birth to people," thereby affirming that man is born by Heaven. "Heaven and Earth are the origins of life," and "the union of Heaven and Earth gives birth to all things," thereby affirming that man is born by Heaven and Earth. Tung Chung-shu says: "Heaven, Earth and Man are the origins of all things. Heaven gives them birth. Earth gives them nourishment and Man gives them perfection." This attitude affirms, on the one hand, man's initiative and acknowledges, on the other, that Man is born of Heaven. Liu Yu-xi says: "The capability of Heaven is to give birth to all things while the capability of man is to rule all things," acknowledging thereby both man's initiative to rule all things and his birth of Heaven and Earth.

Chang Tsai elucidates the relationship between Heaven, Earth and Man in more figurative language. He writes in *Xi Ming (West Inscription)*, that "Qian (Heaven) is Father while Kun (Earth) is Mother. . . . People are born of the same parents as mine; and things are my companions." He compares the relationship between Heaven and man to that between parents and children, vividly illustrating the fact that man is born of Heaven and Earth.

In the meantime, most thinkers affirm that mankind has a higher value than birds and beasts. *Xiao Jing (Classic of Filial Piety)* thus records the remarks of Confucius: "Man is the most valuable according to the nature of Heaven and Earth." Although it is not certain whether these are the remarks of Confucius himself, nevertheless they represent the basic viewpoints of the Confucian school. Mencius affirms that "Everybody has a value appropriate to himself," that is, everybody has his own inherent values.

Hsun-tzu clearly points out the similarities and differences between man and inorganic matter and those between man and all other living things, thus illustrating man's value. He says:

> Fire and water have energy but no life; grass and trees have life but no sense; birds and beasts have sense but no righteousness. Man, however, has all of

them: energy, life, sense and also righteousness. So man is the most valuable under Heaven.

Beings existing in the world fall into 4 levels: water and fire are inorganic matter, they are material being with no life; grass and trees are vegetable, they have life but no sense; birds and beasts are animals, they have sense but no moral consciousness. Man has material being, life, sense and also moral consciousness, so he is the most valuable.

Tung Chung-shu explains in more detail man's moral consciousness:

> Man receives his Mandates from Heaven, so he is different from and superior to all other living things. At home he has the kinship of fathers and sons and brothers; outside the family he has the relationship of monarchs and subjects, superiors and subordinates; in daily encounters and gatherings, he acts according to the order of old and young, senior and junior; he gracefully observes ceremony in social intercourse and joyfully harbors kindness in loving others--that is why man is so valuable.

This attitude considers the major content of morality to be the ethical relationship between father and son, monarch and subject old and young. Here the hierarchical relationships between monarch and subject, superior and subordinate are regarded as human values. Though this clearly indicates the limitations of that era, it is of great significance in characterizing human life as the ethical relationships between father and son, old and young.

Yi Zhuan (Book of Changes), a theoretical work of the Confucian school in the Warring States period, regards Heaven, Earth and Man as "the three gifts," clearly affirming man's significant position between Heaven and Earth. *Lao-tzu*, the representative work of the Taoist school, regards Tao (the way of nature), Heaven, Earth and Man as "the four greatest": "Tao is great, Heaven is great, Earth is great, and Man is also great. That Man is one of "the four greatest within the realm" affirms man's outstanding position as distinguished from other things.

This ideological trend to affirm man's significant position between Heaven and Earth also represents the common views of thinkers in the Tang, Song, Ming and Qing Dynasties.

WHAT ATTITUDE SHOULD MAN TAKE TOWARDS NATURE?

How should man handle his relationship with nature, that is, what attitude should one take towards nature? This is the first question to be solved in human life. Concerning such a question there are three doctrines in ancient Chinese philosophy: first, Chuang-tzu's doctrine of letting nature run its own course and following it; second, Hsun-tzu's doctrine of transforming nature; third, the doctrine of the harmony of Heaven and man in *Yi Zhuan*.

Chuang-Tzu

It is Chuang-tzu's belief that nature was originally harmonious and perfect but that after man acquired knowledge and invented quite a few techniques, nature's harmonious and perfect state of being was destroyed. Hence, the basic principle of life is to clear away all artificiality and return to primitive nature. Chuang-tzu's ideological program is as follows: "Do no damage to Tao by intellect and give no aid to Heaven through human resources." "Follow the course of nature instead of adding anything to it artificially."

Chuang-tzu makes use of the horse as a metaphor to reprimand the fault of doing damage to nature. According to him, "the hoofs of a horse are able to tread on dew and snow, while the hairs of a horse can protect it from wind and chill"; it eats grass and drinks water and raises its hoofs to jump--originally it led a leisurely and carefree life. But then Bo Le claims to be good at handling horses and uses many methods to train them: running, galloping and adorning them. First, they suffer from the bit and tassels held in their mouths, then they are threatened by whips. The horses can no longer lead a leisurely and carefree life, and many of them die of injuries. People in remote antiquity "weave to dress and plough to eat, leading a carefree and unrestrained life. But ever since the sages invented *Ren* (human-heartedness) and *Yi* (righteousness), man began to go after knowledge and wealth; they entered into rivalry with each other and there has been no peace for them."

Chuang-tzu thus comments on the distinction between Heaven and man: "What is Heaven? What is man"? "Oxen and horses have four legs--that is heaven; to halter up the horse and pierce through the muzzle of the ox--that is human." To be natural is heaven and to change nature is human. Chuang-tzu and his school totally deny man-made values, and demand a return to the original state of nature.

Hsun-Tzu

Hsun-tzu's position is opposite to, and critical of, Chuang-tzu: "Obsessed by Heaven Chuang-tzu has no knowledge of man." Where Chuang-tzu sings the praises of Heaven but cannot comprehend the meaning of man's initiative, Hsun-tzu stresses the importance of transforming nature. He says:

Is it not far better to foster and manage Heaven as a thing than merely to wonder at its greatness? Is it not far better to subdue the Mandate of Heaven in order to use it than merely to follow it and sing its praises? Is it not far better to deal with the present season and use it than merely to watch and wait for the proper seasons? Is it not far better to give full play to one's initiative and transform things than to follow the natural course of things and highly praise it? Is it not far better to take actual control of things in order not to miss them than merely to think about them as external objects?

Here the ideal is that of 'subduing Heaven,' 'transforming things' and 'handling things' that is to insist on transforming and harnessing nature.

It is Hsun-Tzu's belief that the ideal of human life should be as follows: "To form an overall view of both Heaven and Earth and make full use of all things there"; "to utilize to the full all things covered by Heaven and carried by Earth"; to transform nature and make use of all things in nature in order to improve human life.

Hsun-tzu puts forward the ideal of transforming nature, yet he pays no attention to research on nature. He says: "To be good at the utilization of things but not to strain oneself to probe into their whys and wherefores: that is a gentleman's attitude towards Heaven and Earth and all things thereof." As a matter of fact, it is essential to have a good knowledge of the laws of things in order to use them; it is impossible "to be good at the utilization of things" without comprehending their whys and therefores. Such is the drawback of the theory of Hsun-tzu.

Yi-Zhuan

Quite different from Chuang-tzu and Hsun-tzu, *Yi Zhuan* puts forward the idea of the harmony of Heaven and man. According to the ancient tradition, *Yi Zhuan* is attributed to Confucius and its ideas had been taken belong to Confucius. Yet in recent years most historians of philosophy believe that *Yi Zhuan* belongs to the Warring States period--or rather that it does not belong to one person and one period but is the joint work of Confucian scholars who taught *Zhou Yi (The Book of Changes)* during the warring states period; some of its chapters were written before Hsun-tzu and others after him.

Xiang Zhuan (The Book of Signs) in *Yi Zhuan* puts forward the principle of "handling the ways of Heaven and Earth and helping towards the readjustment of Heaven and Earth." Its main implication is to adjust the role of natural laws and assist nature in its change. In the same book Xi Ci Zhuan puts forward the ideal of "having a good knowledge of all things and applying Tao to all the land under Heaven"; of "encompassing all the changes between Heaven and Earth and bringing all things to fulfillment." This latter expression has a definite meaning, i.e., to adjust the changes of nature and to help bring all things to perfect fulfillment.

Wen Yan Zhuan in *Yi Zhuan* describes an ideal personality as "sharing the same virtue with Heaven and Earth." Wen Yan Zhuan says: "A noble gentleman is one who shares the same virtue with Heaven and Earth; . . . he precedes Heaven, yet Heaven does not go against it; he succeeds Heaven and follows it." A noble gentleman is actually a great and lofty personality; his virtue coincides with that of Heaven and Earth. To precede Heaven is to guide nature before it undergoes any changes, and to succeed Heaven is to conform to nature after its changes. Being able both to guide the changes of nature and to be suited to the changes, he realizes the harmony of Heaven and man.

Yi Zhuan contains such ideas as "handling the ways of Heaven and Earth and helping towards the readjustment of Heaven and Earth," and also "encompassing all the changes between Heaven and Earth and bringing all things to fulfillment." These are quite simple propositions, but they put forward a comparatively comprehensive dialectical viewpoint, e.g., that we must both grasp the functions of natural laws and adjust the processes in the changes of nature; that we must acknowledge the objectivity of natural changes and their laws, on the one hand, and affirm the initiative of the subject, on the other.

Chuang-tzu demands a return to nature. Yet, as a matter of fact, it is quite natural for man to evolve from a simple primitive state to a sophisticated era of civilization. On the contrary, it is quite unnatural for man to reject civilized life and return to primitive simplicity--this is the inherent paradox of Taoism. Nevertheless, the Taoists demand that no damage be done blindly to nature and that "no destruction be inflicted upon things" is a significant warning to civilized society.

Hsun-tzu's ideal of transforming nature is quite a brilliant idea, but he fails to find any effective means of doing so.

Yi Zhuan puts forward the principle of "handling the ways of Heaven and Earth and helping towards the readjustment of Heaven and Earth." This is described mainly in terms of agricultural production, and in its 2,000 years of history this principle has been applied mainly to agricultural production: different measures being taken according to the changes of the four seasons. The practical significance of the principle is to maintain ecological balance.

In ancient China, none of the theories concerning the relation between man and nature, whether of the Confucian or the Taoist school, regarded that relationship as antagonistic. Rather, the two are seen as interdependent and the perfect harmony of Heaven and man is held to be the supreme ideal. This viewpoint, even from the perspective of the present day, has profound meaning.

Peking University
  Beijing, People's Republic of China

CHAPTER II

ON THE UNITY OF MAN AND HEAVEN

TANG YI-JIE

If philosophical ideas treat the problems of the true, the good, and the beautiful, does traditional Chinese philosophy make a valuable or unique contribution in this regard? I think it does, and very remarkably. We can approach this issue from two aspects: one is the content of its thought, the other is its attitude toward life; both aspects are closely related.

Regarding the issue of the true, the good, and the beautiful, three propositions in traditional Chinese philosophy have exerted an extended influence over Chinese thought: namely, the "integration of heaven with man," which inquires into the unity of the world; the "integration of knowledge with practice," which concerns the problem of an ethical norm; and the "integration of feeling with scenery," which involves the creation and appreciation of artistic works.

THE INTEGRATION OF HEAVEN WITH MAN

How to define the two concepts of "heaven" and "man" varies with different philosophers. Nevertheless, the "Way of Heaven" refers to the basics of the universe or the universe as a whole; the "way of man" often refers to the society of man or man himself. The relationship between heaven and man has always been the fundamental issue studied by Chinese thinkers.

Sima Qian called his *Historical Records* a book that "probes into the relations between heaven and man." Dong Zhongshu described what he saw as a branch of learning that "studies how man is related to heaven." He Yan, one of the founders of the metaphysics of the Wei and Jin dynasties, called another founder, Wang Bi, a philosopher "qualified to discuss the relations between heaven and man." Tao Hongjing, the true founder of the Maoshan sect of China's Daoism, said only Yan Huan, another Daoist leader, understood that "what he had in mind" was the problem "between heaven and man."

The "relationship between heaven and man" has been explained by different theories in traditional Chinese philosophy. For example, Xunzi required that a "distinction be made between heaven and man." Zhuangzi theorized that "those who are ignorant of heaven know nothing about man." Furthermore, the question of "relations between heaven and man" has often found expression in the discussion about the relation between "nature" and the "Confucian ethical code." Nevertheless, the mainstream of traditional Chinese philosophy has taken as its main task the demonstration or explanation of how "heaven is integrated with man."

Confucius said more about "human affairs" and less about "the Mandate of Heaven." Nonetheless, he also believed that "what the saint says" is in keeping with "the Mandate of Heaven." Mencius, is the first philosopher to propose the idea of the "integration of heaven with man" in a complete sense. For example, he said: "Do with all your heart, know your lot, and understand heaven"; "keep up with heaven and earth above and below." Even though Xunzi advocated that a "distinction be made between heaven and man," his fundamental goal was to "bend the will of Heaven to our use" so that "Heaven" would be integrated with man. Laozi of the Daoist school urged: "Man follows earth, earth follows Heaven, Heaven follows the Way, and the Way follows nature." Even Zhuangzi who was "ignorant of heaven and knows nothing about man" had this to say: "Heaven and earth live side-by-side with me and all things on earth are identified with me." He also said that the superior man can "communicate with heaven, earth, and spirit." Dong Zhongshu preached the idea that "heaven and man respond to each other"; he argued that the two were integrated.

Metaphysics during the Wei and Jin dynasties focused its discussion on the relationship between "nature" and "the Confucian ethical code." Even though Ji Kang and Ruan Ji advocated that the "ethical code be overstepped and nature followed," the mainstream of the metaphysical school stressed that the "ethical code" be reconciled with "nature." As Wang Bi embraced the idea that "the intrinsic and the extrinsic are like one," he urged that "the essentials (Nature and the Way of Heaven) be upheld to rule the nonessentials (ethical code and mundane affairs). In stressing that "the intrinsic and the extrinsic are like one," Guo Xiang believed "there is no intrinsic beyond the extrinsic." Therefore he concluded that "heaven is the general term for all things on earth."

By the time of the Song Dynasty, the Confucian philosopher Zhou Dunyi noted in more explicit terms: "A saint shares virtue with heaven and earth," and "a saint aspires to heaven." Zhang Zai stated in his *West Inscription*: "That which exists between heaven and earth is my intrinsic being; that which commands heaven and earth is my character." The two Chengs theorized that "the intrinsic and the extrinsic come from the same source" and stated: "In heaven it is destiny, in man it is character, and it is the heart that commands the body. They are actually one and the same." Zhu Xi held that "Heaven is man, and man is heaven. Since this man is born, heaven rests in him." He added: "A saint . . . is integrated with heaven."

Wang Yangming said: "The heart is heaven. Stressing the importance of the heart upholds heaven, earth, and all things." "Man is actually one with heaven, earth and all things." "The heart has no intrinsic content but takes the response of heaven, earth, and all things its content." Later Wang Fuzhi advanced the idea that man moves along with the vaporization of Heaven to explain why Heaven is integrated with man. "Destiny is realized by days and character is formed by days." "There is not a day that heaven stops thinking of destiny, and there is not a day that man does not submit his destiny to Heaven."

In traditional Chinese philosophy the major thinkers, whether materialist or idealist, all talked about the problem of "integration of Heaven with man" An analysis of their theories brings us to the following general conclusions:

> First, in traditional Chinese philosophy, the concept of the 'integration of Heaven with Man' expresses the idea of observing things in their entirety. It is a direct description, rather than a detailed analysis. We can call it a directly perceived 'overall concept.'

> Second, in traditional Chinese philosophy, the basic argument for the idea of the 'integration of Heaven with Man' is that 'The intrinsic and the extrinsic are like one.' The unity of the ways of Heaven and man is 'both intrinsic and extrinsic.' The Way of Heaven serves intrinsically and the way of man extrinsically. The result can be termed an 'absolute' of 'unity.'

> Third, traditional Chinese philosophy does not see the 'way of man' as something rigid. Furthermore, it sees in the 'Way of Heaven' liveliness and unending vitality. 'Heaven moves along a healthy track, and a gentleman should make unremitting efforts to improve himself.' That human society should move forward and man should improve himself is due to the necessity of keeping up with the development of the 'Way of Heaven.' This can be termed the unlimited 'concept of development.'

> Fourth, in traditional Chinese philosophy, 'Heaven' is object, and the 'way of man' must be brought in line with the 'Way of Heaven.' However, 'man' is the heart of heaven and earth; he should install a heart for heaven and earth. Without 'man,' heaven and earth would have no vitality, rationality or morality. This can be called the 'humanistic concept' of ethics.

> The four above-mentioned concepts comprise the total

implication of the idea of "the integration of heaven with man" in traditional Chinese philosophy.

THE INTEGRATION OF KNOWLEDGE WITH PRACTICE

The problem of "knowledge and practice" is an issue of the theory of knowledge. In traditional Chinese philosophy, however, it is more a problem of ethics and morality. If the question of the theory of knowledge had not been linked to the question of ethics, it would have been difficult for it to be passed down as a part of the traditional Chinese philosophy. Therefore the problem of a theory of knowledge is often also the problem of ethics. This is why the philosophers advocated that man not only seek "knowledge" but also pay special attention to "conduct" (practice).

What is the "good"? The criterion for the "good" can vary, but, according to traditional Chinese philosophy, a unity of "knowledge" and "practice" must be regarded as a prerequisite. From the history of Chinese philosophy contains many explanations of the relationship between knowledge and conduct. In *History Classic* [Chapter I, "On Destiny"] it was said long ago that "it is not difficult to know, but difficult to put into practice." Later the two Chengs advocated: "Knowledge precedes practice." Zhu Xi was of the opinion that "knowledge and practice each give rise to the other." Wang Fuzhi theorized that "practice precedes knowledge." And Sun Zhongshan advanced the idea that "to know about a thing is more difficult than to do it."

Taking things as a whole, however, the concept of the "integration of knowledge with practice" actually has run through traditional Chinese philosophy from beginning to end. Starting from the time of Confucius, the "agreement of one's words with one's deeds" has always been used as an ethical criterion to differentiate a gentleman from a villain. Said Confucius: "A gentleman feels it a shame not to be able to match his words with actions." Mencius stressed "intuitive knowledge" and "intuitive ability." Even though he regarded the four factors including the "sense of pity" as inherent, he thought it necessary to "foster and enhance" benevolence, righteousness, rite and wisdom, which had already become moral codes. As they could be acquired only through moral practice, he advocated that "a noble spirit be cultivated." Xun Zi stressed "practice" as the purpose of seeking "knowledge"; at the same time, he also admitted the guidance "knowledge" provided for "practice": "One who practices it knows it; one who knows it is a saint." As a saint, therefore, one must "integrate knowledge with practice."

By the Song Dynasty, the Confucian philosopher Cheng Yi,

regardless of his opinion that "knowledge precedes practice," argued in terms of morality and self-cultivation that "one who knows but cannot practice is one who does not truly know." Therefore Huang Zongxi noted: "Cheng already had the idea of integrating knowledge with practice" [*Academic Files of the Song and Yuan Dynasties*, Volume LXXV]. Zhu Xi inherited Cheng Yi's theory that "knowledge precedes practice," but he stressed in particular that "knowledge and practice are mutually dependent" and that "efforts on knowledge and practice should be pushed forward side-by-side." He reasoned: "In terms of sequence, knowledge precedes; in terms of importance, practice is more important." Therefore some people described Cheng and Zhu as theories of "integration of knowledge with practice, with emphasis on the latter." Even though "knowledge" is the foundation of "practice," "knowledge is shallow when knowledge has just been acquired and is yet to be put into practice." "When one personally experiences it, his knowledge will be deeper, different from what he knew before." Zhu Xi stressed "practice" because he basically regarded "knowledge" and "practice" as an issue of morality. This is why he remarked:

> Wherever the good is, one must practice it. Having practiced it long enough, it will become identified with oneself. Having identified with it, it will become a part of oneself. Failing to practice it, the good remains the good, and oneself remains oneself; they have nothing to do with each other.

Traditional Chinese philosophy often advocated "practicing the Way." This idea had perhaps a twofold implication: One was to "take the Way as the intrinsic content," another to practice the "intrinsic way," namely, earnestly to practice the "intrinsic way" one advocated, for it is not merely an issue of understanding.

Wang Yangming's theory of "integration of knowledge with practice" is broadly known, but the common understanding of it is not totally correct. By quoting his remark, "Practice begins once an idea is struck upon," people often describe him as "ascribing practice to knowledge" and "taking knowledge to be practice." In fact, Wang Yangming did not equate "knowledge" with "practice" completely. The remark that "practice begins once an idea is struck upon" was made in the context of morality and self-cultivation. Immediately after that, he added: "If the idea is not good, we have to overcome it so that the not-good idea will not lay hidden in our hearts." He also said: "A close and solid knowledge is where practice lies and a conscious and precise practice is where knowledge lies. Efforts for knowledge and practice were originally inseparable. Only scholars in later ages split them into two and lost the essence of knowledge and practice. In regard to the relations between knowledge and practice, Wang explained clearly: "Knowledge gives idea to practice, and practice is the effort made by knowledge. Knowledge is the beginning of practice and practice is the end result of knowledge." From the angle of the theory of knowledge, Wang Yangming could be suspected of "including practice in knowledge." In the perspective of morality and self-cultivation, however, his emphasis on "the integration of knowledge with practice" had a positive significance.

Between the Ming and Qing dynasties, Wang Fuzhi advanced the idea that "practice precedes knowledge" and "practice can also gain knowledge." However, he still stressed "the integration of knowledge with practice when addressing the issue of ethics. He opined that "knowledge and practice complementing each other is use, and the two progressing alongside each other constitutes achievement." He criticized Wang Yangming's idea of "the integration of knowledge with practice" and called Wang "ignorant of the fact that they each have their own use and complement each other." Nevertheless, Wang Fuzhi, too, was an advocator of "the integration of knowledge with practice." He said:

> In saying that someone is engaged in pursuing knowledge and practice we mean he devotes himself to the pursuit of knowledge and makes every effort to practice. Because of his devotion and efforts, achievements can be made and divided. Since achievements can be made and divided, an order of succession can be established, the antecedent and the subsequent can complement each other. From knowledge one knows what is being practiced, and from practice one practices what is being known. Thus it can be said that the two progress alongside and therefore produce achievements.

That knowledge and practice can progress alongside each other arises because in the final analysis the two constitute the moral realm. According to Wang Fuzhi's opinion:

> A wise man is one who knows the rites. A man of ritual is one who practices knowledge. In practicing knowledge, all rituals will be properly performed; in knowing the rites all essentials will go to the mind. Thus one will improve oneself with each passing day and there will be no end to it.

A saint "combines his intelligence with sincerity. He
what he knows and what he practices becomes his knowle..
This is how a man should behave as envisaged by traditional
Chinese philosophy.

In the study of traditional Chinese philosophy the presently
prevailing viewpoint asserts that "since the Song and Ming dynasties the neo-Confucianists, when discussing knowledge and practice, often confuse this issue of the theory of knowledge with the issue of ethics," and insists that this is where the limitations and mistakes of ancient Chinese philosophers lay. Here, I feel, two questions must be discussed.

First, neo-Confucianists since the Song and Ming dynasties did not regard knowledge and practice merely as an issue of the theory of knowledge. They thought the issue important precisely because it was related to morality and self-cultivation. The final purpose of their discussion of relations between knowledge and practice was to improve moral cultivation. Therefore it is out of the question to assert that the neo-Confucians confused the issue of the theory of knowledge with that of morality. Second, as an issue of morality and self-cultivation, the theory and viewpoint of unity between knowledge and practice cannot be without positive significance. Ethically, knowledge and practice cannot be separated into two ends, for it is necessary that "knowledge be integrated with practice." The remark, made by Wang Yangming, that "knowledge is the purpose of practice and practice is the work of knowledge; knowledge is the beginning of practice and practice is the end result of knowledge" can be seen as the best summary ever made by ancient Chinese philosophers on this issue.

THE INTEGRATION OF FEELING WITH SCENERY

"The integration of feeling with scenery" is an aesthetic issue. Wang Guowei discussed it thoroughly in his *Random Talks About Poetry*. He said: "Realm is the most important quality in poetry writing. Having realm, a poem is naturally of a high quality and carries famous lines."

What does "realm" mean? Wang explained:

> Realm does not refer to scenery alone. Delight, anger, sorrow, and joy are also a realm in man's heart. Therefore a poem that can depict true scenery and true feelings can be said to have realm.

Obviously the term 'realm' refers not only to scenery, but to "sentiments" as well. In *Jialing Manuscripts Discussing Poetry*, Ye Jiaying made a very perceptive explanation about Wang Guowei's realm theory. According to Ye:

The generation of realm depends entirely on our sense of perception. The existence of realm depends entirely on what our sense of perception can reach. Therefore the outside world cannot be called realm before we can reproduce it through the function of our sense of perception. Judging by such a conclusion, the theory of realm as advocated by Wang, as a matter of fact, can be traced to the same origin as the theory of interest by Canglang and the theory of romantic charm by Yan Tingzhi.

Bu Yentu, after Wang Guowei, also said in his *Questions and Answers on the Methods of Painting*: "Landscape painting is no more than portraying feeling and scenery, and feeling and scenery is realm." This is why Wang Guowei remarked: "When people in the past discussed poetry, they divided the verses into those describing scenery and those depicting feeling. They did not know that all verses describing scenery depict feeling." Obviously, Wang Guowei regarded as the most creative writing literary pieces that "integrate feeling with scenery." However, this aesthetic viewpoint of "integration of feeling with scenery" did not begin with Wang Guowei. Generally speaking, it was in the period of the Wei and Jin dynasties that the theory of China's literature and art truly became an independent branch of learning, and by that time the idea of "integrating feeling with theory" had already emerged. In the *Introduction to the Grades of Poetry* Zhong Rong said:

> Four-characters-to-a-line poems, can be useful if they imply more in fewer words and are modeled upon works of literary excellence. However, the problem is they often involve many words, but connote little content. Therefore few people learn to write them. The five-characters-to-a-line poems occupy the primary position in writing and stand out as the most meaningful among a variety of genres, thus winning the praise of being popular. Isn't it because they are the most detailed and truthful in narrating events, conjuring images, expressing feelings, and portraying things? Therefore there are three approaches to writing poetry: First, implication; second, comparison; third, narration. The idea that there is more to the poem than the words state is what we call implication. Citing things to indicate one's intention is comparison. A direct account of the happening, thus embodying the idea, is narration. Take the three approaches into consideration and choose the most ap-

propriate, enhance it with charm and force and polish it with color so that those who read it will find unlimited meaning and those who listen to it will be stirred. This will be a poem of top quality.

That a "masterpiece" or "superb work" should "express feelings and portray things" was the forerunner of the idea of "the integration of feeling with scenery." Xie Zhen, one of the Later Seven Scholars of the Ming Dynasty, said in *Four Seas Poetic Discussions*: "Writing poetry rests on feeling and scenery. Neither can work without the other or conflict with the other." He said also: "Poetry is the tool for the portrayal of feeling and scenery. Feeling melts inside, running deep and long; scenery shines on the outside, stretching far and wide." In *Poetic Discussions from the Ginger Studio* Wang Fuzhi put it even more clearly: "In name feeling and scenery are two things, but in fact they are inseparable."

Those skillful in writing poems have unlimited opportunities to write good ones. In an ingenious piece there is "scenery in feeling and feeling in scenery." "Feeling is generated from amid scenery and scenery is generated from amid feeling. This is why we say scenery is the scenery of feeling, and feeling is the feeling of scenery." "Once feeling is integrated with scenery, witty expressions are readily available." This last sentence perhaps constitutes the basic proposition for China's traditional theory of art and literature, manifesting its basic view of "beauty." In the traditional thinking in China, what is beautiful has always been linked to what is good.

That "the substantial is called the beautiful" refers to a spiritual realm in which one takes noble enjoyment. Having listened to the music of "Wu," Confucius commented: "It has all the beautiful, but not all the good." After listening to the music of "Shao," he remarked: "It has all the good and also all the beautiful." Only music that "has all the good and also all the beautiful" can be regarded as the highest and most ideal. This was said of music, but should apply to other arts as well. An art that "has all the good and also all the beautiful" is designed to elevate man's spiritual realm and help him derive therefrom the highest enjoyment of beauty. Because of this the creator of artistic and literary works must be one who has "realm," and his works must "integrate feeling with scenery."

CHINESE PHILOSOPHY AS THE INTEGRATION OF HEAVEN WITH MAN: GOAL AND RENEWAL

In regard to the issue of the true, the good and the beautiful, why does traditional Chinese philosophy keep pursuing the three "integrations"? In my opinion, it is because the basic spirit of Chinese philosophy is to teach how one should behave like a a human person. To be a "human person" one must have set a standard for oneself, an ideal of the true, the good and the beautiful. One who has attained such an ideal realm in which "heaven is integrated with man," "knowledge is integrated with practice" and "feeling is integrated with scenery" is a saint. Therefore the prospective for traditional Chinese philosophy lies in bringing the demand for being human in line with the need for the program of modernization and realizing it. One's ideal may find expression in an immense variety of ways, but it is essential to have such an ideal and noble spiritual realm. The three integrations advocated by traditional Chinese philosophy, in fact, constitute a unified realm by which one is human; at least theoretically, they cannot be separated.

The proposition of "the integration of heaven with man," though designed to illustrate the relations between man and the entire universe, was made on the basis of man being the center of the universe. *The Golden Mean* states: "Honesty is the Way of Heaven; to be honest is the way of man." "An honest man who hits the target without difficulty, arrives at the right idea without brain-wracking, and conforms to the Way without hurry, is a saint." The role of a saint is to "foster a heart for heaven and earth, create a life for living creatures, carry forward peak insights for posterity, and open the way to peace for thousands of generations to come." Therefore a "man" (mainly, the saint) must behave according to the requirements of the Way of Heaven which he should assume it his responsibility to fulfill. Being alive in the world, one must not take a passive attitude; rather, one should "make unremitting efforts to improve oneself" so as to embody the evolution of the immense universe. In this way, one will set oneself a goal, find a reason for one's being, and foster a noble spiritual realm. Since one has set a goal for oneself and has a reason for one's being, the most important thing is to "integrate his knowledge with practice." One must have an ethical standpoint for unifying the two. The three programs and the eight items listed in the *Great Learnings* tell us the precise reason for this. It says:

> The Way of the great learning lies in shedding light on the bright moral principles, being close to the people, and reaching the utmost good. Those in ancient times who wanted to shed light on the bright principles for the world had first to bring order to their own kingdoms. To bring order to their kingdoms they had first to bring their own families to order. To bring their families to order they had first to cultivate their own moral character. To cultivate their

own moral character they had first to set their minds straight. To set their minds straight they had first to foster a sincere desire. To foster a sincere desire they had first to carry knowledge to the utmost degree. To carry knowledge to the utmost degree they had first to inquire into the properties of things. Having inquired into the properties of things, they were able to carry knowledge to the utmost degree. Having carried knowledge to the utmost degree, they were able to foster a sincere desire. Having fostered a sincere desire, they were able to set their minds straight. Having set their minds straight, they were able to cultivate their own moral character. Having cultivated their own moral character, they were able to bring their families to order. Having brought their families to order, they were able to bring order to their kingdoms. Having brought order to their kingdoms, the whole world would be at peace.

"Knowledge" must be integrated with "practice." From "inquiring into the properties of things, to carrying knowledge to the utmost degree," to "bringing order to their kingdoms and peace to the world" is a process of cognition and, more importantly, a process of moral practice. Man must have an ideal, and the highest ideal is to "achieve peace" and thus enable human society to attain a realm of "Great Harmony." The basic demand of a society of "great harmony" is that everyone should set for himself a demand, find a reason for his "being," and "not do to others what he does not wish done to himself." Said Confucius: "My way is consistent; it is nothing more than honesty and forbearance." Leading a life in this world, one should behave like a "man," enjoy the pleasure of "being a man" and appreciate the creation of the universe.

In order to have a genuine appreciation of the creation of the universe, one should have the ability to display human creativity, thus reproducing "the creation of the universe." One should display the spiritual realm of man--the why and how a man exists as a man--thereby making it possible for a writer to produce a "masterpiece," for a painting to be a "superb work," and for music to be the "sound of nature." Art requires "integration of feeling with scenery" whereby "feeling is generated amid scenery and scenery is generated amid feeling."

When one enters the realm of creation, one will reach a situation in which the true, the good, and the beautiful are integrated. There lies the meaning of life and the man's highest ideal. Confucius professed: "At the age of seventy, I can do everything as my heart pleases without violating the rule." What he described was probably a realm in which all one did and said was in harmony with the universe, human society, the others, and oneself, both body and mind, inside and outside. This realm of life is, of course, that of the saint.

In my opinion, traditional Chinese philosophy still bears the value of existence precisely because it tells us the way to be human. To be a man is by no means easy. It is even more difficult to be in harmony with nature, society, other people, and oneself in both body and mind, inside and outside. As this is a necessary requirement for life in today's world we cannot underestimate traditional Chinese philosophy; nor should we ignore where its value lies. However, precisely because traditional Chinese philosophy tells us only the reason for being a man, it is inappropriate for us to set undue demands upon it in other respects, nor should it come as a surprise that it is inadequate in certain areas. For example, it does not emphasize issues of logic and the theory of knowledge, nor does it provide a well-conceived demonstration of the structure of its own theory. We should not be overly critical of this.

Under such circumstances, can we further develop traditional Chinese philosophy while appreciating its value? We should and we can. The pre-Qin Dynasty Confucians, aside from the *Book of Changs*, seldom touched upon problems of ontology. Under the impact of Buddhism, however, neo-Confucians of the Song and Ming dynasties founded a very significant theory of ontology, which made great progress and became neo-Confucianism. As the mainstream of China's traditional philosophy, thinking and culture, Confucian philosophy today has sustained an even heavier impact than in the past. Having profoundly critiqued it, we are now reexamining its value. Is it inconceivable that we redevelop it once again; under the new impact could there not be established a new system with its own logic and theory of knowledge?

Traditional Chinese philosophy should have a third-phase of development because "one must have a reason for being a man." Whether or not this can be developed depends on whether or not it can establish for itself a new system of logic and theory of knowledge. "Man can enhance the Way; not the Way can enhance man": the outcome depends upon our efforts.

Peking University
 Beijing, People's Republic of China

CHAPTER III

LIU ZONGYUAN AND LIU YUXI THEORIES OF HEAVEN AND MAN

FANG LI-TIAN

A deeply philosophical debate concerning the relation between Heaven and man took place among the ideological elite early in the ninth century. Han Yu (768-824), a literati and thinker, provoked this debate by advocating the theory of Heavenly Decree (*Tian ming*). He held that people should be obedient to the Decrees of Heaven and submit themselves to the Will of Heaven (*Tian Yi*). The development and multiplication of humankind would be against Heaven and Earth since people's productive activity did harm to the primordial material force (*Yuanqi*) and broke the balance of *Yin* and *Yang*. His words warned mankind against immoderate multiplication of population and excessive exploitation of nature. Liu Zongyuan (773-819), another great literati and philosopher, wrote an article criticizing this position of Han Yu. Afterwards, Liu Yuxi (772-842), a poet and philosopher, came to write a treatise to supplement Liu Zongyuan's opinion. However, as Liu Zongyuan did not entirely agree with the supplement, he wrote to Liu Yuxi to express his dissent. Finally, Zong Mi (780-841), a Buddhist scholar belonging to both the Hua Yan and Chan schools, denied all the theories held by Han Yu, Liu Zongyuan and Liu Yuxi. In the chapter commenting upon "Doctrine Concerning Heaven and Man" in his famous work *A Treatise on Man*, Zong Mi used the Buddhist theory of principal and subsidiary causes to expose the conflict between the theory of Heavenly Decree and that of primordial material force, and enunciated his own solution to the problem of man's origin. Seven documents recording the above argument are extant:

(1) "Tian Shuo" or "A Speech on Heaven," by Liu Zongyuan;

(2) "Da Yuxi Tian Lun Shu" or "A Letter to Reply to Liu Yuxi's 'Treatise on Heaven'," by Liu Zongyuan;

(3) "Tian Dui" or "Answers to Questions on Heaven," by Liu Zongyuan;

(4) "Tian Lun" or "A Treatise on Heaven," by Liu Yuxi;

(5) "Yuan Ren" or "On Man," by Han Yu;

(6) "Yuan Dao" or "On Tao," by Han Yu;

(7) "Yuan Ren Lun" or "A Treatise on Man," by Zong Mi.

In our view, Liu Zongyuan and Liu Yuxi's explanations of the relationship between Heaven and man by and large are correct. The following is a commentary upon their conceptions in four parts.

HEAVEN AND MAN NEVER INTERVENE WITH EACH OTHER

Up to the Tang dynasty, the word "Tian" or Heaven in theoretical writings had three main meanings:

(1) A conscious and anthropomorphic God;
(2) The sky in contrast with the earth;
(3) The whole natural world including the earth.

In Liu Zongyuan's works "Heaven" often contrasts with the earth. For instance, he said, "That which is above and dark, people call 'Heaven', while that which is below and yellow, people call 'Earth'."[1] In Liu Yuxi's works, "Heaven" is used as a concept in contrast with man: "Heaven is the largest of those having forms; man is the most perfect of animals."[2]

Therefore the meaning of Liu Zongyuan's "Heaven" seems not unlike that of Liu Yuxi's considering their common point that Heaven implies, not God, but a physical thing, namely, the object of astronomical study. Speaking precisely, however, the meaning of Heaven in Liu Yuxi's works is wider, for it refers not only to heavenly principles and regulations, but also to man's physical constitution and power.

Liu Zongyuan asserted that "Heaven and man never intervene with each other," saying, "Both the production [of myriad things] and the happening of [natural] disasters are affairs of Heaven, while both [good government according to] laws and regulations and social disorder are affairs of man. They are obviously two kinds of things and go respectively on their own ways without interactions."[3] In other words, he emphasized that Heaven and man all have their positive and negative facets and that there is a strict line of demarcation between Heaven and man; hence each goes its own way without interaction. Furthermore, he said, "It is rather by our efforts than by the Decrees of Heaven that the unlucky is changed into the lucky and the unjustifiable transformed into the justifiable."[4] According to his point of view, the above-mentioned transformations are decided by the efforts of man and have nothing to do with the Decree of Heaven. His opinion was an objection to the theory of Heavenly Decree advocated by Han Hu, and also a dissent from Liu Yuxi's idea that Heaven and man predominate over each other in their respective spheres."

HEAVEN AND MAN PREDOMINATE OVER EACH OTHER IN THEIR RESPECTIVE SPHERES

Liu Yuxi was of the opinion that "A Speech on Heaven" by Liu Zongyuan had not yet completely elucidated all aspects of the relationship between Heaven and man; hence he wrote "A Treatise on Heaven" to discuss this relationship more deeply. Drawing for the first time a clear line of demarcation between the two major schools of thought concerning Heaven, he asserted that there were two approaches to Heaven in the world. One insisted on the "Providence" of Heaven (or Heaven as conscious) and on the "true and accurate interactions between Heaven and man"; the other stuck to the unconsciousness of Heaven, to the sharp difference between Heaven and man, and to the spontaneity and "absence of unnatural action" (Wu Wei) on the part of Heaven, which then, of course, had nothing to do with social affairs.

Liu Yuxi himself was against the former approach while in favor of the latter. Based on the recognition of the discrepancy between Heaven and man Liu Yuxi made his statement: "The capability of Heaven is to produce myriad things, while the capability of man is to govern them."[5] What Liu Yuxi called the "capability of Heaven" means the natural shift of the four seasons, the natural properties of metal, wood, water, fire, etc., the natural endowment of man--his physical constitution--and the natural change of his physical powers in accordance with his age. In short, "Heaven" means all the natural properties and the non-artificial conditions. What Liu Yuxi called the "capability of man" means the control, recognition and government of both the natural world and human society, namely, the capability of utilizing the four seasons, metal, wood, water, fire, and other natural things, and the capability of establishing various regulations and laws by which to govern society.

Therefore, on one hand, "Heaven always holds what it can do and thus looks down at those beneath: it is not that it has anything to do with [human] order or disorder. Man always holds what he can do and so looks up at Heaven: it is not that he has anything to do with the cold and heat."[6] In his opinion, Heaven by no means could change the social laws which determine whether the society is stable or not, nor could man vary the natural course of turn and return between the cold and heat, and the objective order that plants always sprout in the spring, grow in the summer, are harvested in the autumn and are stored in the winter. Therefore, Heaven and man do not intervene with one another.

On the other hand, "what Heaven can do is just what man certainly cannot: what man can do is just what Heaven cannot. Therefore, I (Liu Yuxi) say, 'Heaven and man predominate over each other in their respective spheres'."[7] Since the property of Heaven is different from that of man, Heaven in some spheres predominates over man, while man in other spheres predominates over Heaven. In this sense, it is not an absolute law that Heaven and man never intervene with each other.

In further explanation, Liu Yuxi said, "the way of Heaven manifests itself in production and generation; it functions through the predominance of the strong over the weak. The way of man manifests itself in laws and regulations; it functions through the discrimination of the right from the wrong (by rewarding the good and punishing the evil)."[8]

Liu Yuxi gave the following example: When a group of travellers come to a wilderness and want to rest under leafy trees and drink sweet spring water, the strong and powerful certainly will take precedence. When they come to a city and seek shelter under decorated eaves, and eat their fill from the sacrificial feasts, however, the sages and worthies will certainly take precedence. The former case should be called "predomination of Heaven" while the latter "predomination of man." Liu Yuxi opined that physical strength and power are endowed by Heaven, whereas sageness and worthiness are gained through ceremonies and righteousness. If the country which the travellers visit holds ceremonies and righteousness in reverence, he added, even when they come to the wilderness the case will not be unlike that in a city. But if the country which they visit neglects ceremonies and righteousness, even when they come to a city, the case will be the same as that in the wilderness.

This example shows that man can predominate over Heaven in some spheres, while Heaven can predominate over man in other spheres. What Liu Yuxi called "predomination of Heaven" implies the predomination of natural conditions, while "predomination of man" implies predomination of conditions gained through man's efforts. During travel, there are possibilities for the predomination of both Heaven and man in accord with changing circumstances.

By analogy, Liu Yuxi stated that, living in a stable society in which the laws, regulations and discrimination of the right from the wrong are evident, people will have no faith in the Decree of Heaven; this suggests the predomination of man over Heaven. Living in a disorderly society in which laws, regulations, and discrimination all lose their effects, people have to attribute their fate to the Heavenly principle; this suggests the predomination of Heaven over man.

To explain this, Liu Yuxi used another example: When a boat sails on small rivers, the people in the boat can easily grasp the natural regulations pertinent to sailing and hence can have them well in hand: this implies a predominance of man over Heaven. When the boat sails on large rivers where the natural regulations can hardly be recognized, the people in the boat will have to submit themselves to Heaven and its Decrees; this implies a predominance of Heaven over man.

This example suggests that both Heaven and man are restricted by certain stipulations (numbers) and tendencies. In some cases people can grasp them, but in other cases they cannot; this results in alternating the predominance of Heaven and man over one another.

Dissenting from Liu Yuxi's concept that Heaven and man predominate over each other in respective spheres, Liu Zongyuan criticized that Liu Yuxi failed to draw a clear demarcation between Heaven and man. In his opinion, both strength and sageness are within man's sphere, so that it is unacceptable to attribute the strength of man to Heaven. On the contrary, abolition of laws and regulations and the prevalence of disorder are purely human affairs which have nothing to do with Heaven. When people cannot recognize the regulations, the problem lies within themselves and it can not be said that Heaven has predominated over man. If the social disorders and people's ignorance of the natural regulations are regarded as a predomination of Heaven over man it will lead to the misunderstanding that Heaven has certain moral attributes and a mystic ability to reward or punish people.

Thus, Liu Zongyuan's definitions of Heaven and man, as well as his understanding of "predomination," differed from those of Liu Yuxi. Liu Zongyuan's emphasis upon the difference between Heaven and man and between social laws and natural regulations--as well as his emphasis upon the subject of humankind itself which can grasp and make use of the natural laws-- was reasonable. His over-emphasis on the contradiction between Heaven and man, however, was rooted in a latent mechanistic factor.

In contrast, Liu Yuxi failed to recognize that man's physical strength also includes his effort, and his relation of social disorder to the predomination of Heaven is liable to misunderstanding. These were the main shortcomings of his theory. His recognition of the correlation and interpenetration between Heaven and man, however, seems more comprehensive and profound than does Liu Zongyuan's concept. His observation that people will turn to the belief that the will of Heaven predominates over man when they cannot foresee their fate during social disorder or when they are subjected to Nature whose regulations they fail to grasp is, in fact, a correct identification of the social and epistemological roots of theism.

Had Liu Yuxi and Liu Zongyuan's theories complemented each other, the theoretical cognition of the relationship between Heaven and man in ancient China would have reached a new stage.

HEAVEN AND MAN MAKE USE OF EACH OTHER

Closely related to the concept that "Heaven and man predominate over each other in respective spheres," another concept, "Heaven and man make use of each other," was stated by Liu Yuxi, indicating that Heaven can make use of man while man can also make use of Heaven. In fact, however, Liu Yuxi laid emphasis on the latter alone, saying people "can use the heavenly advantages to establish the regulations of man"[9] and thereby make Heaven benefit humankind. For example, Heaven has both seasons favorable for plants to grow and seasons for withering them, water brings both the advantages of irrigation and the disaster of flooding, and fire contributes illumination but also damage from conflagrations. Through practice people have learned to take the advantages and avoid or gradually regulate the disadvantages--taking advantage of the spring and summer to sow and grow plants, and that of the autumn and winter to harvest and store them; using water for irrigation and fire for illumination.

The concept that "Heaven and man predominate over each other in respective spheres" represents the contradiction and struggle between man and Nature; this is but one aspect of the relationship between the two. The concept "Heaven and man make use of each other" represents the other aspect of the relationship, namely, that man and Nature are united and interdependent. As it kept in view both the contrast and the "correlation" between Heaven and man, Liu Yuxi's theory more comprehensively elucidated the dialectical relationship between humankind and Nature.

MAN'S PREDOMINATION OVER HEAVEN IS CERTAIN

In Liu Yuxi's opinion, though Heaven and man predominate over each other in respective spheres, the situations of the respective predominations are somehow different. He said, "Heaven's predomination over man is uncertain. Why? Because it is only when people cannot dominate their own fate that they attribute it to Heaven. On the contrary, man's predominance over Heaven is certain. Why? Because Heaven has no self-interest [to resist man's predominance], hence it is certain."[10] Contrasting with the unconsciousness of Heaven, man "is the most perfect of animals," "his wisdom is supreme." In addition, Liu Yuxi said, "It is the law by which man can predominate over Heaven."[11] The main reason for this is that he has established a system of regulations. Furthermore, through an analysis of the three possible social situations--(1) the system of regulations goes well, (2) the system is partly broken, or (3) the system is completely abolished--Liu Yuxi showed that how social regulations are carried out can decide not only whether the society is orderly or not, but also whether the theory of Heavenly Decree prevails or not. The above arguments explain how man necessarily can predominate over Heaven in view of the difference between man and other animals and Heaven.

Liu Zongyuan did not agree with Liu Yuxi's idea, saying, "Now that it (Heaven) does not want to compete with us, how then could we be said to 'predominate' over it"?[12] Liu Yuxi's statement that man predominates over Heaven gives "too much favor to man, but too much disfavor to Heaven."[13] Here Liu Zongyuan feared that an idealist error would result from the use of moral categories to discuss the relationship between Heaven and man.

CONCLUSION

The debate concerning the relationship between Heaven and man, which took place in the Mid-Tang dynasty in China, referred to a series of relations: between the Decree of Heaven and the power of man, between spontaneity and man's effort, between society and Nature, between social and natural properties, and between social laws and natural regulations. Of the very complicated arguments regarding these relations the most important ones were:

What was the real nature of Heaven?
What was the correct attitude of man towards Nature?
What was the reason for social disorder and how would the people's thought be influenced by it?

All of these are significant problems both philosophically and practically.

Insisting on the theory of Heavenly Decree, Han Yu fell into mysticism. In a sense, however, his pointing out that excessive exploitation of Nature deserved punishment was important. Liu Zongyuan objected to Han Yu's theory of Heavenly Decree, and disagreed with Liu Yuxi's concept that Heaven and man predominate over each other in their respective spheres. He emphasized that Heaven and man never intervene with each other. Liu Yuxi also objected to Han Yu's theory, while he praised Liu Zongyuan's concept that Heaven and man predominate in their respective spheres, that Heaven and man can make use of each other, and that man, the most wise, should necessarily predominate over the unconscious Heaven. It can be said with certainty that Liu Yuxi's main point of view is more comprehensive and profound, though he made his own mistakes.

From this concise analysis of the above scholars' theories on the relationship between Heaven and man there emerges the suggestion that there was indeed a basic line of demarcation between the right and the wrong among the ancient scholars whose concepts were sharply contradictory. Nevertheless, none of the contradictory concepts are mere nonsense. In other words, these concepts all have certain reasonable aspects which can be assimilated either simply or after some adjustment.

The sense of the history of this discussion on the relation between man and Nature is that as Nature supplies resources for human life man should exploit and make use of it. However, the exploitation cannot be thoughtless and excessive, but should be done with conservation and moderation. Man ought to transform the disadvantageous factors of nature into advantageous ones. This must be done in a scientific way in order that the natural environment be improved, not worsened. Therefore, the fundamental conclusion regarding the relationship between man and nature which should be drawn from the history of the question seems to be a combination of utilization and conservation, of exploitation and improvement.

People's University of China
 Beijing, China

NOTES

1. *A Speech on Heaven*, in *Collected Works of Liu Zongyuan* (Beijing: Zhong Hua Book Store, 1979), vol. 16, pp. 441-443.
2. *A Treatise on Heaven*, Part I, in *Collected Works of Liu Yuxi*, vol. 12, pp. 6-8.
3. *A Letter in Reply to Liu Yuxi's 'A Treatise on Heaven'*, in *Collected Works of Liu Zongyuan*, vol. 31, pp. 816-817.
4. *Collected Works of Liu Zongyuan*, vol. 2, pp. 65-67.
5. *A treatise on Heaven.*
6. *Ibid.*
7. *Ibid.*
8. *Ibid.*
9. *A Treatise on Heaven, Part III*, in *Collected Works of Liu Yuxi*, vol. 12, pp. 11-12.
10. *A Treatise on Heaven*, Part. II in *Collected Works of Liu Yuxi*, vol. 12, pp. 8-11
11. *A Treatise on Heaven.*
12. *A letter in Reply.*
13. *Ibid.*

CHAPTER IV

PARADIGMS OF NATURE IN WESTERN THOUGHT

KENNETH L. SCHMITZ

In the present condition of mankind, it is no longer possible to ignore the variety of human cultures and the potential of each to contribute to our common understanding. Cultural exchange presupposes mutual respect, of course, and calls for a growing appreciation of the special character of each culture and of what it can contribute to our shared humanity. The present colloquium is of the greatest interest, therefore, because it promises an exchange between philosophers situated in different cultural and social milieus.[1] Nevertheless, since it is best to speak of what one knows best, I will speak of the relation between man and nature as it has been understood in so-called "Western" societies and cultures.

I ought to say from the outset, however, that I find the equation often made between "modernity" and so-called Western ideas to be both premature and presumptuous. The resilience of some non-Western cultures today in the face of the pressures of what is called "modernization" indicates that the present and the future remain open to significant developments within a variety of cultures, and that no one present culture may lay claim to the whole future of mankind. My own remarks are offered, then, as a modest contribution to our common reflection.

The way in which a society relates to the natural world both expresses its life-situation as a whole and shapes that situation. Now, I take metaphysics to be the most comprehensive and fundamental study of the whole scope of reality, and so I find that the relation between man and nature has metaphysical significance. The specific question to be considered in this essay, then, may be put into metaphysical terms as follows: Is there at present in *Western* society and culture a basic, comprehensive understanding or dominant *paradigm* of the relation between man and *nature*? In putting the question in these general terms, I hope that it can be adapted to other social, cultural and individual backgrounds.

Before beginning, however, several terms need to be clarified. By the short-hand term "Western," I mean the societies of Eastern and Western Europe, South and North America, and of Australasia, as well as some parts of the Middle East and a few enclaves throughout the world. Moreover, I use the term not only to indicate ideas and values rooted in the *present-day*

Euro-American cultures, but also to refer to ideas and values which have their original source in several earlier civilizations, societies and cultures of the Mediterranean basin. These civilizations no longer exist as such, but they do form the basis for later Western civilization. The earliest stratum of this basis is formed by two of the original civilizations: by Mesopotamia (including Sumeria and subsequent societies) and by Ancient Egypt.[2] Until recent archaeological explorations, these early Mediterranean civilizations were very imperfectly known, except through the Hebrew Bible, whose materials reach back to about 1400 B.C. (before Christ). The influence of these ancient, non-extant civilizations is, therefore, largely implicit and indirect, but nonetheless real.

On the other hand, the next stratum or stage of Western culture--the Hebraic and the Hellenic--has been explicit in two ways. First of all, the Biblical narrative has been enormously influential; it has continued to shape Western society through the Christian understanding of the New and Old Testaments, as well as through the continuing presence of Judaism in the West and the indebtedness of the medieval West to Islam. Secondly, the civilizations of early and classical Greece, and of Republican and Imperial Rome, as well as of the Hellenistic culture of Asia Minor, have been, along with the Bible, part of the *actual memory* operative in the formation of Western Euro-American culture. For that memory reaches back by way of the *Psalms* of David, and the poetry of Homer and Hesiod into the second millennium B.C. In sum, the twin influences of Biblical religion and Greek philosophy, drama and literature have become inseparable from and constitutive of the Euro-American cultures. Indeed, they have been the main, even though not the only, pillars upon which later ideas, values and orientations were consciously developed. Or, to change the metaphor, Israel, Greece and Rome provided initial and enduring patterns on the basis of which later events and personalities, material forces of production and spiritual energies have been, and continue to be, woven in order to constitute the fabric of later Western societies and cultures. The use of the term "Western", then, contains three stages: the most ancient is implicit, the next is explicit, and the third is its present modern form.

By "nature" or the "natural world" I mean to include living as well as non-living things, and humankind itself insofar as it is a part of nature. I say, "insofar as humankind is a *part* of nature," for Western culture is characterized by a tension between humanity and nature, which has been brought about by two sources. The first source of tension is the Biblical understanding that humankind is made in the image and likeness of

God, and has, therefore, a certain transcendence about it; and secondly, by the stance of disengagement brought about by Greek discourse. This double tension has been at the origin of much of Western culture's energy for good and for ill. For good, insofar as mankind assumes responsibility as steward of nature, or more rarely (as with St. Francis of Assisi) takes nature as its companion; but for ill, insofar as it has thought of itself as absolute master of nature and destined to dominate it by force.

By "paradigms" I do not mean patterns of thought which depict the natural world by a direct isomorphism, as would a scale model. Indeed, in that sense these basic paradigms are not direct models at all, but are more like what have been called indirect or analogue models.[3] The paradigms I have in mind are primarily and properly contexts, elaborated by thought, for the interpretation of nature. They do not picture the world so much as give direction within it and in relation to it. These basic ways of understanding nature touch upon all aspects of human life,--social, cultural and spiritual as well as physical and biological; for these paradigms are rooted in an even more fundamental orientation towards reality itself, an orientation that gives them their metaphysical importance. Moreover, it is characteristic of dominant paradigms of nature that they can captivate the intelligence and imagination of society as a whole for a very long time.

Every society and culture has one or more dominant conceptions which set forth the relation of man to nature, or within nature.[4] Now, given its complex and variegated beginnings, it is not surprising that there have been several basic paradigms of nature within Western society itself. Undoubtedly, there are common characteristics in these various paradigms that mark them as distinctively Western,[5] but their differences are equally important. Several conceptions of the relation of man to nature have gained the status of eminent paradigms, though not without competition from concurrent alternative paradigms. Nevertheless, these eminent paradigms have set the agenda of things to be done and of thought for centuries at a time. Some of these conceptions are still attractive to many individuals and groups within Western societies. For that reason, as well as for their intrinsic meaning, they are important resources to be used creatively and critically in the examination, re-direction or transformation of existing trends.

What is more, not only have there been several paradigms of the relation of man to nature in Western society in the past, there is some evidence that Western attitudes towards the natural world are in flux today. As a result, several older conceptions have once again become "live options," or at least significant resources, for the current discussion about the "nature of nature." I mean that no single conception of nature at present holds the Western intelligence and imagination *completely* in its grip. The West seems to be in a period of transition in this regard. Indeed, several older conceptions show a resilient staying power and may even have the capacity to help re-formulate a fresh paradigm of nature.

It is the aim of this paper to sketch broadly and generally the character of four basic conceptions of nature which have been dominant or eminent paradigms in Western society; and to do this in order critically to assess the problems and opportunities facing Western societies and cultures today in regard to the relation between man and the natural world. Using a very broad brush, then, I shall consider the following five paradigms: (i) from the Greek, that of *physis* (or physical nature); (ii) from the Latin, that of *natura* (or nature); (iii) from the French, that of *la nature* (or the system of nature as a machine); and (iv) from the German, that of *die Natur* (or the system of nature as an organism). To this I would add a current paradigm: hominization. The linking of a particular language and culture with each of the paradigms may seem somewhat artificial a mnemonic device. Nevertheless, it is true that each paradigm is in fact associated rather closely with the designated language and culture, without in any way being its sole possessor. Thus, for example, the French (e.g. Descartes, de la Mettrie, D'Holbach and Condillac) gave clear expression to the philosophical underpinnings of mechanism; but, of course, it remained to the English genius, Isaac Newton, to present it as a full-fledged "System of Nature." Moreover, in his great work, he brought together the achievements of Polish, Danish and Italian astronomers and physicists (Copernicus, Kepler and Galileo, respectively). In a word, these paradigms were by no means insulated from mutual influence, development, alteration and transformation. Still, each of the four represents a rather stable *core intuition* into the nature of reality and of the relation between man and the natural world within that reality.[6] So much, then, by way of introduction. Now, I shall consider each of the four paradigms in their chronological order.

A COSMOLOGICAL PARADIGM

I turn first to the Greek conception of *physis*. Greek culture originally expressed its understanding of man and nature in the mythical and poetic terms of cosmogony and theogony. The Greek mythical heritage was from the beginning a mixture of quite diverse sources and versions, myths of nature, of society and of the gods and was formed out of the experience of quite diverse racial stocks. In a very influential composite version (Hesiod's *Theogony*, 700 B.C.), the darker divinities of the under world and the gods of the upper-world took shape through the mythic imagination as vague personifications which at the same time were thought of as different regions of the world: *Gaia*, the earth goddess, was both the earth and yet a goddess; *Ouranos*, the sky-god, was both god of the sky and the very sky itself; *Okeanos* was a kind of personification of the fast-flowing river that bounded the solid earth; and *Chronos* was both crafty, shadowy Titan and relentless principle of division (time itself).

Through this mytho-poetic process of representation an ordered whole took shape; out of a latent Ur-*chaos* there emerged a *Cosmos*. This primordial sense of order must not be thought of as a merely theoretical, "value neutral" description. On the contrary, the early expressions of it in Hesiod, in the Attic tragedians and in the earliest Greek philosophers included what today we might call--too precisely perhaps--moral and aesthetic concerns as well as metaphysical and scientific ones. Thus, for example, Anaximander rebukes things for staying too long lest they offend justice (*dike*), and Parmenides deprecates motion, difference and plurality as unworthy of genuine being (*on*).

But there was also incipient rationality in this value-laden cosmos of the poets and philosophers. Rationality has its own history in other cultures, such as in the Chinese and in the Indian; in Greece, it took shape as *logos*. By *logos* I mean a twofold process of *conceptualization* or concept-formation and of *objectification* by which the thinker and speaker gained a certain "distance" from his or her immediate absorption in the world, while at the same time remaining physically involved in it. This process of *logos* took form in Greece from the eighth century B.C.E. and soon developed a fourfold pattern of rational discourse: in philosophy (concerning being), in mathematics (concerning number), in history (concerning temporal actions). and in linguistics (concerning grammar, logic and rhetoric). Now, this "logical" or "rational" view of cosmic order arose with the adaptation of Phoenician writing and with the formation of a unique social institution: the *polis*, which is neither a city in our sense nor a state in our sense. Moreover, this incipient rationality (*logos*) remains fixed in the cultural memory of Western society and provides it with an initial understanding of nature as *cosmos*. As *cosmos* the universe is understood to be the ordered arrangement of the various regions, parts, elements and forces of a totality which is to be analyzed and explained in terms of principles and causes (*archai*) and (*aitiai*). In sum, the cosmos is accounted for by means of rational discourse; and rationaldiscourse is the *logos* of the *cosmos*, in a word: *cosmology*.[7]

Among the various understandings of nature presented by the Greek philosophers, including those of Pythagoras, the Atomists, Plato and the Stoics, the most influential for later cultures is arguably that of Aristotle. What caught his attention about nature was, first of all, its movement, its change, its coming to be and passing away. And he gave to all of physical nature just this paramount name: *physis*. and to its study was given the name *physike*.[8] The word comes from *phuo*, meaning: to bring forth, to produce, to cause to grow; also: to generate, to beget; but also: to be formed in a certain way, to have a definite shape or structure or constitution. Aristotle thought of this structured unfolding (*physis*) as an inborn dynamic feature of things. According to Aristotle each thing possesses within itself its own orientation (*telos*) towards realizing its nature, and each thing comes to be by nature (*kata physin*) insofar as it comes to be in accordance with the natural order of the cosmos. This natural order stands in contrast with what comes about either by positive human decree (*kata nomon*), or by violence or chance (*tyche*), i.e. accidentally. Chance, however, is not due to the absence of causes but to their conflict. The opposite of natural order, then, disorder, comes about either by vice or by chance. This basic paradigm of ordered movement underlies the Aristotelian doctrine of the four causes (the productive or efficient, the constitutive or formal, the material or elemental, and the final or teleological); and it underlies the doctrines of the four elements (earth, air, fire and water), of the fifth element (aether), and of the orientation of all movement towards the imitation (*mimesis*) of the separated intelligences (*noesis noeseos*).

Greek culture was possessed of a fine sense of limit, not least in their tragic sense awakened by its transgression. The Greek ideal of virtue was moderation ("nothing in excess"); and tragedy for them came about through an action--committed either knowingly (e.g. Antigone) or unknowingly (e.g. Oedipus)--which exceeds the limit set for mortal beings (*thnete physis*: mankind, those born to die). Among artefacts we still admire Greek sculpture and architecture for its vibrant symmetry. Finally, their concept of nature expressed a just sense of the due proportion and limitation of things, a cosmic order already pre-determined in its fundamental character by the causes which make it up. Indeed, so firmly did the Greeks embrace the principle of limit, that it may well have prevented them from fashioning a political union beyond that of a loose and warring set of independent, small city-states.

A THEOLOGICAL PARADIGM

For the ancient Greeks, then, nature was the field of limited, well-proportioned beings; indeed, even the gods were limited in shape and power. It may seem surprising, therefore, to insist that the ancient Greeks with their emphasis upon limit knew nothing of what the medieval Latin Christians spoke of as *finitude*. Nevertheless, it is true that the terms "limited" and "finite" are not, strictly speaking, synonymous.[9]

In order to translate what is *limited* (ancient Greek: *horos, peras*; ancient Latin: *finis*) into what is *finite (esse finitum)*, one must take up a position that is at once both "beyond" the finite and "within" it. Such a position is assumed originally as the faith-response to a divine revelation, in which the finite believer is placed by grace within the infinite horizon of the divine life itself. For the revelation is taken to disclose an eternal, personal being, who is no part of the created world, not even its highest part;[10] and *for that very reason* this infinite being is the intimate and necessary continuing support of all finite being. To use the technical terms: in relation to nature God is at once and *through the same relation* both transcendent and immanent, but he is immanent because he is transcendent.[11]

This paradoxical position is at the root of the second paradigm, according to which nature is viewed as *creation*. While the second paradigm does, indeed, draw upon the Greek and Roman heritage, its principal source is Biblical religious faith. If the ancient Greek paradigm is cosmological, the medieval Latin paradigm is theological: at its center is the personal God, who is the creative source and providential lord of all that exists, and without whose active sustenance nothing would exist. In Europe the form of this paradigm is predominantly Christian, but it also has its Judaic and Islamic parallels. It continued as the dominant, and all but exclusive, paradigm for almost 1500 years during the European Middle Ages, from about 300 A.D. (anno Domini, from the beginning of the Christian era) to about 1800 A.D. Indeed, it is still a remarkably powerful paradigm in the West, though it has been in contention for the past two or three centuries with more recent paradigms associated with the European Enlightenment. While its central insights are religious, it inspires an extraordinary intensity of rational speculation, and has borne remarkable fruit in philosophy, science, social organization, and art.

In the 17th century A.D., towards the end of the period of the exclusive dominance of this second paradigm, René Descartes helped to launch what came to be known as "modern" philosophy. "Modern" philosophy is supposed to be the work of an autonomous reason, separated rigorously from Christian theology.

Nevertheless, an historian of Western thought[12] has pointed out that Descartes was concerned about ideas which were quite unknown to the ancient Greek philosophers, but which he had taken over from medieval thought: and especially the idea of an infinite, omnipotent, omniscient, wholly free personal Being, who creates the world out of nothing except his own power and love (*creatio ex nihilo*).[13] According to this theological paradigm, then, the very being of the natural world (as well as of man) is completely dependent upon a Creator who brings it into being out of nothing (*ex nihilo*).

It is this lack of ultimate resources within nature itself that sets it off as not merely limited but as actually *finite*. In place of an eternal, unbegotten and self-sufficient cosmos, nature is at once both poorer (when considered in itself alone) than the Greek cosmos, yet richer than it by far (because its very being is sustained and suffused by the presence of the divine Glory to it). On the one hand, the natural world is not self-sufficient, but has to be begotten (*natura* from *nascitur*: to be born, to emerge from, to come to be); on the other hand, it is born of an infinitely glorious parentage. As a consequence, nature is perceived to have an interiority and depth of which the ancient Greeks were unaware, and also a touch of infinity that transcends the limits of the Greek cosmos. Man, too, made in the image of the infinite Creator takes up his stewardship over such a nature: creature facing creature within the divine creative abundance.

Out of this encounter between God, man and nature have come significant philosophical conceptions, such as: a new sense of wonder, bearing upon the question of existence as such; the conception of person as the highest embodiment of being; the consequent conviction that nature being created by the divine person was meant to sustain personal values; and a new sense of human liberty and human possibility. With the help of rational discourse, this paradigm brought to the fore the philosophical questions of the origin of the universe (Why anything at all? Why not rather nothing?), the fundamental nature of being (the primacy of existence: *actus essendi*), the status of nature (as a created world receiving its being through its relation to God), and the tension between the determinations of nature and the limited freedom of man (the problem of nature and history).

THE GENERAL CONCEPT OF SYSTEM AND MECHANISM

Nevertheless, although Descartes owed much to the medieval paradigm which preceded him,[14] he also played a role in the formation of a new very general paradigm which emerged in European society during the 16th and 17th centuries. It drew upon conceptions and motivations in the first two paradigms, but--in conjunction with certain religious, socio-economic and political changes,[15] and in association with certain cultural, scientific and philosophical developments--this new paradigm reached its definitive formulation in the conception of nature as a *system*.

Now, the ancient meaning of *systema* was that of a composition or arrangement of elements or parts which formed a whole (cf. Lucretius: *concilium*, assemblage). The modern sense of system has a stronger coherence, however, for it takes a system to be a whole in which the reality and significance of the parts consists principally in their function within the whole. This added power operative within the modern conception is undoubtedly due in part to the determining role played by mathematics in the formation of the modern conception of system. For its completion, the modern conception of system required the explicit formulation of a mathematically systemic concept of space, to be followed eventually by a systemic understanding of time. The work of Newton contributed greatly to such an undertaking, and Kant's conception of an architectonic system[16] certainly gave articulation to the stronger modern conception.

To be sure, the melding of mathematics and physics in the study of nature was not unknown in ancient and medieval times, especially in those circles influenced by the atomism of Epicurus and the idealizations of Plato; but it took the form of an unprecedented collaboration in the 16th and 17th centuries. The need for a more unified conception undoubtedly arose also in order to accommodate the modern demand for experimental control in scientific enquiry, a control to which mathematics lent its precision. Moreover, the mathematization of the conception of system provided an idealization that served the anthropocentric turn which has been so influential in modern Europe from the Renaissance period onwards. Indeed, along with a genuine theoretical interest among scientists and philosophers (many of whom were practicing scientists), the study of nature was often justified practically for the sake of a higher utility: the "commodity," "commodiousness," or "comfort" of humankind (thus, for example, Descartes, Bacon, and Hobbes).[17] And so, the unprecedented *mathematization* of science and technology, as well as the related effort to *control* the conditions of enquiry, served the theoretical and practical aims of the *anthropocentric* turn and led to the formation of the specifically modern, stricter sense of system. The modern systemic paradigm has played an important role in the modern West over the past three centuries, but during that period it has taken shape in two quite different versions.

The early modern investigation of nature in the 16th and 17th centuries took place under the hegemony of mathematical astronomy and physics, and more precisely of mechanics; so that the first versions of the paradigm were mechanistic. The term *"mechanism"* expresses the initial intuition and conviction that nature is best interpreted when viewed as a "machine," albeit an extraordinary one. By extension, then, the term designates a general *philosophical* position that understands the natural world to be a system produced by more or less discrete particles of matter, existing in space and time, and moving in accordance with deterministic physical laws. It was the dual task of science to discover the fundamental units of reality and the laws which govern them and to present the whole in the form of a system. The classical statement of the mechanistic system was given by Isaac Newton in *The Mathematical Principles of Natural Philosophy*. Although he voiced caution about taking his account as the final and fundamental reading of reality, it has served just such a metaphysical purpose for many scientists and non-scientists in the West during the past three centuries. Now because modern mechanism is more cohesive (through the power of its systemic laws) than ancient atomism (with its blind necessity), one of the achievements of modern mechanistic systems has been to contain randomness, which was gradually rendered more explicable (more rational or reasonable) by the laws of probability. The system, then, presents nature as a totality of discrete units externally related to one another in space and time in accordance with mathematically formulated laws.

A SECOND SYSTEMIC PARADIGM: ORGANICISM

Although the mathematization of nature proceeded brilliantly in the spheres of physics, astronomy, chemistry and cognate fields, nevertheless its mechanistic formulations seemed less satisfactory when applied to the sphere of biology proper (as distinct, that is, from bio-chemistry). And so an alternative, non-mechanistic version of the system of nature came to the fore about two centuries ago. Of course, its roots lay more broadly and deeply in the cultural traditions of the West, as, for example, in the various conceptions of the world-soul (*anima mundi*). More recently, it was also discernible in Leibniz and certain Scholastics in the later 17th and the 18th centuries as a kind of residual Aristotelianism. And it even assumed a quasi-scientific form as "vitalism," though the latter did not meet with wide acceptance among scientists. In the face of the fragmentation brought about by the very success of mechanism, however, poets, philosophers and others sought to express a more intimate degree of unity in nature than mechanism represented. Among these thinkers was Goethe, poet, philosopher and amateur scientist. But, for the most part, the poets were Romantics, and the philosophers were Idealists. They deliberately sought to recover the sense of the immanent unity of nature found in the ancient Greek cosmological paradigm by translating the Greek cosmos into modern systematic form. Some even went so far as to rehabilitate the Platonic notion of the world-soul.

Against mechanism they argued that, although life *can* be interpreted in mechanical principles, it *cannot* be reduced to them without losing what is distinctive about life. Positively, they argued that, if nature is the all-inclusive system from which and within which all that is takes its origin and plays out its existence, then nature must include within itself *all* of the resources for generating modes of being higher than that of bodies moving mechanistically in space. They argued that, as the source of all that is, nature must include within itself life in all of its multiple forms and levels: vegetal and self-reproductive, animal and sensitive, human and rationally conscious. In a word, if nature is the source of various forms of life, it must be understood in organic terms: the alternative to mechanism, then, is to represent the system of nature according to the paradigm of *organicism*. Thus, in *Ideas on a Philosophy of Nature*, Schelling claims that the idea of nature as a self-enclosed purposive totality arises in us out of the necessity of thought.[18]

The paradigm of nature as a sort of "super-organic" unity represents nature as a more integrated system than that of mechanism, with its loose collectivity of law-governed particulars related to one another functionally and contextually (i.e., operating upon one another externally in space and successively in time in accordance with the system of laws). In the organicist paradigm, on the other hand, the individual beings of nature are bound to one another by deep, internal relations, for they receive their meaning and reality from their membership within nature as a whole. This emphasis upon unity and harmony has proven attractive to those who find in it an anti-dote for excessive pre-occupation with individualism. Above all, they find in the organicist paradigm a key to the harmony between man and nature that is obscured, if not lost outright, by the exaggerated dualism so pronounced in the modern West. This dualism was expressed by the Kantian antinomies between sense and intellect, appearance and reality, necessity and freedom, faith and reason, and also by the antinomies of mind and body, individual and community, man and nature.

The organicist version of the third paradigm has proven more attractive to literary and humanist scholars than to scientists and technologues; this provides at least some basis for what the British novelist, C. P. Snow, called "the two cultures."[19] The one "culture" is scientific and technological, and is cultivated mostly by scientists, mathematicians and engineers; the other "culture" is literary and humanistic, and is cultivated mostly by scholars, writers and artists. Although somewhat overdrawn, this rough division within Western culture as a whole is not entirely inaccurate.

A CURRENT PARADIGM: HOMINIZATION?[20]

The present situation of Western society, however, is more complex and transitional; for it exhibits a certain ambivalence regarding the role of scientific technology in shaping man's relation to nature. In place of the indiscriminately positive attitude that has generally inspired public confidence in science and technology over the past three centuries in the West, many people now look upon scientific technology as an endeavour that produces serious new *problems* as well as *solutions* to old ones. Except for a few earlier prophetic voices, mostly philosophical, the first great shock to the public mind undoubtedly came with the contribution of "pure" science to the production and deployment of the atomic bomb. The confidence of many (including not a few scientists) in the purported "innocence" of modern scientific enquiry was shaken by this collaboration. Despite the long-standing symbiosis between modern Western society and scientific technology, some scientists (along with others) have organized groups for reflection upon the possibilities for good *and* evil that are implicit in basic and applied research. Among non-scientists, some current expressions of mistrust even suggest the possibility of an irrational reaction against scientific technology on a broad front, not wholly unlike that of the Luddites of early industrial times. Of course, if such a sudden reaction were to become general, it would greatly disrupt Western society, since it has committed itself so single-mindedly to reshaping the human relation to nature by means of the present scientific technology.

The notion of continuous progress has been rightly challenged in some spheres of human life, such as that of art, but there is no denying that over the long history of mankind there has been gradual *technical* progress. The precarious stance of early man was one of adaptation to the environment. Relatively primitive traditional technologies usually strove for a prudent relation between man and nature, if only because the limits of human survival had to be carefully observed and the demands of nature respected. Only gradually, here and there, were human groups able to emancipate themselves progressively from immediate and direct domination by nature. This seeming emancipation came about technically in pre-historical times through the control of fire, the cultivation of plants, the domestication of animals, and through the exploitation of minerals, chemicals and inorganic forces. Further technical development occurred in historical times. In the past three centuries, however, the basic process has been greatly accelerated. Industrialization has been propelled by a technology guided by modern scientific research; and this technology has thereby achieved an insistent momentum. The momentum has produced an almost *exponential* increase of human power over nature; so that we can speak without exaggeration today of a radical *shift* in the immemorial relationship between man and nature.

What has happened is that there has been a transformation and re-emergence of the first (mechanistic) version of the systemic paradigm, but in the form of a new technology. Now, like the first version (mechanism), this new technology addresses itself above all to the inorganic levels of nature. It is, therefore, a return to physics, and to a technology based upon physics, but not a return to Newtonian physics. It is rather a turn to the physics of electronic forces and chemical energies, drawing upon the elementary particles and field theory of sub-atomic physics. Interestingly, a number of theoretical physicists are attempting to reformulate the contemporary post-Newtonian physics in non-mechanistic, holistic terms, such as the concept of "implicate order" in the work of David Bohm.[21] In biology, there are attempts to re-introduce a limited version of the teleological principle within a more holistic approach to the study of life. Nonetheless, the formal language of the sciences remains mathematical, and the inorganic realm of particles and fields continues to contribute the formative materials to the new paradigm for man's relation to nature.

One of the most notable applications of contemporary *physics* to technology has been made, of course, in the development of nuclear energy, along with the development of electronic systems, telecommunications, computers, automation and space exploration. All of these take their origin from sub-atomic physics. Perhaps the most notable technical application of *chemistry* is in the combination of fertilizers and insecticides which has revolutionized food production; but the development of food preservatives and additives is closely associated with the processing and marketing of that food. In *biology*, one is struck by the rapid strides taken in bio-genetics, at first in the breeding of domesticated animal stock by artificial insemination, and more recently by the applications of certain techniques to human reproduction. In *medicine*, new medicaments, organ transplants, by-pass surgery and the like have succeeded in all but eradicating some diseases, reducing others, and generally prolonging life. These remarkable achievements of scientific technology have transformed the lives of individuals and the fabric of society, and their genuine contribution to human well-being must not be under-estimated.

At the same time, as with all rapid social change, they also have brought about new problems and reactions. Nuclear energy has brought with it not only the possibility of genocide and the malfunction of power plants, but also the problem of the disposal of nuclear wastes. Even more drastically perhaps, the chemical revolution has produced not only regional pollution, but also the possibility of global pollution, including the weakening of the protective ozone layer about the earth, acid rain, deforestation, and soil erosion. In medicine, the very success in prolonging life has led to problems of aging; new medicaments often enough have side-effects; drug-resistant strains of viruses develop, and stubborn low-grade infections make their appearance in hospitals. A complex of causes has led to the withdrawal of productive land to meet the insistent pressures of urbanization and conurbation. The list of problems and negative phenomena can be extended further. Because the problems are too complex and pervasive to be solved by traditional technologies, a simple return to less developed technologies seems neither wise nor likely. In the face of this ambivalence of scientific technology, it is not surprising that practices and social movements have developed, ranging from critical concern to outright rejection of certain technological developments.

I have spoken of an exponential increase in human power over nature. Nevertheless, it is important not to over-state the case. Nature can still inflict great damage upon puny man: through storm and flood, fire and drought, plague and pollution. What is more, in any contest between man and nature, nature will be the ultimate victor, since it can survive in some fashion even if all life is destroyed, even if mankind mismanages *itself* to death. But the special state of nature which is the support and companion of humankind what we usually think of when we speak of "nature" *must now receive protection from mankind itself*, if only to ensure the continuation of human life. We have been moving not only in the West but on a planetary scale across a threshold, towards an increase in technological power that is putting humankind in a *qualitatively different relation to technical power itself*. In an increasing number of ways nature itself has become dependent upon humankind for its present "habitable" condition. It is now no exaggeration to speak of nature itself, i.e. in the present condition in which it can support human life, as being held in jeopardy by mankind. Of course, this means that mankind holds its own life hostage in its uncertain hands. The relation between humankind and nature is rapidly becoming, and in some aspects already is, one whose basic quality is to be determined by what mankind will do or fail to do.

It is not too much to speak of the present shift as a *reversal* in the age-old relation of man to nature. For better and for worse, and within the ultimate limits set by nature, a new reciprocity has begun to emerge in which more and more of the regions and processes of nature are subject to human power, and in which the initiative is passing over from nature to man. We may be in transition, therefore, to a new paradigm which as I have suggested might be fittingly called: *hominization*. Unlike the previous paradigms which situated human life within nature, hominization places the significance of nature as habitable within the concerns of human life. The new paradigm tends to center its attention primarily (though not exclusively) upon the natural world of our planet.[22] The danger in the new situation is that the horizon of concern may be drawn too narrowly and may center too exclusively upon immediate human concerns.

What is called for is a broader and less self centered attitude towards nature, which values it in and for itself as well as for its service to humankind. The term "hominization" is not meant to promote a sense of human power, but to call us to a new sense of responsibility. For it requires us to recognize human power within a larger context in which nature is not thought of primarily as either an enemy to be conquered or as a mere slave to every human desire. Instead, it calls us to break free of the slavery of the master-slave attitude toward nature, in which we are supposedly master and nature our slave. It calls upon us to place technical knowledge (*techne*) at the service of wiser modes of knowing (*sophia*). It is just here that reflection upon the earlier paradigms can provide the West with the possibilities for enlarging and deepening the scope of this new paradigm, for example, through further studies of the nature of space and time, and of the nature of life, as well as through reflection upon the ultimate questions of origin and destiny.[23] It is here that we can still learn from older paradigms in orienting ourselves towards nature: *inexorability* from a cosmic order, *trans-human values* from a created world, *pre-human stability* from mechanism and the *insistent recursiveness* of life from organicism.

Certain current movements of concern in Western society manifest this new sense of responsibility and take on added significance when interpreted according to the paradigm of hominization. Thus, for example, the preservation of endangered wild species of animals. For some time now, there have been conservationist groups interested in reforestation, preservation of wet lands and sanctuaries, and the protection of endangered species. But perhaps the paradigm of hominization is most strikingly illustrated by the programs which seek to save certain species of animals by breeding them in zoos, with the intention of keeping them there, or of releasing them if their habitation still exists. An even more striking illustration of the reversal of the relation between man and nature is afforded by the establishment in northern Canada of wilderness parks. These are quite different from the domesticated "wildparks" of 18th century European aristocrats, for the new wilderness parks are vast areas from which humans are excluded except under strictly controlled conditions. This is an ironic reversal, since the very concept of "wilderness" is precisely of a region in which man has no proper place and in which *he* would stand in need of protection, whereas the concept of "wilderness parks" is, on the contrary, that of a region that *itself* stands in need of protection by man from man.

A related phenomenon is that of social movements concerned with the "rights" of animals. Of course, the domestication of animals is an ancient practice. It consists in assimilating a few amenable kinds of animals to the purposes and conditions of human living. The relationship has often been characterized by a high degree of utility, but it is not uncommon for there to emerge elements of trust and even of affection between master and animal. In the last several centuries, however, the concept of pets has become widespread, i.e., of animals kept purely as household companions, without serving the utilitarian functions of farm animals, watch dogs, etc. No doubt the association with animals as pets has contributed to the formation of associations for the protection of animals, beginning with the various "humane" societies. (These are societies for the prevention of cruelty to animals, but which were initially for the prevention of cruelty to children as well, especially against industrial abuse.) More recently, however, social and even political movements have arisen, such as the Greens in Germany, or the Greenpeace movement; while others have organized to secure the protection of what has come to be known as "animal rights." Some of the latter have taken a very strong stand against the use of animals in medical research, even going so far as to release animals from their cages or laboratories, so that a conflict is dramatized between the perceived needs of medical research and the perceived rights of the objects of that research.

The paradigm of hominization and the concomitant sense of responsibility seems to function in the West today within two limiting principles. First, as already mentioned, there is the growing caution that technological successes may well be attended by new problems, so that there are few problems which are solved absolutely, without residue. Relative success is thought to be attained if the new problems (e.g. medical side-effects of a cure) are less serious than the problem solved. But there is a recognition that the new problems may well be of a different order (e.g. chemical fertilizers increase specific crop production but may cause long term pollution). At times the new problems are more difficult to resolve than the original ones they "solved" (e.g. the increase in food-production through a reduction of mortality may be attended by an increasing population-density).

The second limiting principle within which hominization functions is the growing awareness that, not only the technological development that results from basic research, but research itself is socially determined in important ways. Science and technology do not operate in a vacuum, but are the joint product of technical, social, economic and political forces. For this latter reason, in addition to building upon recent scientific and technical achievements, the paradigm of hominization must make room within itself for ethical concerns.[24] Further, it must provide for continuing study of the cultural and historical past of the society within which public policy is being made regarding scientific research and technological development: ignorance of the past foreshortens our concern for the future.

As in most human affairs, there are moderate and immoderate actions. What is clear, however, is that the increased pressure upon the earth's resources is not likely to be solved by the renunciation of the positive possibilities inherent in the new knowledge once it is placed in the service of wiser human attitudes. Nostalgia for past ways is tempting, but it is no general solution. What is best in these current phenomena is not an effete sentimentalism, but a new sense of responsibility in the face of what seems to be a reversal in the traditional relation between man and nature. This calls for the courage to see through and beyond the problems in order to realize the opportunities in the new knowledge. To the degree that a reversal is actually at work in the contemporary situation, the paradigm of hominization gives these disparate phenomena a coherence and suggests to human beings certain lines of action.

The danger inherent in the paradigm of hominization is that it may settle too narrowly and functionally upon what constitutes "livable" nature, and too immediately upon present needs and wants. The value of the older paradigms is that they suggest that the "fragile complicity" between man and nature can be preserved and nourished only on two conditions: first that something of the vastness of the mechanistic and the intimacy and mutuality of the organicist systems can be incorporated into the paradigm of hominization; and second that the priority of nature to man in the cosmic paradigm and the transcendence and tension between man and nature in the paradigm of creation inspire humankind to a genuine respect for, and reciprocity with, nature. Hominization will deteriorate into one more form of human *hubris* unless technical power is subordinated to the metaphysical, social and ethical good of humankind as a whole.

Finally, to the extent that the achievements and problems have a global impact, the question and its answer cannot be confined to Western society. It remains to the West to look into its own resources for a reflection upon the relation, and to look with hope to other societies and cultures for their contribution to resolving this unprecedented challenge to all humankind.

Trinity College
University of Toronto

NOTES

1. The present version of this paper has benefitted from the general discussion which followed its presentation, and among others from the remarks of Professors Li and Tang Yi-jie (China), Tomonobu Imamichi (Japan), Margaret Chatterjee (India) and George McLean (USA).

2. China is itself, of course, another original civilization, and the only fully extant one, although that of the Indus Valley and the Mayan retain tenuous lines of descent, respectively to existing Indian and Latin American cultures.

3. Cf. Max Black, *Models and Metaphors* (Ithaca: Cornell, 1962), especially pp. 219, 243. Nevertheless, he stresses more than I do an underlying, deeper isomorphism in what he calls "analogue models." Nor do I quite use the term "paradigm" in its simple meaning (cf. Black, *op. cit.*, pp. 156ff.) of a clear case which can serve as an example. The paradigms I have in mind are much more than examples; they provide what Kant might have called a generative *schema* for further thought and action, as when we are given the paradigm for the declension of a type of noun or the conjugation of a type of verb. We think *within* the paradigm and *by means of* it. -- Finally, I use the term "paradigm" in a metaphysical sense broader than that of Thomas Kuhn in *The Structure of Scientific Revolutions*, nor am I committed to the epistemology implied in that work.

4. I have added the last phrase in order to accommodate as far as possible an African colleague's insistence (on a later occasion) that "there is no [distinct] concept of nature [as such] in African thought" (Prof. M'Bedy, W. Germany, Cameroun). Indeed, the exaggerated divorce of the human *from* nature, epitomized by Cartesian dualism, for example, has contributed greatly to the false emancipation of technology from nature, and has even led to what Adorno and others criticize as merely "instrumental" rationality. (See Horkheimer and Adorno, *The Concept of Enlightenment*.) Prof. Imamichi has remarked that for the Greeks *techne* is contained within nature itself, and indeed is one of the several kinds of knowledge by which human nature reaches its fulfillment. At the same time, the energy of Western technology arises in part from the tension between the human and the non-human already mentioned, a tension expressed by such phrases as "the relation *between* man and nature," or "the relation of man *to* nature." Professors Tang Yi-jie and Chen Kui-de reminded us that the central concern of classical Chinese philosophy was not the relation between man and nature, but that between man and man, within which the understanding of nature is to be situated.

5. Professor Quiles (Spain) observed (on a later occasion) that all of the paradigms mentioned are paradigms of *discourse* (*logos*) and in that respect are "Greek." Discourse is, undoubtedly, one of the sources of that tension that is characteristic of the "Western" relation between man and nature. (See footnote n. 7.)

6. These paradigms are, it seems to me, more than metaphors (cf. S.C. Pepper, *World Hypotheses* [Berkeley: University of California, 1942]). They do not arise by selection of an already existing meaning which is then transferred to a larger and different medium, but arise out of the convergence of many insights, experiences, values and actions that pervade a society as a whole.

7. I have developed the concept of discourse (*logos*) in more detail in "Gibt es fuer den Menschen Wichtigeres, als zu ueberleben? Das Erbe Griechenlands: Rationalitaet," *Das europaeische Erbe unde seine christliche Zukunft* (Koeln: Hanns Martin Schleyer-Stiftung, Bd. 16, 1985), pp. 95-105 (English text, pp. 348-356).

8. As well as "Lectures on Physics" (*physike akroasis*), Aristotle also refers to some of the books on physics under the title: "the books about motion" *(ta peri kineseos)*. -- Professor Imamichi has correctly observed that the term *physis*" cannot be translated in any direct way from the Greek; the more so, if we consider the important variations among the Greeks themselves.

I can consider here only the most general sense of the term with some emphasis upon Aristotle's influential meaning. It is worth remarking that so many of the terms we use in Western philosophy remain transliterated in their Greek form rather than translated (e.g., "philosophy," "school," "economy," "politics," "ethics," etc.). The question may be asked: whether the transformations of meaning which they have undergone have left only an empty shell of their original meaning, or whether a Greek residue remains that contains the still germinal seeds of discourse (*logos*). It seems that a Greek root does remain as an abiding determinant, and with it the logical weight of discourse.

9. Hegel has drawn the difference very sharply in his discussion of the finite and the infinite in the first book of the *Wissenschaft der Logik*, 2d. edn. The distinction can be accepted without having to accept his whole system.

10. Cf. Robert Sokolowski, *The God of Faith and Reason* (Notre Dame: Univ. of Notre Dame Press, 1982).

11. See K. L. Schmitz, "Le transcendance coincidente: fondement de l'interrogation religieuse," in: *Urgence de la philosophie* (Quebec: Presse Universitaire de Laval), pp. 591-597.

12. Etienne Gilson, *The Philosopher and Theology* (New York: Random House, 1962), p. 90.

13. See, for example, St. Thomas Aquinas, *Summa Theologiae*, Part 1, Question 44, especially Article 2. See also my own consideration of the topic: *The Gift: Creation* (Milwaukee: Marquette U.P.; Aquinas Lecture, 1982). It might be well to differentiate such a philosophical and theological view of creation (which is quite compatible with scientific theories of evolution) from the current Christian fundamentalist views of "creationism," which are based upon a crude, anachronistic and literalist reading of *Genesis*.

14. Gilson in *The Philosopher* remarks: "This philosophy that Descartes had found in scholasticism, how did it get there? Through Greece, no doubt, and especially owing to Aristotle; but Aristotle happened to be precisely what Descartes detested in scholasticism, the Christian conclusions of which were the only points he retained. The existence of a unique God, infinite, simple, supremely free, Creator of the universe as an all-powerful efficient cause, and of man himself, made to His image and likeness, endowed with an immaterial soul capable of surviving its body: not one of these notions could be found in Aristotle. But they all were easy to find in any scholastic theologian and Descartes inherited all of them. It is therefore a fact that Greek philosophy came out of the middle ages other than it had been in the minds of the ancient philosophers. On every one of these points Descartes came after the middle ages almost as if

the Greeks had never existed."

15. I mean respectively: those brought about by the Reformation and Counter-Reformation, the rise of mercantile capitalism, and the rise of bourgeois liberalism.

16. See *Critique of Pure Reason* A832 B860ff.

17. I have developed this interpretation somewhat more at length in "Analysis by Principles and Analysis by Elements," *Graceful Reason: Essays in Ancient and Medieval Philosophy Presented to Jos. Owens, CSSR*, ed. L. P. Gerson (Papers in Medieval Studies, 4; Toronto: PIMS, 1983), pp. 315-330.

18. An English translation by Priscilla Hayden-Roy has appeared in *Philosophy of German Idealism*, ed. E. Behler (The German Library, vol. 23; New York: Continuum, 1987), pp. 167-202; based upon the second edition of 1803.--Schelling continued the "organicist" line of interpretation in the *System of Transcendental Idealism*, but there he looked to art as the "sole true and eternal organon as well as document of philosophy" (Alfred Hofstadter's translation of the concluding section of the *System* appears in the volume just cited, pp. 203-216.)--Already in Leibniz, as contrasted with the Scholastic "vitalists" and their Aristotelian emphasis upon quality, it seems to me that more is at work than an interpretation using organism as its key. For the meaning and prominence Leibniz gives to *perceptions* and to *appetition* points to the ideality of human consciousness present within his account, rather than to the distinctively pre-conscious, qualitative nature of organic life. In Schelling, too, it is clear that his talk about organism and art work is subordinated to his attempt, on the one hand, to break out of the limitations of Kant's and Fichte's conceptions of consciousness, while yet, on the other hand, to preserve an enlarged sense of the "unconscious-conscious." And so, the unity which he seeks is still in function of consciousness, whose limitations Schelling tries to overcome with dubious results in his later work. If the foregoing is correct, then, the most influential forms of the so-called "organicist" version are idealist.

19. *The Two Cultures (1959): and A Second Look (1964)* (Cambridge: Cambridge U.P., 1964).

20. I take the term from the Jesuit anthropologist, Teilhard de Chardin (who worked upon "Peking Man"), but use it in a somewhat different sense than he did.

21. More recently he has preferred the term "integrative" order.

22. "Not exclusively:" indeed, the exponential increase in power has produced in astronomy and astrophysics a remarkable extension and refinement of our knowledge of distant stars and planets, and in geology a remarkable prolongation of our know-

ledge of the history of our planet. Professor Chatterjee remarked upon the new sensibility towards the earth experienced by space-travellers as well as by those who view the pictures of "mother earth" transmitted by television from afar.

23. Professor Imamichi gave expression to the deeply rooted Japanese insight into the fruitfulness of nature as a privileged teacher of mankind; and Professor Chatterjee remarked that nature still provides us with paradigms of interconnection. So that, although the future may rest in our fragile hands, we are not without recourse beyond ourselves.

24. One of the most promising developments in medical technology is the appointment of "ethicians" to the consulting teams in major hospitals in North America. In addition, the most rapidly expanding field in North American philosophy is that of professional, medical, legal and environmental ethics, along with bio-ethics.

PART II

HERMENEUTICS AND THE APPLICATION OF CLASSICAL PHILOSOPHIES TO CONTEMPORARY LIFE

CHAPTER V

HERMENEUTICS AND HERITAGE

GEORGE F. McLEAN

This paper concerns the relation between cultural heritage and hermeneutics. Here heritage refers especially to the cumulative sense of human dignity and appropriate social relations which lies at the heart of the culture(s) we inherit. Hermeneutics refers to the understanding of the nature and application of this heritage as well as to its critique.

This raises a cluster of problems:

I. In what does a cultural heritage or tradition consist: that is, how is it constituted; on what basis is it a point of reference for human action?
II. Can this culture have new meaning for these changing times: that is, how does it both live through time as a tradition and in each new age make specifically relevant contributions?
III. Can a culture critique the past which it inspired and be a guide to yet unknown pathways of peace: what is the basis for a transforming critique which will enable the culture to be an authentically liberating, rather than an enslaving, force?

This paper will consider each of these questions in sequence.

THE NATURE AND ORIGIN OF A CULTURAL HERITAGE

It is characteristic of modern times--and possibly foundational to our problematic--that tradition has progressively ceded its standing to technique. This may be traced to Descartes who, at the end of the Renaissance, resolved to sort through its tumultuous accumulation of knowledge, new and old, in order to select and order that which was clear and distinct to the mind's intuition. Further, though a conclusion once clearly seen by someone did not have to be rejustified by that person each time it was used, this dispensation was non-transferable.[1] Hence, the image of the thinker became that of a solitary hero working out the interconnections of ideas. That these are best seen in isolation, while life is always lived with others, forces one to ask whether this understanding has not lost sight of the relevance of thought to life--as Marx was keen to observe.

Correlatively, tradition, as arising from the community, as providing an initial sense of the truth, and thereby as laying a foundation for insight and judgment--that is, heritage as fore-understanding or pre-judgment--gradually assumed the ever more

58 *Hermeneutics and Heritage*

pejorative connotations presently conveyed by the term 'prejudice.'[2] But if our heritage be useless, upon what are we to base our efforts correctly to evaluate and respond to present issues? It has become necessary therefore to rebuild the value, and to assure the reading, of tradition, in part through a major critique of the rationalistic character of modern thought. This has been undertaken by Prof. Hans Georg Gadamer in continuation of the phenomenological work of Martin Heidegger. In *Truth and Method,* Prof. Gadamer undertook to reconstruct the notion of a heritage as: (a) based in community, (b) consisting of knowledge developed from the experience of living through time, and (c) possessed of authority.

Because tradition is sometimes interpreted as a threat to personal and social freedom I would like to focus especially upon the way our cultural heritage is a reflection of our life as free and responsible members of a concerned community.

Community

Autogenesis is no more characteristic of the birth of knowledge than it is of persons. Just as a person is born into a family on which he or she depends absolutely for life, sustenance, protection and promotion, so one's understanding develops in community. It is from one's family, and in one's earliest weeks and months, that one does or does not develop the basic attitudes to trust and confidence which undergird or undermine one's capacities for subsequent social relations. It is there that one learns care and concern for others independently of what they do for us, and that one acquires the language and symbol system in terms of which to conceptualize, communicate and understand.[3]

Similarly, through the various steps of one's development, as one's circle of community expands through neighborhood, school, work and recreation, one comes to learn and to share personally and passionately an interpretation of reality and a pattern of value responses. For the phenomenologist this implies that life in community is a new source for wisdom. Hence, rather than turning away from daily life in order to contemplate abstract and disembodied ideas, the place to discover meaning is life in the family and in the progressively wider circles into which one enters.

Time and the Building of Tradition

If it were merely a matter of community, however, all might be limited to the present, with no place for tradition--literally, that which is "passed on" from one generation to the next. The wisdom with which we are concerned, however, is a not a matter of mere tactical adjustments to temporary concerns; it attends rather to the meaning we are able to envision for life and which we desire to achieve through all such adjustments and over a period of generations. Hence, contemporary interchange needs to be complemented by the historical depth of accumulated human insight predicated upon the full wealth of human experience.

The process of trial and error, of continual correction and addition, in relation to the evolving sense of human dignity and purpose, constitutes a type of learning and testing laboratory for successive generations. In this laboratory of history the strengths of various insights and behavior patterns can be identified and reinforced, while deficiencies are progressively corrected or eliminated. But this language remains too abstract, and is limited to method or technique. While it can be described in general and at a distance in terms of feed-back mechanisms, what is being spoken about are free acts, expressive of passionate human commitment and sacrifice in responding to concrete danger, building and rebuilding family alliances, and constructing and defending one's nation. The cumulative result of this extended process of learning and commitment constitutes the content of a tradition.[4]

The impact of the convergence of cumulative experience and reflection is heightened by its gradual elaboration in ritual and music, and is imaginatively configured in epics such as the Mahabarata or in dance. All conspire to constitute a culture which, like a giant telecommunications dish, shapes, intensifies and extends the range of our personal sensitivity, free decisions and mutual concerns.

Tradition then, is, not simply everything that ever happened, but what appears significant. It is what has been seen through time to be deeply true about human life, along with the values to which our forebears freely have given passionate commitment. It appears either in specific historical circumstances or over time in works of literature whose worth progressively emerges as something upon which character and community can be built. Tradition constitutes a rich source from which multiple themes can be drawn, provided it be accepted and embraced, affirmed and cultivated. Hence, it is not because of personal inertia on our part or arbitrary will on the part of our forbears that tradition serves as model and exemplar. On the contrary, the importance of tradition derives both from the cooperative character of the learning by which wisdom is drawn from experience, and from the cumulative free acts of commitment and sacrifice which have defined, defended and through time passed on the corporate life of the community.[5]

Authority

Perhaps the greatest point of tension between a sense of one's heritage and modern liberal thinking relates to authority. Is it possible to recognize authority on the part of tradition and still retain freedom through time; could it be that authority, rather than being the negation of freedom, is the cumulative expression of, and the positive condition for, authentic human freedom?

One of the most important characteristics of the human person is one's capability for development and growth. One is born with open and unlimited powers for knowledge and for love. Life consists in developing, deploying and exercising these capabilities. Given the communitary character of human growth and learning, dependence upon others is not unnatural--indeed, quite the contrary. Within as well as beyond our social group, we depend upon other persons according as they possess abilities we lack, but need, in the process of our own growth and actualization. This dependence is not primarily one of obedience to their will, but is based upon their comparative excellence in some dimension, whether it be the doctor's professional skill in healing patients, or the wise person's insight and judgment in matters where profound understanding is required. The preeminence of wise persons in the community is then not something they usurp or with which they are arbitrarily endowed, but is based rather upon their abilities as these are reasonably and freely acknowledged by others. The role of the community in learning, the contribution of extended historical experience, and the grounding of dependence in competency combine to endow tradition with authority for subsequent ages.

There are reasons to believe, moreover, that tradition is not a passive storehouse of materials simply waiting upon the inquirer, but that its content of authentic wisdom plays a normative role for life in subsequent ages. On the one hand, without such a normative referent prudence would be as relativistic and ineffective as muscular action without a skeletal substructure. Life would be merely a matter of compromise and accommodation in any terms, with no sense of the value of what was being compromised or of that for which it was compromised. On the other hand, were the normative factor to reside simply in a transcendental or abstract vision, the result would be an idealism devoid of existential content.

In history, on the contrary, one finds vision which both transcends its own time and stands as directive for time that follows. The content of that vision is a set of values and of human and social goals which, by their fullness and harmony of measure, point the way to mature and perfect human formation and thereby orient the life of a person.[6] Such a vision is historical because it arises from the life of a people in time and presents an appropriate way of preserving that life through time. It is also normative because it provides a basis upon which past historical ages, present options and future possibilities are judged. The fact that humans do not remain indifferent before the flow of events, but dispute bitterly over the direction of change appropriate for their community or shared life reflects the fact that every humanism is committed to the realization of some common--if general--model of perfection. Without this even conflict would be impossible for there would be no intersection of the divergent positions. A shared vision of what is desirable for life, at least in some broad terms, is the condition of possibility for personal interchange and dialogue.

As such a classical model one's heritage or tradition is not chronologically distant in the past and therefore in need of being drawn forward artificially. It lives and acts in the lives of all whom it inspires and judges; through time it is the timeless dimension of history. Rather than reconstructing it, we belong to it--just as it belongs to us. Such a tradition is, in effect, the ultimate community of human striving, for human understanding is implemented, not by isolated individual acts of subjectivity, but by our situatedness in a tradition. By fusing both past and present this enables us today to determine the specific direction of our lives and mobilize a community of consensus and commitment.[7]

This sense of the good or of value, derived from the concrete experience of a people through its history and constituting its cultural heritage, enables it in turn to appreciate the real impact of the achievements and deformations of the present. In the absence of tradition as the cumulative lived experience of a people, present events would be simply facts of the moment, to be succeeded by counter-facts. The succeeding waves of such disjointed happenings would constitute a history written in terms of violence. In these terms such violence could be reduced only by a Utopian abstraction built upon the reductivist limitations of a modern rationalism. By eliminating all expressions of freedom, past and future, this constitutes the archetypal modern nightmare, *1984*.

In ebulliant contrast stands one's heritage or tradition as the rich cumulative vision evolved by men through the ages to a point of classical and normative perfection. Exemplified architecturally in a Parthenon or a Taj Mahal, it is embodied personally in a Confucius, Gandhi, Bolivar, or Lincoln, a Martin Luther King or a Mother Theresa. Superseding mere historical facts, they express that harmony of measure and fullness which is at once classical and historical, ideal and personal, uplifting and dynamizing--in a word, liberating.

The truly important concern at the present time is, then, to enable peoples to draw on their heritage of personal vision, evaluation and free decision, elaborated through the ages and in their various communities, as a basis for deliberating and working out the response they decide to make to present circumstances. That these circumstances are often shifting and difficult in the extreme is important, but what is of definitive importance is that this people's response be truly theirs; that it be part of their history and not simply the automatic effect of someone else's history, or--worst of all--of abstract, impersonal and depersonalizing laws or ideals.

APPLICATION: HERITAGE AND THE PRESENT

There exists a second set of problems regarding tradition. These concern directly, not its nature and origin, but its relation to the present. For, to the degree that one recognizes the validity and even authoritative character of one's heritage, one would seem to be in danger of diminishing the significance and even the freedom of present efforts to find answers to the new issues which arise in our personal, and especially our social, life. Indeed the very reality of novelty is at issue, for if our present life were but a simple repetition of what had already been known life would lose its challenge, progress would be rejected in principle, and hope would die. Let us turn then from the construction and content of a cultural heritage to its application in our days through dialogue which grows out of care and concern.

In brief, this is the correlative of the problem faced above. Just as the classical ideal is constituted from the concrete expressions of the freedom in the past, rather than in abstract depersonalized law, so the challenge of the present is how to understand the application of this ideal in a manner that promotes, rather than suppresses, the creative exercise of freedom in our day.

Novelty and Application

To understand this we must, first of all, take time seriously, that is, we must recognize that reality includes authentic novelty. This implies that tradition, with its authoritative or normative character, achieves its perfection not in opposition to, but in the temporal unfolding of, reality. Because persons determine their changing social universe and its values, for an adequate sense of culture one must attend to the truly new elements introduced by historical acts of encounter in community.

As response to the good takes place in concrete circumstances, the guiding principles of human action, even in ethics as a science, must be neither purely theoretical knowledge nor a simple historical accounting from the past, but must provide help toward moral consciousness in one's concrete circumstances. This implies an important difference of ethics from techné. In the latter, action is governed by an idea as an exemplary cause which is fully determined and known by objective theoretical knowledge. Skill consists in knowing how to act according to a well understood idea or plan. When this cannot be carried out some parts of it are simply omitted in the execution.

In contrast, in ethics the situation, though similar in being an application of a practical guide to a particular task, differs in important ways. First, in moral action subjects make themselves as much as they make the object; agents differentiate themselves by their actions. Hence, moral knowledge as understanding of the appropriateness of one's actions is not fully determined independently of the persons involved. Thus, the identity of a person or people, as constituted through a past (or tradition) and exercised through present free acts, is a central factor in the determination of what is appropriate. This does not override what can be known in the general terms of one's specific nature; rather within one's nature one's culture specifies the implications of nature for the actions of those involved. Secondly, adaptation by moral agents in applying the law do not diminish, but corrects and perfects it. In itself the law is imperfect, for in a relatively unordered world it cannot contain in any explicit manner responses to the concrete possibilities which arise in history. It is precisely here that human freedom and creativity come into play in shaping the present according to a sense of what is just and good; this they do in a way which manifests and indeed creates for the first time more of what justice and goodness mean.

That the law is perfected by its application in the circumstances is driven home by the experience that a simple mechanical replication of the law works injustice rather than justice. If ethics is to be an instrument of realizing the good it must be not only knowledge of what is right in general, but also the search for what is right in the situation. For this, epoché and equity are required in order to perfect the law and complete moral knowledge.[8] This is particularly essential in situations of personal and structured inequality in which an ordinary application of general and abstract laws can be expected only to extend and deepen the injustice. Hence, special attention must be paid to the concrete circumstances of persons in their mesh of psychological, economic and social interrelations.

Concern for Others

The question of what the situation asks of us is answered in the light of what has been discovered about appropriate human action and exists normatively in the tradition. This is properly the work of intellect (*nous*) with the virtue of prudence (*phronesis*), that is, thoughtful reflection which enables one to discover the appropriate means in the circumstances. In order to be appropriate, however, the means must truly fit all who are engaged in the situation. Hence, it is essential to be finely tuned to other persons, and this precisely as they are persons with their own freedom, feelings and understanding. Such an assessment of what is truly appropriate will require also the virtue of sagacity (*sunesis*), that is, concern for others, because in order adequately to appreciate the situation one must undergo it with the affected parties. Truly ethical knowledge can be had only by one who is united in mutual interest or love with the other. Such knowledge is profoundly social and metaphysical.

This goes notably beyond simply a concern for justice, that is, for rendering to others what is clearly due them by right. It is true that an ethical or moral situation cannot exist without justice. Nevertheless, justice is based upon persons as distinct. It distinguishes and even opposes one to the other in a mutual relationship of rights and duties as each party tends to look more to their rights and to what others owe to them, rather than to their responsibility and to what they owe *to others*. The result of a relationship based only upon justice is more likely to be strife than harmony and peace. This can be overcome and justice rendered only when concern for self is broadened to concern for others as well, that is, when sagacity (*sunesis*) is added to prudence (*phronesis*).

In sum, the application of the heritage or tradition is not a subsequent or accidental part of understanding; rather it radically co-determines this understanding. Social consciousness must seek to understand the good, not as an ideal which is known independently and then applied to the circumstances, but as related to the concerns of all. In this light our sense of unity with others begins to appear as a condition for applying our tradition, that is, for enabling it to live in our day. Let us look more closely then at the hermeneutic process by which social understanding creatively articulates the meaning of one's cultural heritage in present circumstances.

HERMENEUTIC AS DIALOGUE OF HORIZONS

Horizon and Historicity

If one's horizon is the totality of all that can be seen

from one's vantage point, then the application of a living tradition involves a dialectic of the horizons of different times or groups or cultures. One such dialectic is had in reading a 'text' from the past--this could be a document, such as "The Declaration of Independence" or of "The Rights of Man," or even the broad pattern of values which constitutes a tradition or cultural heritage. Such a dialectic of horizons is involved in the process of being stimulated by contact with other cultures to discover needed new meaning in our own culture in order to face such problems of the present as technology and urbanization.

We do not enter upon this task of understanding with a blank mind as Locke supposed or proceed to suspend all judgment under a pervasive Cartesian doubt. Instead, we summon up all our resources to construe an initial or prior conception of the meaning of our culture or that of the one with whom we are in dialogue. Gadamer terms this a 'fore-understanding', or 'pre-judgment', and hence 'prejudice' in a non pejorative sense. This is a tentative projection of the general meaning of our culture and the meaning of our interlocutor. The content of this anticipation is not an objective, fixed content to which we come; but what we produce as we participate in the evolution of the tradition and thereby further determine ourselves. For our horizon reflects not only the content of the past, but the sensibility of the time in which we stand and the life project in which we are engaged. This pre-judgment is gradually corrected in the process of reading our culture in detail until we unveil the meaning our cultural tradition has in distinctive relation to our circumstances to its present problematic. In this manner there is a creative unveiling of the content of the culture or tradition as this comes progressively and historically into the present and, through the present, passes into the future.[9]

In this light, time is not a barrier or separation, but rather a bridge and opportunity for the process of understanding; it is a fertile ground filled with experience, custom and tradition. The contribution of time lies in opening new sources of understanding, whether contemporary challenges or meetings with other cultures, which reveal unsuspected elements and even whole new dimensions of meaning in our tradition. How does this take place?[10]

Questioning and Openness

Horizons are not limitations, but vantage points, for the mind as open or mobile is capable of being aware of its present horizon and of transcending this through the acknowledgement of other horizons and of the horizons of others. Indeed, historic movement implies precisely that we not be bound by one horizon, but move in and out of horizons. It is the very act of becoming aware of one's horizon which establishes historical consciousness, puts one's horizon at risk in dialogue with others, and thereby liberates one from the limitations of his and her horizon. When our initial projection of the meaning of the 'text' or of the other will not bear up under progressive questioning we are justified in making needed adjustments in our projection of meaning and in the horizon from which we were thinking.

It is important then that we retain a questioning attitude. Rather than simply following through with our previous ideas until a change is forced upon us, true openness or sensitivity to new meaning requires a willingness continually to revise our initial projection or expectation of meaning, that is, our horizon. This is neither neutrality as regards the meaning of the tradition, nor an abandonment of passionate concern regarding action towards the future. Rather, to be aware of our own horizon and to adjust it in dialogue with others is to make it work for us in our effort to discover the new and rich implications of our tradition required for our times.

Because such discovery depends upon the questions, the art of discovery is the art of questioning. Consequently, whether working alone or in conjunction with others, our effort at finding the answers should be, not to suppress a question raised by contact with another culture, but to reinforce and unfold the question. To the degree that its probabilities are intensified it can serve as a searchlight to bring out new meaning in one's own culture. In contrast to opinion which suppresses questions and to arguing which searches out the weakness of the others' argument, conversation as dialogue is a mutual and cooperative search for truth. Through eliminating errors and working out a common meaning, truth is progressively unveiled.[11]

Further, it should not be expected that the text or tradition will answer but one question, for the sense of a culture or a text reaches beyond what even its authors intended. Because of the dynamic character of being emerging in time, the horizon is never definitively fixed. At each step a new dimension of the potentialities of one's culture is opened to understanding, for the meaning of a culture lives with the consciousness, not of its author, but of the many persons who live it with others in history and pass it on in new ways (*tradito/traditio*). This dialectic of our horizon with that of the others intensifies our ability to question our heritage and to receive answers that are ever new.[12]

Finally, this openness consists not merely in receptivity to new information, but in a recognition of our historical, situated, and hence limited vision. Real escape from that which has deceived us and held us captive is to be found, not through those who are well integrated into our culture and social structures, for dialogue with those of similar horizons opens one only to a limited degree. Real liberation from our most basic limitations and deceptions comes only with a conscious effort to take account of the horizons of those who differ notably. This might be another nation, or a distinct culture which might co-exist with our own in the same geographic region, or--still more definitively--which might exist on the margins of all of these societies and be integrated into none.

Such openness is directed primarily, not to others as persons who are to be surveyed objectively or obeyed unquestioningly, but to ourselves. It opens our horizons, extends our ability to listen to others, and assimilates the implications of their answers for changes in our own positions. In other words, it is an acknowledgement that our cultural heritage has something new to say to us. The characteristic hermeneutic attitude of effective historical consciousness therefore is not methodological sureness, but openness or readiness for experience.[13] Seen in these terms our heritage is not closed, but the basis for a life that is ever new, more inclusive, and more rich.

HERITAGE AND CRITICAL HERMENEUTICS

The relation between hermeneutics and social critique is dialectical. The social sciences provide an indispensable element of awareness and hence of emancipation in the world of increasingly technical and convoluted structures. But heritage and tradition must provide an essential context and the basic principles for the critique to which these sciences contribute. Paul Ricoeur has attempted to codify some contributions of the tradition.[14]

First, critique is carried out within a context of interests which establish the frame of meaning. The sequence of technical, practical and emancipating interests reflects the emergence of man out of nature and corresponds to the developmental phase of moral sensitivity. Habermas studies Kohlberg closely on this and employs his work.[15] To the question of the basis of these interests, however, no adequate answer is provided. They are not empirically justifiable or they would be found at the level of technical interests. Neither do they constitute a theory as a network of working hypotheses for then they would be regional and justified at most by the interest in emancipation. But this would leave them entrapped in a vicious circle.

The only proper description of these interests as truly all-embracing must be found in the direction of Heidegger's existentials and hence of Being Itself with its unity, truth and goodness. These are hidden only in being so present that they are in need of being unveiled by hermeneutic method. Thus, Gadamer's hermeneutic project on the clarification of fore-understandings or 'prejudices' and Habermas' critical work on interests by the social sciences, though not identical, share common ground.

Secondly, in the end, critiques of ideologies appear to share characteristics common to those of the historical hermeneutic sciences. Both focus upon the development of communicative action by free persons. Their common effort is to avoid a reduction of all human communication to instrumental action and institutionalization, for it is there that manipulation takes place. The success or failure in extending the critique of interests beyond instrumental action to communicative action determines whether the community will promote or destroy its members. Such critique is unlikely ever to be successful, however, if we have no experience of communication with our own cultural heritage. For in a dialogue distortions can be identified as such only if there is a basis of consensus. This, in turn, must concern not only an empty ideal or regulative idea, but one that has been experienced, lived and shared. "He who is unable to interpret his past may also be incapable of projecting concretely his interest in emancipation."[16]

Thirdly, today communicative action needs more than a model to suggest what might not otherwise occur to our minds, for the rationalization of human life has become such that all of its aspects are controlled pervasively in terms of instrumental action. Whereas Marx could refer in his day to surplus value as the motive of production, this is true no longer. Instead, the system itself of technology has become the key to productivity and all is coordinated toward the support and promotion of this system; it is the ideology of our day. As a result the distinction between communicative action and instrumental action has been overridden and control no longer can be expected from communicative action.

This raises a new type of question, namely, how can the interest in emancipation be kept alive. Undoubtedly, communicative action must be reawakened and made to live if we are not to be simply subjects--indeed 'slaves'--of the technological machine. But how is this to be done; whence can this life be derived if the present situation is pervasively occupied and shaped by science and technology as the new, and now all-encompassing, master? It can be done only by drawing upon our heritage in the manner suggested by Heidegger. We need to retrieve or reach back into our heritage--now as never before--in order to find the radically new resources needed for emancipation in an increasingly dominated world.

Finally, there is a still more fundamental sense in which critique, rather than being opposed to tradition or taking a questioning attitude thereto, is itself an appeal to tradition. Criticism appeals unabashedly to the heritage of emancipation it has received from the Enlightenment. But this tradition has longer roots which reach back to the liberating acts of the Exodus and the Resurrection. "Perhaps" writes Ricoeur "there would be no more interest in emancipation, no more anticipation of freedom, if the Exodus and Resurrection were effaced from the memory of mankind."[17]

According to the proper norms of communicative action, these historical acts should be taken also in their symbolic sense in which liberation and emancipation express the root interest basic to traditional cultures. In this manner they point to fundamental dimensions of being, indeed to Being Itself as the unique existent in whom the alienated can be reunited, to the logos which founds subjectivity without an estranging selfishness, and to the spirit through whom human freedom can be creative in history. Remembrance and celebration of this heritage provides needed inspiration and direction both for any in power who might be indifferent to the needs of the poor and alienated and for the alienated poor themselves. On this basis they can reach out in mutual comprehension, reconciliation and concern to form a social unity marked by emancipation and peace.

The Catholic University of America
Washington, D.C.

NOTES

1. *Discourse on the Method of Rightly Conducting the Reason and Seeking for Truth in the Sciences*, Parts I and II; and *Meditations on the First Philosophy*, Meditation I, in *The Philosophical Works of Descartes*, E.S. Haldane and G.R.T. Ross, trans. (Cambridge: At the University Press, 1969).

2. Hans-Georg Gadamer, *Truth and Method* (New York: Crossroad, 1975) pp. 241-45.

3. John Caputo, "A Phenomenology of Moral Sensibility: Moral Emotion," George F. McLean, Frederick Ellrod et al., eds., *Act and Agent: Philosophical Foundations for Moral Education and Character Development* (Washington: The Council for Research in Values and Education and The University Press of America, 1986), pp. 199-222.

4. *Ibid.*, pp. 245-53.

5. *Ibid*. Gadamer emphasizes knowledge as the basis of tradition in contrast to those who would see it pejoratively as the result of arbitrary will. It is important to add to knowledge the free acts which, e.g., give birth to a nation and shape the attitudes and values of successive generations. As an example one might cite the continuing impact had by the Magna Carta through the Declaration of Independence upon life in North America, or of the Declaration of the Rights of Man in the life of nations on a number of continents.

6. *Ibid.*, p. 254.
7. *Ibid.*, p. 258.
8. *Ibid.*, pp. 278-86.
9. *Ibid.*, pp. 261-64.
10. *Ibid.*, pp. 267-71, 235-38.
11. *Ibid.*, pp. 325-32.
12. *Ibid.*, pp. 335-40.
13. *Ibid.*, pp. 324-25.
14. Jurgen Habermas, *Zur Rekonstruktion des Historischen Materialismis* (Frankfurt: Suhrkamp, 1976), pp. 72-73; *Knowledge and Human Interests* (Boston: Beacon, 1971), pp. 196-209; Thomas A. McCarthy, *Critical Theory of Jurgen Habermas* (Cambridge, Mass.: The MIT Press, 1978).
15. Lawrence Kohlberg, "From Is to Ought," in T. Misbel, ed., *Cognitive Development and Epistemology* (New York: Academic Press, 1971), pp. 151-236.
16. Paul Ricoeur, "Hermeneutics and the Critique of Ideology" in J.B. Thompson, ed., *Paul Ricoeur, Hermeneutics and the Human Sciences* (New York: Cambridge Univ. Press, 1981), pp. 90-97.
17. *Ibid.*, pp. 99 and 100.

CHAPTER VI

TOWARDS AN HERMENEUTICS OF NATURE AND CULTURE

GHISLAINE FLORIVAL

Nature and culture constitute the object of a twofold analysis, one in terms of concepts and the other in terms of reality itself. The distinction between these two levels and their basic relation determines both our world-view and the objective value of any scientific knowledge. Is there a cosmic process which exists independently and in its own right--a nature (*physis*) broadly speaking--or would any positive answer to this question derive from the words of the one who enunciates it? If there is such a reality, it must be related to the meaning in which it is expressed. And if this be the case, how can one speak of "nature" without this very concept being bound up in the entire cultural history of mankind? Nevertheless the givenness (*Esgibt*) or existence of reality--the cosmos as such--obliges the mind to apply itself to the facts. How then could we justify the objectivity and, consequently, the value of the human sciences as distinct from the positive sciences?

These questions have been widely debated for the last century in the history of philosophy. We will review them with the help of two methods: one, phenomenological, which retraces the process genetically beginning from perception; the other, hermeneutic, which concerns the problem faced by the historical sciences. As in each of these methods the given cultural reality appears as the basic milieu of meaning, we will treat the problem of culture against the background of this relational experience with the aid of the concept of *praxis*, or lived action, in relation to meaning.

Thus, there are three parts in what follows:
1) the phenomenological approach of Husserl, with the concept of constitution;
2) the hermeneutic approach of Gadamer, with the concept of horizon; and
3) cultural action, which will permit us, in conclusion, to take up the question of intercultural meaning.

THE PHENOMENOLOGICAL APPROACH: THE CONSTITUTION OF NATURE AND OF CULTURE

In his *Ideas Pertaining To a Pure Phenomenology and a Phenomenological Philosophy*, Book II, which was written gradually from 1912 to 1925 and published well after its author's death, Husserl applied the theory of constitution which he had presented in the first volume of *Ideas*.[1] There he wished to provide a foundation for the objectivity of the positive sciences and to justify their unity. The first two sections of the work describe the constitution of nature on its material and animate levels. Both things and the soul as the form of living things pertain to physical nature, whereas the spiritual (*Geist*) pertains to culture which is studied, or constituted, in the third section of his work.

The Constitution of Physical Nature

Examining the natural sciences, Husserl contrasts them to the sciences of the spirit (*Geisteswissenschaften*) and shows that they can be established only in terms of the opposition--already present in Dilthey--between "explaining" and "understanding." Whereas the natural sciences do nothing but "explain" on the basis of objective linear causality, the sciences of the spirit must be constituted in function of an "understanding" which, in turn, depends upon the lived realization of meaning. Husserl does not reject the objectivity of the sciences, but wishes to give them a foundation in perception.[2]

Let us begin with the constitution of nature as a process moving from matter to spirit. One might be tempted to see this merely as a traditional analysis were it not, for Husserl, the origin of meaning, that is to say, the constitution of nature for the conscious subject, and hence at least methodologically of transcendental priority. This is not an idealism, however, because it sees consciousness as open to exterior reality given in experience, and because consciousness directs its attention to the perceived object as its phenomenal correlate. Consciousness receives its capacity to signify only from the object given in perception, that is to say, from the manifestation of the phenomenon in its own right. In this orientation to the object the consciousness passes beyond itself to grasp, through a succession of profiles, the invariant sense of the object or the *eidos* which fills to the object.

Husserl's first intentional analysis applies to nature. As his point of departure he takes a global idea--which has meaning for the mind--in order to elaborate the multiple senses or intentions found in the one object or nature. Beginning from this primordial correlate unfolding before the *Ego*, that is to say, from the universe as a totality of possible experiences, Husserl constitutes successively the thing, the soul and the body, that is, both material and living or psychic natures.

In approaching the natural object consciousness first takes up a doxo-theoretical point of view to the exclusion of such other attitudes as the aesthetic or the practical (praxis), thereby excluding all such factors as the beautiful or the useful. In this naturalistic attitude, the thing or object is constituted in terms of the first attribute of nature in general (in the strict sense), extension. What is thus extended has a form, but this scheme by itself remains ghostly; it can affirm its materiality only in function of circumstances which, despite constant variation, manifest certain permanent properties.

Materiality reflects the durable essence or substantial unity of the thing, which, in turn, is constituted through the standard concrete causal interaction proper to normal or habitual circumstances by the *aistheta* which sensibly affect organic bodies. Thus, in sense experience substances present themselves through multiple sense qualities to the intuition of the *Ego*, which sensible qualities of the material thing "depend upon the body of the subject having the experience."

To the relative stability of circumstances there corresponds a balanced organization of bodily dispositions which, in turn, depend upon the motor and kinesthetic processes of the subject. Perception is related also to the abilities of the subject. But the body itself, as condition of perception, is subject to changes, produced or undergone, which can give way to anomalous states. This dependence regarding its changes underlines the physical character of the body as well as the contrast between the normal and the pathological. Because a radical perturbation of perception calls methodologically for some recourse of others to the perceptions, Husserl's passage from the relativity of an object to the subject, and thence to the objectivity of the thing is regulated by what is normal in everyone's perception. Hence, according to Husserl, this actual intersubjectivity becomes constitutive of theoretical objectivity.

In sum, in this section Husserl has constituted the specific trait of the object, namely, objective space as a relational system of orientations--an ideal frame in which every form and every movement is inscribed. This is physical, mathematical space which determines the objectivity of physics and is subordinated, in turn, to intersubjective determinations.

The Constitution of Animate Nature

In the second section, Husserl treats the constitution of animate nature--the psychic order. Though a part of nature, this domain emerges from the material structure of mere things to which it adds the soul as a new layer of meaning. The ego pole of the pure self has as its counterpart the animation of the body-object. Transcendental reduction makes it possible to bring to light both the reality of the *Ego* as a constituting source and thereby its parallel reality, the living body, which stands out from among things. Thus, psychism is ambiguous, being linked at the same time both to the objectification of a subject-object and to the level of autonomous experience.

Here the analysis of the body proper as actually lived permits Husserl to rely upon the field of experience which includes a perduring temporal reality, the Ego and the concrete fragments of actuality they live in their spatio-temporal context or world. This incarnation poses the problem of interweaving consciousness and world inasmuch as the "psyche" is a flux rather than a schema or thing and therefore depends upon historical rather than causal circumstances. The soul is a quasi nature or dual reality "in which physical nature is elevated by a layer of meaning by which it is interiorized and made immanent." In this context Husserl describes a double experience: at the solipsistic level it concerns the body proper, at the intersubjective level it is one of intropathy--the correspondence of our perceptions and feelings (*Einfühlung*).

The body proper--which I am--is revealed in acts of perception which interrelate the perceiving organ and its action. Thus, my hand as touching and as touched constitutes a reflexivity in which the body is revealed both as object and as actor. As both localized and spontaneous this is manifestly my body so that the psyche experiences itself in the lived space of the body, which acts as an organ of my will, being linked to my feelings and intentions, and open to others or intimate. Though the tactile sense is not the act of touching and is localized only indirectly, nevertheless what constitutes my "presence" remains the point of view from which all other points of view are organized. As a thing the body has sensations, but it is also a center inhabiting a place around which things find their orientation. It is not a natural object in the same manner as are things, but belongs to an idio-psychic order.

Husserl clarifies the difference between this original presence to oneself and the perceptive discovery, in appresentation, of another body and subjectivity present to me. The process of affective "transfer" allows me to localize in the other his own perceptions, as if I lived them in him and his expressive and affective gesture; through intropathy I am able to grasp the psychic life of the other objectively from his bodily expression. By a ricochet effect, I become an other for him (as I am also body for him) while discovering my own incarnate subjectivity. In this manner my psychic and physical identity becomes also a perceptive, intersubjective co-presence.

Thusfar, Husserl's methodology relies upon the original lived perceptions of things in order gradually to move back to the psycho-organic reality, and finally, by a lived intropathy, to actual intersubjectivity. Throughout, this constitution of nature is always in relation to transcendental consciousness.

Culture

In the third section Husserl completes what remained ambiguous in the natural self by introducing the dimensions of person and community. He describes *Geist* or spirit as the empirical counterpart of the pure subject with the cultural world and the *Ego* (man, the objective self), reacting against the scientific milieu of his time which had naturalized man without taking account of the *Geisteswissenschaften* or the sciences of the spirit. Phenomenological reduction brackets such a naturalistic attitude and by changing perspectives looks disinterestedly into each human attitude.

The naturalistic attitude constituted the person or *Ego*-man as one appears bodily. Though not localized, the soul was considered to be so integral to the body that the psychic was inseparable from the qualities of the physical body. Thus, the states of consciousness were seen to coincide with physical or measurable time. As susceptible to measurement, man was defined by the naturalistic attitude merely as an animated being or a zoological entity.

Here Husserl returns to the question of method, observing that the ultimate attempt to reduce man to nature produces a reversal of attitude which, in turn, makes manifest the absolute consciousness which constitutes nature. By "virtue of the eidetic correlation between the constituting and the constituted all nature must be relative." Hence, the transcendental reduction of man focuses no longer upon man as nature, but upon our life in common. In our daily life the world which surrounds us and which we inhabit contains not simply things, but objects for our use, works of art, literary products, juridical and religious symbols and institutions. The persons we encounter are members of our family, state, Church or community, all cooperating toward the same political and social goals. The people we encounter are not mere beings of nature, but beings of culture located in surroundings or *Umwelt* which can be attained by the natural attitude.

Thus our convergent motivations bind us into mutual person-to-person relationships in common activities directed toward the constitution of works of culture. Scientific objectivity, in turn, is constructed on the basis of this common cultural world, which is the original or basic context expressed by the term *Lebenswelt*.

The other attitudes depend upon this constituting consciousness. Husserl returns "to the eidetic context of consciousness in its primordiality and plenitude." In the doxo-theoretical attitude we had bracketed the beautiful and the useful--all that belongs to the practical, axiological and affective attitudes--whereas here opening once again to our entire context changes the way we look at what we experience. Husserl underlines the loss which had been sustained in objectifying the cultural given, reduced thereby to the same level of abstraction as the natural sciences. Psychic acts or states were treated inductively, rather than as lived modes of feeling or of will. In The objects we use and social structures were considered according to their attractiveness, exchange value or potential for conflict, so that in sociology human groups were analyzed in terms of causal links.

On the contrary, the new method converts our aperception of the world of things into a world of persons according to an intuitive rather than an inductive approach. To perceive our everyday world in terms of the actions of persons with whom I am dealing enables it to take on a continually developing meaning in a reciprocal production of sense. This world emerges as the horizon of our mutual existences in which objects have personal meaning and, like symbols, a motivating power. Thus, a flag can be the sign of an entire people aware of the interrelationships they have built. Here the person is no longer reducible to an object of nature, even if one finds one's bearings physically in the surrounding world and in relation to other persons. He/she dwells in the sphere of the spirit and of intentional sharing so that the world is no longer merely nature or what is there in front of one but what is organized according to a process of mutual understanding. In its evaluations and interactions the cultural world is based upon the motivations which produce its meaning.

This world is not for one individual, even though it is through the Ego that the others, each for him/herself, exists within cooperative action. To be a person is to be an Ego freely motivated by the presence of the other. The world of persons manifests this capacity of social subjects for mutual promotion. This is true also in the preparation of people for the future on the basis of a living tradition as experienced through language, style and art. Science itself does not exist but is supported by the intention to learn through action which, in turn, is supported by reason and hope in what is reasonable.

Thus, the environing cultural world is first of all an understanding of the universe of persons and from this motivating intuition the spirit or *Geist* descends upon "things" and permits the constitution of explanatory science.

Ghislaine Florival 77

THE HERMENEUTIC APPROACH: CULTURAL HORIZONS

In his study of hermeneutics and ideologies, referring to the discussion between Gadamer and Habermas regarding historical science,[3] Ricoeur underlines the opposition between critical and hermeneutic consciousness understood in terms of Gadamer's *Wahrheit und Method*. This analysis is important for our reflection upon culture because it introduces a critical conception of objective knowledge as tied to culture and locates therein the role of reason.

Gadamer's original conception of the impact of culture upon science recalls Husserl's analyses. According to Gadamer, scientific knowledge, being based upon objectification, supposes that the facts under study be placed at some distance. Ricoeur notes that this position of Gadamer reflects the influence of romanticism as a turn to the past, in contrast to Habermas who, in facing the same problem of objectivity, followed the Enlightenment tradition of rejecting tradition. For Gadamer history would have no object unless persons were primordially related: we are immersed in history and this, in turn, calls into question our capacity for radical objectivity.

In order to demonstrate this, Gadamer proposes three forms of distancing: aesthetic, historical and linguistic. Focusing mainly upon the historical, Gadamer places himself resolutely in the German tradition of the human sciences (or *Geistwissenschaften*), a new romanticism in the sense of Dilthey and, in a way, of Heidegger.

The romantic tradition enables Gadamer to rehabilitate the notion of prejudice, which had been disparaged by the Enlightenment as authoritarian and opposed to pure reason. Gadamer wants to restore a sense of prejudice which is not opposed to reason. Where the romantic solution failed by interchanging the truth-value of the two antithetic terms, *mythos* and *logos*, Gadamer displaces the question by redeveloping the meaning of prejudice.

Dilthey had first pointed to this in the essay he wrote to provide a foundation for the human sciences (or *Geistwissenschaften*), but he remained imprisoned in a traditional theory of knowledge based upon the primacy of the subject. Gadamer criticizes this primacy of subjective consciousness as a reflexive return upon oneself. "History precedes me and goes ahead of my reflection,"[5] writes Ricoeur, adding "I belong to history before belonging to myself." This clearly differentiates his position, not only from all idealistic philosophies, but equally from philosophers of the Frankfurt School as heirs of the Enlightenment. Thus, we escape from the traditional point of view which founds ontology on epistemology and, following Heidegger's *Vorstruktur des Verstehens*, look for what Ricoeur calls "the structure of anticipation in the very situation of our being in Being."[6]

This Heideggerian conception influences Gadamer, who notes especially its two dimensions of pre-understanding and temporality as the integral power-to-be of *Dasein* or the human manner of being in the world. This redirects our attention from the history of historical facts to the meaning of Being, which is connected intimately to the destiny of Western metaphysics. Following Heidegger Gadamer underlines the structure of anticipation for "prejudice" is rooted in the history of metaphysics itself: the "history of Being" is the "prejudice" which is always already there; it is the historical anchoring whence every reflection--especially hermeneutic reflection--arises.

Analyzing the dimensions of this foundational metaphysical prejudice in every historical search for meaning, Gadamer presents them under three headings: (1) the phenomenological link which connects prejudice with tradition, and through this to authority; (2) the ontological link which unites prejudice, tradition and authority on the basis of the "consciousness of the efficacy of history" (*Wirkungsgeschichtliches Bewusstsein*); and (3) the metaphysical consequence of this state of affairs. We shall consider in sequence each of these steps in Gadamer's historical hermeneutics.

(1) The phenomenological essence of prejudice or pre-understanding is linked to the historical character of human beings as such. This is what had been rejected by the rationalist critique due to its more fundamental prejudice, namely, its identification of authority with violent domination. It is fundamental for Gadamer that because authority belongs to persons, far from being a degrading act of submission, an abdication of reason or blind obedience, authority is "the link through which we recognize in the other a judgment or aperception with priority over our own."[7] In this sense, tradition is endowed with authority, even where it has become anonymous, for it molds our understanding and behavior: "tradition is continually a factor of liberty and of history itself." Between reason and tradition there is, therefore, not a fissure, but a relationship in which tradition supports the work of reason by opening the mind to the realm of the reasonable. Between the spirit of innovation and the spirit of tradition there is dialogue rather than opposition as between *Verstand* and *Vernunft*.

(2) Gadamer goes on to show that prejudice is legitimate because we cannot extract ourselves from the historical process, but must take charge of ourselves within this process. Though we must distance ourselves in history through a process of objectification, history acts upon us through this distance and it

would be an illusion to believe that we could master it completely or render it objective. Because it is not possible to escape the effects of history inasmuch as a part of us is always engaged therein, history cannot be recovered as an objective past: "An historical being," says Gadamer, "never knows itself."

On the other hand, there is no absolute limit, because the historian can always take another point of view. Nevertheless--and it is here that Gadamer's thought is the most interesting--the historian can never acquire an "objective vision." For were a text to be treated as an object it would lose its intentionality and hence its claim to tell us by a word-in-act some living truth. The word cannot be understood unless there is previous agreement about the subject of this word; without this it dies, crushed upon itself for lack of an horizon of meaning to sustain it.

Gadamer shows thereby that history is not reducible to the absolute point of view of Reason which contemplates all from above; but neither can it be reduced to the punctual analysis of limited facts. Rather, the horizon carries us along with it for we are implicated in it: the event is not a fact, but keeps its value as an horizon by which we are continually engaged.

Thus, we are not closed in an horizon for we can move to another point of view or another culture. In doing this, however, we do not cease to be ourselves, for then we would not "understand" what "the other" means. Though there is no absolute knowing, there is prior understanding because every point of view exists only against the background of other points of view. Thus, there is a fundamental "fusion of horizons" which has the form not of an objective totalization of all, but of living relationality linking one horizon with the other. Gadamer thus rehabilitates the prejudice of tradition as the horizon of my present in its openness to the future.

(3) The meta-critical consequence of such an hermeneutics is the impossibility of an exhaustive criticism of prejudices and, with them, of ideologies. As there is no absolute horizon and as it is always from a tradition and our present position that history is understood, we are induced by a kind of criticism of the critique itself to speak of a living universality. This is not the universality of a totalizing and objectifying reason, but the kind of universality which in everyday experience founds the becoming of the world as an openness of horizon. It precedes and envelops the very possibility of the sciences, because historical time of history is always already there: the historian or philosopher fights to distance him/herself for purposes of objectivity from that in which they already are implicated. Gadamer's hermeneutics plays upon this methodological paradox by inserting

distance in our understanding of the meaning by which we are borne along. Even our failures of mutual understanding become apparent only in this founding horizon which is constituted by language and art as the living flux of historical time.

THE APPROACH OF PRAXIS: ACTION AND WORD

Thusfar we have interpreted culture in its relation to nature from a phenomenological point of view. According to this the objectivity proper to the sciences of nature is founded upon the *Lebenswelt* which supports all cultural works. Further hermeneutic critique shows that we are always involved in a basic horizon which is becoming or changing in a manner which precludes any possibility of absolute observation. It is in the relations between our points of view that we are differentiated one from another. In mutual implication we can take the measure of our own points of view without any of us being privileged over others in the historical process.

The two methods, the phenomenological and the hermeneutic, have opened up the field of mutual cultural understanding. We must now work out a concrete realization of this understanding, not merely in terms of the general meaning of culture, but in historically situated existing cultures, East and West, North and South.

In *The Human Condition*[8] Hannah Arendt speaks of the "vita activa" as the essential political dimension of the human condition. In this context she writes:

> Human plurality, the fundamental condition of action and of speech, has the twofold characteristic of equality and of distinction. If men were not equal, they would not be able to understand each other, nor would they be able to understand those who have preceded them, nor would they be able to prepare the future and to anticipate the needs of those who will come after them. If men were not distinct, each human being distinguishing himself from any other being, present, past or future, they would need neither language nor action in order to make themselves understood. Simple signs would suffice to communicate the immediate and identical needs. . . . Now man only communicates himself, . . . and human plurality is the paradoxical plurality of unique beings.[9]

For Arendt the Greek city is the model of the "polis," that is, of the place where free men are allowed to speak in the "agora" or public market and, through this interchange of words, overcome physical violence and bring it under control. The essence of liberty is in political action through the use of words.

For people to free themselves in action, however, they must take initiatives so that something new happens in their world, that is, something is produced through direct contact in the community. Persons reveal their identity in this work, which becomes the work of all. This active word is the mediation which imposes itself in relations with others; it is the place of interrelation and communion, and the expression of freedom. By analogy, every particular culture is the product of a community and can be linked to the choice of a singular innovative action which promotes the entire cultural field.

Similarly, every culture presents itself in its properly historical identity as the act of a singular community. Just as the identity of every culture is related to a tradition which precedes it as an horizon, always open to a future understanding, the same is true of all existing cultures. They are not juxtaposed wholes without doors or windows, but are co-determined in their relations to the horizons of others. Just as words are exchanged in a universe of meaning which already exists, cultures are constituted in a lived context or *Lebenswelt* in which the singular points of view are interchanged. There, each one finds him/herself already engaged in the whole inter-related history of the world and implicated in the becoming of all humankind. No all-embracing view is possible because that too would be part of this history. Hence, cultures can in no way objectify each other, for as in a mirror they themselves are implicated in the horizon of others.

There remains then our initial requirement for the specific character of human interrelation. Is language this indispensable point of political action, the pre-cultural dimension upon which every culture constitutes itself? To be sure, we are not dealing here with a common linguistic rootedness--a syncretic basis of all cultures or some practical esperanto. Rather, we are suggesting a relation whose pre-understanding enables everyone to remain themselves while opening in a reciprocal horizon to all others. Merleau-Ponty defined language by reference to "body" as no more than bodily behavior elevated to expression through an interweaving of meaning by which we are united to each other. From the point of view of Being language is this relationality of meaning. It is neither nature nor culture, but the juncture of the two at which meaning is born.

CONCLUSION

In referring to the "Lebenswelt," the historical horizon and action as operative word, we linked together many concepts in order to describe the mutually related meaning of "nature" and "culture." "Nature" exists only in terms of man who, in turn, is understandable only in nature. There is then but one meaning which gradually unfolds itself.

Meaning is the radical outcome of the phenomenological and hermeneutic methods themselves. It is elaborated through a lived temporality, which exists, in turn, within the cosmic givenness of time. To be sure, persons in nature alone are capable of encompassing in one glance this becoming from which they are emerging and on the basis of which the whole cultural process progressively takes shape. Nevertheless, the problem of time clings to the cosmos. Kant said, "Give me matter and I will build from it a world, that is to say, give me matter and I will show you how the world has emerged." (Preface to *General History of Nature and Theory of the Heavens*).[10]

However, it is always from my lived time, from the present word, that I re-read the meaning of history, the paleontological meaning whence we draw our present reality. It is always from a world which is already acquired culturally and from a language which is already constituted that we can designate what nature and matter are. The "in-itself" is but an idea projected backwards through a time that is already full of meaning.

The same reasoning with respect to cultural action suggests a similar process of reverse constitution for cultures. Just as the origin of time has meaning only with respect to the present, it is from the present that the look backward tries to recover the archeology of the first man or the appearance of the first atom. Similarly, we can change the present only on the basis of a future which calls us to self-understanding. Hope for progress through intercultural cooperation would seem then to lie in the compenetration of our horizons, in the inter-relation of a living plurality of meanings differentiated according to the differences between cultures: each is unique and nevertheless part of the horizon for the others. Is not this metaphor of meaning that is to come, and which manifests itself as the progressive unfolding of historical time, that pole of every human action which Kant called the "City of ends"?

Institut Supérieur de Philosophie
    Louvain-la-Neuve, Belgium

NOTES

1. E. Husserl, *Ideas Pertaining to a Pure Phenomenology and a Phenomenological Philosophy*, trans. F. Kersten (The Hague: Nijhoff, 1982), Book II.

2. P. Ricoeur, "Analyses et problèmes dans *Ideen II* de Husserl," in *Revue de Métaphysique et de Morale*, 56 1951, p. 359.
 3. P. Ricoeur, "Herméneutique et critique des idéologies" in E. Casteli, *Demythisation et idéologies* (Paris, Aubier-Montaigne, 1973), pp. 25-64.
 4. G. Gadamer, *Wahrheit und Method* (Tübingen: Mohr, 1969).
 5. P. Ricoeur, *Du Texte à l'action. Essai d'herméneutique II*, Paris: Seuil, 1986).
 6. Ibid. p. 341.
 7. Ibid. p. 344.
 8. H. Arendt, *La Condition de l'homme moderne* (Paris: Calman-Levy, 1982); *The Human Condition* (Chicago: Univ. of Chicago Press, 1958).
 9. *Ibid*. pp. 197, 198.
 10. Kant, *Histoire générale de la nature et théorie du ciel*, (1755), Préface; *Allgemeine Naturgescbichte und Theorie des Himmels* (Leipzig: Engelmann, 1898), Preface.

CHAPTER VII

MAN AND NATURE IN THE INDIAN CONTEXT

MARGARET CHATTERJEE

INTRODUCTION

It is perhaps significant that thinkers in many parts of the world are searching for a meaningful relation between man and nature at a juncture in history when, at one and the same time, we are conscious of the growth of human control over nature and yet brought up short by the frightening ways in which this very control can boomerang upon us. In part we are looking for an "alternative to the purely secular and pragmatic desire for material betterment."[1] This secular and pragmatic desire in our day cuts across national boundaries. It would be foolish merely to decry it, for there can be no denying the claim of all to have their rightful place in the world order. This claim passes over into something more, a desire to have a more fair distribution, and this especially when it becomes evident that the distribution of goods and services is hardly equitable within national boundaries, let alone on an international scale.

The second consideration which encourages thinkers to re-explore the relation between man and nature comes out of a heightened sense of national identity. There is a connection between the two. The very forces which propel a people towards greater material prosperity, invite a rethinking of the specific, of what makes one people different from another.

The third consideration arises when we compare these specificities and often experience a desire to share, however imperfectly, the heritages of our neighbors. Social realities today tend to transform themselves rapidly, whether through economic changes or political shifts in the locus of power, and this rapidity often prevents a taking stock of cultural traits, of the corpus of values known to our fathers but of which we are aware only as faint echoes. Our thinking, and especially our valuations, have not kept pace with the course of events, which often are opaque to understanding. It is as if we found ourselves on an island of history and wish we could regain the shore of the mainland. The intellectual grasp of reality in our times, that is to say, is fed by a sense of economic and historical facts, but veiled by a sense of 'unknowing' as to the whither of our venturing as well as, in many cases, a nostalgia about the past. This nostalgia is felt only by the seniormost among us. The young may either experience an optimism propelled by the immediate prospect of more-sense level rewards, or by contrast they may have a sense of vacuum, a sense that amidst the stream of change there is no solid shore in sight.

The nations of Asia are in the poignant position of being betwixt many worlds, wondering to what extent it may be feasible, or desirable, to combine them. We are no longer flattered by being regarded as repositories of exotica, and we view with an ironic eye the tendency in some quarters to find in Asian culture items which apparently are available in a supermarket fashion, but which are not in fact able to be grafted onto the cult of money-making or the acquisitive life in general. Chinese calligraphy, Indonesian batik work, the tea ceremony, handwoven tapestries--all belong to cultures which have characteristic concepts of time and work. The labor involved is not a means to an end, beautiful though the end may be, but valuable in itself as a *discipline*. This discipline mirrors in microcosmic form the *travail of nature* whose very order encompasses something akin to *labor*

This is ill understood as conflict and contradiction; it reminds us in an infinity of ways of the elaboration of interconnections which at one extreme may be manifest in volcanic eruption and at the other in the blossoming of a flower in the desert. In man as creator the very travail of nature becomes articulate. He embodies the seasons in his own process of aging; his breath mingles with the winds and his body becomes dust and ashes. It is the mystery of this articulation upon which philosophers and artists reflect and that the tiller of the field enacts with the sowing of seed and the garnering of the harvest.

PHILOSOPHICAL SCHOOLS ON NATURE

From the foregoing it may be gathered that I see our theme in terms of cultural history and in terms of ontology, and that I see the two as closely related. For this reason I do not find the sole sources of Indian concepts of nature (for there is no single monolithic concept identifiable) in texts, but also elsewhere. However, let us look at the more explicitly philosophical side. We can detect four distinct *theories*:

(a) The Theory of *bhutas* (elements): water, earth, wind, fire and air. This provides a cosmic framework which can link up temperament, food, medicine and virtually all phenomena.

(b) The Samkhya distinction between *purush* (spirit) and *prakriti* (nature). This amounts to the most uncompromising philosophical dualism yet thought out. It has a number of peculiarities. It classifies mind along with *prakriti* which makes it curiously consonant with that contemporary philosophical oddity, physicalism. *Prakriti* is said to be a combination of *sattva* (luminosity), *rajas* (activity) and *tamas* (turgidity), which means that matter includes *sattvik* elements, and also that mind is quasi-material. While this view does not separate consciousness from nature, it involves saying that consciousness is non-sentient (since *prakriti* is non-sentient). However, in granting that *prakriti* is self-propelled and that mind is the product of this self-propelling capacity, mind is granted a certain elan which is nonetheless blind rather than illuminated or illumining.

(c) The theory of *paramanus* (atoms) associated with Nyaya-Vaisheshika. Being pluralist and realist this is compatible with the type of natural science to be found in Democritus and Leucippus.

(d) The Advaitin concept of *mayavada* which sees in the empirical, and therefore in nature, something to be transcended. Drawing a wedge between the phenomenal and the real as it does, it strives to take us beyond nature. Indeed, in the strict sense, it also takes us beyond the concept of man since it sets as a goal for the human being the shedding of those very features which make him human.

Of these four theories of nature the richest is the first, the theory of *bhutas* or elements, found in the Vedas. Two hymns in particular provide material on this, the *Prthivi mahini* (RV V, 84) and the *Bhumi Sukta* (AV XII, I). The former apparently refers to *prthivi* in the sense of earth, rather than in the modern connotation of world: "You in your sturdy strength hold fast the forests, clamping the trees all firmly to the ground." The *Bhumi Sukta* (AV XII, I) begins with the origin of earth from amidst the waters, showing how she bears, carries and sustains all else: "The Earth is mother; I am son of Earth (line 12). The rain-giver is my father; may he shower on us blessings"!

Earth in turn is "sustained by Heavenly Law." Particularly noteworthy is the way in which function, attribute and quality are fused together. She bears "all that has two legs, three, or four," she is the stage "where mortals sing and play," where altars are made, and therefore where Agni the fire-god resides. She is 'patient', and she is "a vessel of gladness." A particularly lovely passage describes the fragrance of the earth, and how this emanates in different ways from plants, water, lotuses, animals, human beings and the gods. One has only to recall that the spouse of earth is Indra, and that the rain-giver is described as father in line 12 to appreciate the prayer made in line 23: "Instill in us abundantly that fragrance, O Mother Earth, which emanates from you." Fragrance is invisible but unmistakable; this is why, in our own century, Gandhi speaks of spirituality through the image of fragrance as the quality which *others* recognize. There can be no lines with a stronger ecological message than these (35):

> Whatever I dig up of you, O Earth,
> may you of that have quick replenishment!
> O purifying One, may my thrust never
> reach right into your vital points, your heart!

The place of man in the cosmos is made clear (line 53):

> Heaven and Earth and the space in between
> have set me in a wide expanse!
> Fire, the Sun, the Waters, the Gods
> have joined to give me inspiration.

Although man's place is what one of our contemporary Indian philosophers has aptly called "the realm of between," how to fulfill this destiny is beautifully exemplified through the elements themselves. Water, from which everything has its source, is betwixt the solid and the ethereal. The power of the invisible is illustrated by the wind. Wind also epitomizes power, mystery, and freedom. Who knows whence it comes or whither it goes. The mind wanders freely. "We bring him our homage, whose voice may be heard, but whose form is not seen" (RV X, 168).

Are natural phenomena then gods? Sometimes indeed they seem to be such. The mythopoeic imagination can move easily from looking on wind as the "breath of the gods" to intuiting its divinity. In so doing one is linking force, power and attribute in ways which invoke respect, indeed emulation. The stability and firmness of earth, of mountains and trees, are models for man. The grass which straightens its back after being trampled on (the image is mine) is a symbol of regeneration and courage. This recalls the way the bamboo is regarded with respect in China, personifying as it does resilience and patience. The *Atharva Veda* (III, 22; VI, 38) celebrates the splendors of nature which for man are objects of quest--the dignity of the elephant, the strength of the lion, and the swiftness of the waters. And when folk literature recounts the not so admirable qualities of some members of the animal kingdom, it is with the knowledge that man is, likewise, a bundle of potencies, good and bad.

CULTURAL THEMES

When we probe into how this near celebratory and certainly participatory understanding of nature developed into something more complex, the Indian cultural experience reveals many facets. The need for discipline and work continues in the idea of *tapasya* which at one extreme is austerity. Exuberance and austerity are embodied in one and the same figure, that of Shiva. The need for acquiring skill from those who know and the realization that this is a process which involves *stages* and therefore time, is contained in the concept of *diksa* or initiation. The agricultural cycle teaches the discipline of collaboration with nature; for example no one would attempt to plough a rockface or expect dry cattle to produce milk. Thus was born the concept of *seva* or service; service to the land, animals, the family, people of other families, and to the gods. Actions must be performed correctly, whether it be the ritual acts demanded upon special occasions or day-to-day duties which must be carefully executed so that the work prosper.

The Indian ethos at its best was able to discern a transcendent meaning in natural phenomena and so was able to create out of a cosmos of elements--plants, animals and gods--a world. In all this the notion of object as *Gegenstand*, or what stands 'over against', strikes an alien note. Perhaps the ancient Indians were protected from seeing the natural as *object*, not by any absence of the scientific temper, but by their ability to see polarities as complementaries. Such an interpretation derives support from ancient Indian systems of medicine where the diagnostic eye is clearly guided by a sense of the need for balance between contraries, a principle which guides the most up-to-date medical practice today.

But the glimpse of transcendence in the many-colored world of nature also beckoned some souls to hunt for something further. It is this further quest, reinforced by a sense of much in life that is sorrowful and hard, that led some philosophers-- of whom Sankara was probably the greatest--to coin a vocabulary which, begins with the cosmic but strives nonetheless to take flight from it. This led to a considerable impoverishment of the original many-splendored Vedic vision. If antique visions are born to fade, it is one thing for them to fade into the light of common day, and quite another for a wedge to be driven between the day-to-day and the transcendent so that the *transforming* of the mundane appears as an impossible task.

In all their rich variety, Indian arts were able to avoid the path taken by some philosophers of forsaking nature for the transcendent delights of infinite seduction but conceptual inaccessibility. That many a time experience exceeds our conceptual nets is a point well taken, but we turn our backs on nature at our peril. Her lessons are infinite, most of all the lesson that cultivation is done in the valleys and not in the isolation of mountain tops and caves. We shall turn to the message of Indian art a little later. But I am at this point making my own stand clear vis-a-vis what seems to be a definite strand in some Indian philosophical schools, namely, the tendency to regard nature in an instrumental way--not as a means for mundane activities, but as a springboard towards a putative state where the 'natural' (especially the gamut of passions, etc., within man) shall have been transcended. Sankhya, Nyaya-Vaisesika, Advaita and Jainism all seem to me to regard nature in this light, whereas I am attempting to highlight *other* resources in Indian traditions which may provide more possibilities in our contemporary condition.

Unity

One of the strands in the contemporary search for a view of man and nature which does not make a rift between the two is the felt need to find a non-utilitarian element in our attitude to nature. The tendency is to assume that the peoples of Asia make more room for this than do those in the West. We need to proceed warily here for the following reason. For centuries the cultures of Asia have been based largely upon agriculture and the farmer least of all is used to regarding nature in a non-utilitarian way. The crops are for consumption, the water for drinking and irrigation; animals provide food and manure and pull the plough, and fire is for keeping warm in winter. The peasant is familiar with battling with nature and with wooing her. But because man endows his activities with multiple meaning he environs his relations with nature with celebration and ritual. He propitiates the powers that can endanger him in a calendar of symbolic practices, and he elicits the fertile potencies of natural elements by nurturing and controlling them. When he consults almanacs he does so in the belief that the planets influence tides in the affairs of men.

My point is that the utilitarian motive of all these activities need not be underrated in our appreciation of this host of symbolical actions which we may tend to view with a nostalgic eye if we live in places where most of this has been lost. We also need, I think, to avoid romanticizing what appears to us strange, rich and meaningful. The agricultural year allows for natural pauses between periods of labor in a way which is excluded in the tending of machines in industrial life. The land must lie fallow before it is ploughed again. The heavy labor of harvesting invites celebration when the work is done. The long winter nights go along with the return of sap to the root, and the gathering in of cattle to the stables. Up in the Himalayas the animals live beneath the first floor, and the very heat they generate helps to keep the living room above warm. These are the months of the year for spinning and weaving, and for storytelling.

Indian life, and Indian rural life in particular, strives to establish not only connections between man and nature but between man and the cosmos. If a textual warrant for this is sought, we can find it in the *Rig Veda* which invokes the natural powers of sun, wind and thunder, recognizing their potency and evidencing a host of man's mythopoeic abilities--praising, propitiating, and enlisting them in the course of mundane human activities. If Agni, the fire god, is given a primary role at the beginning of ritual acts it is in recognition of the volatility of this element, its suitability as a messenger, and the need to keep such a powerful force as a friend and not as an adversary.

It is not only philosophers and poets who try to create confidence in the world;[2] the daily round of actions of ordinary people are shot through with gestures which make it meaningful. I think here of the salutation of the early morning sun, the pouring of water on a tulsi plant growing in the courtyard, the sprinkling of water on the place made ready for *puja* (worship), the offering of the first mango of the season to the household gods. All these can be seen in terms of establishing inter-connections between human living and the world of gods and goddesses and cosmic powers, including also those powers which are intrinsically fearful--disease, the loneliness of the desert, the absence of water, the impassible mountain crag, and the places in the forest where danger lurks. The countryman well understands the polarities of darkness and light, pain and joy, failure and success. But he sees these as complementaries, finding in the rhythm of life a natural place for them all.

This use of the word 'natural' needs pointing up for it means 'how things are, what we must expect to be the case'. Perhaps there can be nothing which so well embodies "isness." Rural life does not inscribe a small circle as might the circumscribed mechanical movement made by the worker on the factory floor and which constitutes his whole day's work. Instead it draws an increasingly wider circle, taking in, as it does nowadays with improved agriculture, the effect of dams far away, the pollution of rivers across frontiers and the melting of glaciers high up in the mountains.

Invocation and Evocation

But in Indian life the natural, what *is*, includes men and animals, gods and other celestial beings and all cosmic powers. It is clear that this totality includes far more than the polarity of mind and matter, a polarity which often seems to be behind many discussions of man and nature. I have stressed the rural background of Indian resources regarding our theme, the pre-industrial setting. I stress also that nature is by no means co-extensive with the concept matter. Man participates in nature through the clay figures made for play or for worship, and in the making of floral garlands for use in the temple or to honor a guest.

The nature of folk art is particularly illuminating here. The materials used are simple--bamboo, clay, rice paste, wood and stone. But the figures, terra-cotta and wood, in no way attempt to imitate nature, for cosmic power cannot be *represented*. In tribal ritual it is the human act which endows the ritual object with power, but the act is at the same time an invocation for the cosmic to be situated therein--to be embodied, however temporarily, in a locus to which due honor can be made. Indian art expresses a quest not just for harmony, but for attunement with a divine principle. The principle is believed to be "the formless that is beyond form." The infinite is expressed through the bounded, but the bounded is seen to encapsulate cosmic rhythm.

Invocation and evocation, rather than the contriving of conceptual frameworks, therefore, seem to me highly significant ways in which the Indian cultural heritage eloquently exhibits its understanding of the relation between man and nature. But, as I suggested earlier, this does not drive out the utilitarian considerations which are natural to people who live in a rural setting, but provides *a context of meaning* for them.

The concept of environment, especially with ecological connotations, is a fairly recent one. What I refer to, however, as a key to Indian attitudes to nature refers to a rather different sense of environing, the environing of mundane activities with dimensions of meaning which are enacted in ritual and festival and told by the story-teller in myths, legends and folktales. The symbols involved are rich in their diversity. Let us take some examples. The wheel is at first sight an artifact, something which is not part of nature; in the history of technology no doubt the wheel has a crucial place. Through the chariot one can traverse space, carry goods in a bullock cart and so forth. But Indian thinkers also saw therein something more. The center of the wheel symbolizes *Brahman* or the Absolute, the constant still point amidst change. The wheel also means the cycle of births and deaths, the insubstantiality of the empirical self, the causal chain of momentary events bent back upon itself. The wheel is akin to the cyclicality of all natural phenomena, the seasons, birth and death. The wheelwright is at the hub of things. The chariot of Surya, the sun god, shoots across the sky; day is followed by night. The human world participates in this cosmic drama; the potter's wheel brings forth vessels which can contain life-giving water; the villager returns home in his bullock cart at the end of the day. The bullet-train propelled by modern technology is joined, through centuries of experiment, to the first inventor of the wheel.

Play and Austerity

If invocation and evocation provide an alternative vocabulary to that of explanation, I would next suggest that *lila* (play) and *tapasya* (austerity) provide an alternative to the concept of *determinism* with which our modern idea of nature so often is associated. Both *lila* and *tapasya* are concerned with the origin of the cosmos and its sustenance. Ancient Indian thought does not accommodate the conception of creation as found, say, in Plato's *Timaeus*. *Lila* and *tapasya* throw their diverse light on how things began. *Lila* literally means play. As a theory about the cosmos it suggests a spilling over of the fullness of being into multiplicity in a spontaneous way, an activity which has no extraneous purpose. This is a theory which springs out of the Vedic perception of the plentitude of Being, a perception which was both metaphysical and aesthetic. The aesthetic aspect of this is seen in the exuberance of detail on the exteriors of Indian temples, an exuberance which includes living things, dancing elephants, chattering monkeys, luxuriant trees with twining creepers and, amidst all this, human activities of every possible kind. While some interpret this as what is to be left behind in quest of liberation (witness the stark interiors of cave temples), I myself doubt whether this later philosophical motif can be read into the 'text' left behind by our artists--a celebratory text, to my way of thinking, which is as free of inhibition as it is of other-worldliness. At most we can, if we like, regard it as one moment in the rhythm of withdrawal and return which is so common to the culture of many peoples.

If we go to folk culture the ethos is thoroughly this-worldly, with ordinary daily use objects exhibiting the artistic impulse, and gods and goddesses, spirits and demons all thoroughly involved with day-to-day activities. Leaves and flowers are brought into daily ritual and man is realized to be very much a child of nature, but without any of the Rousseauesque sentimentality which comes into the picture whenever man-in-nature is seen as counter to something else, i.e., man *vis-a-vis* nature in the context of the 'civilizing' context of cities. The powers by which Rousseau and Hume set great store, the desires, passions, and sentiments, in fact "the sensitive part" of human nature in Hume's phrase, are not thought much of in most Indian philosophical traditions. Their influence, however, is writ large in epic literature where the strength of ennobling sentiments is given ample recognition; surely there is a satirical intent in the portrayal of the holy man as an emaciated figure amidst teeming life in the rock sculptures of Mahabalipuram.

I mentioned *tapasya* as a resource concept, and one which pulls in a different direction from that of *lila*. In the *Brahmanas* the threefold universe is said to emanate from Prajapati, "Lord of offspring or creatures." Now *tapasya* is the inner glow produced by austerity. The *Brahmanas* tell us that a primeval divine being differentiated himself into name and form through *tapasya*. It is not too far-fetched to see these apparently contrary principles of play and austerity at work in artistic activity on a microcosmic scale. These are the principles we need to take into account in contrast to the idea of *poesis* or making, which in some form or other lies at the basis of the theistic concept of creation.

The theme in Indian art which perhaps most vividly embodies cosmic ideas is the Nataraja, Shiva as the Lord of the Dance. He is the dynamic center around which the forces of the cosmos move. In plastic terms the bronze image of Shiva depicts divine truth, beauty and joy. The dwarf demon crushed under his dancing feet is the demon of ignorance. Perhaps no image in the repertoire of world art more eloquently incarnates cosmic activity. The two upper hands symbolize the balance of creation and destruction. They carry a small drum at the sound of which everything began, and a tongue of flame which is the instrument of destruction at the end of a *kalpa* or mundane epoch of time. The lower hands bestow protection. The lifted left foot symbolizes the release of devout souls. The ring of fire surrounding the dancing god symbolizes the life-process of the universe within which the dance of the prime mover takes place ceaselessly. God alone is imperishable. But this does not mean that life is static. On the contrary, the dynamism of the entire cosmic process is made clear in the *Nataraja*. Shaivism, of course, has inspired other paradigms in Indian art. For example, we have the yogi figure in the rock sculptures of Mahabalipuram (illustrating the *tapasya* mentioned earlier), or the androgynous figures which symbolize Shiva and his consort Shakti. As far as Kashmir Saivism is concerned one has only to see the landscape of Kashmir to realize the extent to which the mythic powers of Shiva are writ large in the bubbling streams which flow from the melting snows. Here is the prototype of Shiva's abundant locks. The very geographical features of the landscape indicate the alternation of demoniac powers and benign grace, the torrents and crags of the high altitude regions and the tranquility of the valley. The latter is indeed a tranquility amidst surrounding activity--the centrality of the dancer in the dance, the centrality of the hub in the moving wheel. It is no wonder that the theme of Shiva has inspired some of the most powerful examples of Indian art.

COPARTNERSHIP OF MAN AND NATURE
Inanimate Nature and Man

In common with people of many lands the Indian people find in Mother Earth a powerful symbol. To illustrate this adequately would need a study in itself. But here again the main resources are to be found in the culture itself and not in the theoretical treatises. Some of the finest examples of South Indian metal are the elaborate censers and votive lamps made for ceremonial use or for use at home. The Vedic texts prescribe that the *deepas* (lamps) should have pedestals, for "Mother Earth is accustomed to all sort of sufferings, but she will not put up with the heat of lamps." Herein lies most surely man's primeval fear of fire which causes destruction. But it is fused with man's built-in respect for light and his desire to associate his ritual celebrations with homage to it. If without a pedestal, the lamps are hung from the temple ceiling by means of chains. Since they are symbols of Surya (the sun god) and Agni (fire) they are regarded as auspicious. Earth, air and light are implicitly invoked in this lesser known art form.

Village houses are made basically of mud (along with stones, wattle, etc.). The very substance of which the huts are made is also the medium used for *cleaning* both the walls and the floors. The place for cooking food is also made of mud, the stove being then dried in the sun. In Visva-Bharati, the University founded by Tagore, a special ritual celebrates the time of ploughing the fields and the whole day is given over to festivities.

To this day the Bharatnatyam dancer makes obeisance not only to her guru or teacher, but to the earth--in the modern context, the stage--in apology for stamping on her during the dance. This is a further cosmic reference, in addition to the actual themes of the dances themselves which so often incorporate the miming of natural objects such as the lotus flower, the creeper, the stream, the tall tree, the deer, etc.

The mimetic element in Indian dance forms is well known. The symbolic weight of each gesture needs to be 'read' almost as a text is read, except that the observer is not only decoding but also, presumably, in a state of admiration and enjoyment. The gestures of dance need to be seen against the backdrop of gesture in general. The way in which gesture is of special importance in a culture where there are taboos about touch is a theme itself. I have already mentioned salutation of the sun (this is done with the same gesture of folded hands which serves for greeting friends) and the watering of plants. The latter is described in a beautiful passage in Kalidasa's *Shakuntala* where it is said of the heroine that she would not quench her thirst until the trees had been watered. Act 4 of the drama moreover parallels the loving gestures of the child of nature, Shakuntala, with responses on the part of nature when the time comes for her to leave her friends in the grove. The passage runs as follows: "The deer let fall the morsels of darbha-grass, the peacocks stop their dancing and the creepers, whose pale leaves fall (to the ground), appear to shed tears." The passage recalls the response of the natural world to the music of Orpheus. This example of mutuality of gestures is not a pathetic fallacy, but evidence of a community of feeling which extends beyond the human world. In Vedic times the hermitage was a place of retreat; however, there was never a breach of the close relation which man has to trees, plants and animals, and it was invariably these that were a source of consolation in times of banishment and exile.

Early Vedic literature also draws the inanimate world into the world of meaningful connections. Figures carved from the rock, and caves which house shrines, partake of the substantiality, the thatness, of the inanimate, and at the same time are enlivened by the sculptor's skill and the pilgrim's devotion. Soil, rockface and mountain are indispensable dramatic personae and are often seen as the *embodiment* of values. The parched soil in summer is an image of the long suffering heart, and the mountain personifies immovability in a good sense, that is, *sthirbhava*. The running streams symbolize both flux and continuity. Lotus ponds and lakes, so often featured in Indian paintings, are the abode of Lakshmi and evoke peace and tranquillity. They are shown frequented by flamingoes, cranes and swans and in this way a single painting connects so-called inanimate nature, the animal world, and the realm of gods and goddesses. Indian-painting and music, moreover, show how the concept of nature includes both the weather, seasons, and times of day. The very jungle, which at times in its density and darkness is fearsome, is a potent example of inter-dependence where each part supports the rest, animal and plant life forming a dynamic whole. Indian culture does not show the sensitivity of the Far East towards the beauty of rocks, or the subtle appreciation of the tactile qualities of jade, but the importance attached to *mountains* must not be missed. One of Krishna's exploits is the lifting of a mountain. The Himalayas are the dwelling place of the gods and the birthplace of holy rivers. The notion that mountains possess *merits* provides a most interesting counter theme to the assumption that nature and value are *ipso facto* opposed.

Animate Nature and Man

That the animal kingdom exemplifies merit comes in sharp contrast to thinking which includes concepts such as 'brute', 'beast', 'the animal in us' and the like. Myth and folklore abound in stories of the merits of the elephant--nobility, grace and fidelity. Even where admission of fault is mentioned, this is balanced by the recognition of good qualities. The folklore concerning monkeys, jackals and foxes shows them as being very like us in their combination of qualities, often possessing merits which we lack. It is the animal kingdom which provides paradigms in Vatsyayan's *Kamasutra.*

In an agricultural setting the animal world is not distant from the human. In rural life the horse, cow and buffalo are part of the family. In the city animals are drawn into the family circle only through the institution of pets, an extreme form of domestication where animals of necessity lose their spontaneity. The importance of animal life in India's understanding of nature is nowhere illustrated so well as in sculpture and architecture. The impression that the observer has is one of teeming life and movement. While human figures, trees and mountains can give an impression of stillness and tranquillity, this is certainly not the case with animals. This is why temple friezes abound in dancing elephants, and monkeys leaping from branch to branch. In paintings the tranquillity of lotuses and swans on lakes is balanced by frolicking deer, flitting birds and bees flying from flower to flower. Life is seen as movement and as delight. But all this also goes along with a focus on *human* activities. This focus is probably more central in Indian painting than it is in Chinese landscape (I speak under correction here) where cloud, cataract and mountain hold our attention more than the tiny figures below. One could illustrate the stress on the human element by noting how celestial figures are endowed with multiple arms rather than wings. To go into this, however, would take us into the comparative history of art.

Nature, Man and Divinity

John Passmore suggests that to divinize nature is to underestimate its fragility.[3] This argument would hold only if divinity is identified with omnipotence, but this is not the case if we consider the deities of the Indian pantheon. The fragility of nature is well understood by peoples familiar with the overflowing of river banks, whether of the Ganga or the Yangtze. Crops face a myriad of hazards and the animal world is no less open to suffering than is man. But is nature divinized in the Indian cultural framework? It is not easy to answer this question, cast as it is in a mould which may not be fully congruent with Indian thinking. Yet we must use common terms, however comparative our discourses may be. Let me put it this way. Taking the diverse data referred to so far, a picture gradually emerges of a way of thinking, and more importantly a way of *life*, where there is neither a sharp divide between man and nature, not between nature and the gods. To say this probably needs to be distinguished from 'divinizing' nature simpliciter. Indian thinking somehow manages to steer clear both of the 'object' in all its Latinized and clearly sculpted particularity, and of assuming that nature is for the most part in tune with human feelings and aspirations.

There is a sense in which nature *abides,* while men and other creatures do not. The Himalayas are a powerful symbol of this abidingness. To say that the Himalayas are the abode of the gods is not to say they are gods themselves. Characteristically gods and goddesses are seen as mobile. They descend from the mountains, enter into human houses (Lakshmi), and are associated with favorite trees and flowers. But they are to a certain extent both domesticated and yet set free from man and nature. Such a view, it seems to me, is phenomenologically distinguishable from the one which *locates* divinities in specific places and which is usually the basis for the concept of 'divinization of nature'. My purpose however is not so much to press this point as to suggest, vis-a-vis Passmore's remark, that the Indian worldview is very conscious of the fragility of nature, for fragility and strength are not incompatible. Of course this does not stand in the way of either nature's fecundity or its destructiveness.

The very manner in which forms proliferate and constantly are undergoing transmutation familiarizes the man in the field (as against the city 'man in the street') with "the place of man in the cosmos." He inherits a world and a cosmos rich in divine beings and natural powers, powers of which he is the guardian. Herein lies an intimation of something which goes beyond the idea of 'environment', for man embodies those 'environing' powers in microcosmic form within himself. His body is made of the elements; he is subject to change and decay; his moods mirror the times of day and the seasons of the year; he shares the angers and aspirations of the gods. At its best such a world view can affirm both the dignity of man and the dignity of nature. It still needs reinforcing by a sense of the indispensable link between man and society, and a sense of history. But the basic backdrop remains, an indissoluble co-partnership between man and the elements which nurture him, a co-partnership built into the ancient concept of *rta* (cosmic order), and a pervasive creativity for which both man and the cosmos consisting of all living things provide mutually reinforcing paradigms.

Indian Institute of Advanced Studies
 Rashtrapati Nivas, Simla, India

NOTES

1. Richard Lanney, *The Speaking Tree, A Study of Indian Culture and Society* (London: Oxford Univ. Press, 1979; first edition 1971), Preface, p. xxiii.
2. Cf. Wallace Stevens's essay, "A Collect of Philosophy."
3. "Attitudes to Nature" in *Nature and Conduct*, ed. by R.S. Peters (London: Royal Institute of Philosophy Lectures, 1973-1974), vol. VIII.

PART III

MARXISM ON

NATURE AND MAN

CHAPTER VIII

ON THE RELATIONSHIP BETWEEN MAN AND NATURE

HUANG NAN-SHENG AND ZHAO GUANGWU

While nature contrasts with human society and the outer world contrasts to the individual, the outer world includes both nature and human society. Thus, the relation between man and nature is actually that between human society and nature, not between an individual and one's outer world. Obviously, an individual can form a relationship with nature but, because one is not able to exist without society, in forming a relationship with nature an individual must act as one of the particles of human society.

Human society has two major problem areas: one is the inner relationship of human society, and the other is the relationship between human society and nature (shortened as the Man-Nature relationship). As these two types of problems interrelate with one another things become rather complicated. The handling of the inner relationship of human society is conditioned by the Man-Nature relationship and dealing with it is conditioned in turn by the inner relationship of human society. Generally speaking, or from an historical point of view, the Man-Nature relationship is basically of greater importance than the inner relationship of human society because nature is the prerequisite for the presence of human society and the material concitions of its existence and development. On the whole, the Man-Nature relationship conditions and influences the solution of the problems of inner relationship. Productive forces are the foundation of the whole history and the final determining cause of the development of society. In order to deal with the problem of the Man-Nature relationship properly, a first requirement is to make clear the line of demarcation between human society and nature, and hence what each of these is.

In a broad sense, nature is the entire universe, including human society. In a narrow sense, it is often juxtaposed with human society, though it actually refers simply to the world excluding human society. Therefore, as far as space is concerned, human society is up to now part of the earth which is extremely small, whereas nature includes the earth and the immense universe outside of earth which is boundless. Where then is the dividing line between nature in the narrow sense and human society? Certainly, a clear-cut demarcation can never be found between human society and nature. In space, it is also difficult to point out where the limitation of human society is. We cannot say that cities are equal to society and suburbs to nature. Nor can we say that the inhabited areas are society and uninhabited areas such as forests and fields are nature. Human society exists in such natural objects as fields, mountains and rivers; it lives in houses, towns and cities; it depends upon sunshine, rain, clothes and food; and it travels about by ships, vehicles and machines. Every animate man or woman is first of all a physical being. Without or outside of nature there can be no human society at all. But nature itself is not indivisible; according to the degree of its relationship with human society, it is divided into the following levels or parts:

(1) Nature which is not known. This part of nature is farthest away from man and known least, but its existence can be assured through the development of science and practice. This is the existence of infinitely large and extremely small things. Finiteness and infinity are closely and indivisibly connected. Infinity exists in and through finiteness; finite objects include and are connected with infinity. The so-called finiteness means limitedness, which presupposes transcendence, but if there is transcendence, then there is no limitedness. Limitedness means transcendence and finitude includes infinity. Therefore, though through sensation we cannot directly grasp infinity, we can know infinity through finiteness by abstract thinking, namely through transcending finiteness in order to grasp and determine infinity. As was said by Engels, in thinking we can "find infinity from finiteness, find eternity from temporality, and affirm it." (*Selected Works of Marx and Engels*, Beijing, Vol. 3, p. 554.)

(2) Nature that is somewhat known. This refers to nature that is untouched by man, but known to some extent indirectly by means of practice and science; for example, the stars which have already been seen by people, especially the sun and other planets and stars. Although people have not set foot on those stars and planets, they have more or less known them through the naked eye or by means of a telescope and other instruments.

(3) Nature that has been set foot on by man. This refers to nature that is touched by man but has not been transformed, such as the moon, high mountains, deep oceans, the Arctic and Antarctic Poles, etc. Some traces of man have been left, but these places still remain original and primitive with few signs of man.

(4) Nature that is humanized. This concept was used by Karl Marx in his *Manuscript of Economics and Philosophy in 1844*. This remains under discussion within academic circles both at home and abroad, especially as to its meaning. It refers to

the part of nature which is transformed by man but remains in a primitive state, for example, such products of agriculture and animal husbandry as grain, fruits, vegetables, animals, and the fields, water, pastureland, orchards, forests, rivers and land, which help produce these products. To be sure, the degrees of their humanization are different, but they are deeply touched and even marked by man.

(5) Man-made nature. This includes things which do not exist in primitive nature and are produced totally by man, namely, the so-called materialized intellect, e.g., vehicles and ships in ancient times, trains, steamships and aeroplances in recent times, space rockets and electronic computers in modern times, etc. Nature contains most prototypes of these finished objects which are usually created by man. For instance, desks, chairs, benches, bridges and houses are made in obvious imitation of something in nature, but in nature there are no such ready-made things as desks, chairs, benches, bridges and houses. Some things having no archetypes at all in nature, but are created completely by man to meet his own needs after he masters the laws of nature. If flying birds can with difficulty be said to be the archetype of airplane, it is very difficult to find in nature the archetype of space rockets. Telephone, telegraph and TV are created by man purely and simply.

(6) Nature as the human body. This is undoubtedly a kind of natural substance, and surely the nearest to man, for as far as his natural respects are concerned man is simply human body. The ability to know and reform the human body, however, is not necessarily better than that of knowing and transforming other natural substances. Due to this peculiarity, we view human body as special level of nature.

Obviously, the limits of these six levels are not quite clear and have been changing continuously. Some levels are contained in others. Nature that is somewhat known includes that which bears the footprint of man; this includes humanized nature, which in turn includes man-made nature. Therefore, the difference between them must not be emphasized absolutely, nor should they be regarded as isolated levels. Nature is an integrated whole, every part or level of which has a certain distinctiveness. But as they are all objective realities, and their movements, changes and development occur regularly, they can be known and transformed.

As noted above, human society, which in a broad sense is also a part or level of nature, is the highest level of nature. In a narrow sense, however, it is not nature but exists side-by-side with nature. The relationship of human society and nature takes it in its narrow sense.

No doubt human society is formed by animate individuals. After the apes in the forests changed into human beings under certain conditions, men created productive forces in the course of transforming nature with tools. Meanwhile, people formed productive relations, and on this basis formed social and political institutions and social ideology, i.e., a superstructure; thus, human society came into being.

Social movement has three major levels: productive forces, productive relations and superstructure; among these the level of productive relations is intermediate, linking the other two so that they form two contradictions. Productive relations, combining all the productive elements, contradict productive forces. In connection with superstructure and as the social economic structure, productive relations form contradictions between superstructure and economic base. The fundamental nature of superstructure, however, is decided by its economic base, as it has no direct connection with productive forces. These forces influence superstructure only inasmuch as they reflect the economic base as their intermediate foundation. Therefore, superstructure does not in general circumstances directly contradict productive forces.

Productive forces are the basis of history because people cannot stop consuming for one day, and therefore society cannot stop producing for one day. Production is always social production. People taking part in social production occupy a particular economic position and have their own ideology and socio-political ideas. They also participate in various kinds of economic, political and cultural activities. Therefore, the two contradictions have been in existence since human society came into being, and will exist as long as society continues to exist. They permeate society, determining its nature and pushing it forward. They are the fundamental contradictions of social movement.

Nature is the necessary condition of the existence and development of society. Thus far, the earth is the only planet found suitable to human life; without it man cannot exist at all. Modern sciences have told us that there is no water or air on the moon, but only waste sand and gravel. It is a deathly static planet on which no living things exist. The atmosphere of Mars has too low a pressure; it consists mainly of carbon dioxide with little oxygen. Its temperature often goes down to minus 130 degrees centigrade. Hence, no living things are able to survive there. The atmosphere on the surface of Venus is very thick; its pressure is a hundred times that of earth and consists largely of carbon dioxide. Day and night the temperature is approximately 500 degrees centigrade so that any living things would be burned to ashes. Mercury is as bleak, desolate and deathly static as the moon, without any air. The temperature varies drastically from day to night: at night it reaches minus 160 degrees centigrade, while in the day it may be as high as 330 degrees centigrade. Thus, apart from the earth, we have so far found no places in the solar system with conditions suitable for life. Whether or not other galaxies suitable for life can be found in the future is unpredictable.

On earth the natural surroundings continuously provide human beings with materials for life and resources for production and building. These include ecological or "permanent" resources such as sun radiation, temperature, water, etc. Such resources differ in varying degrees in different regions. If people adapt their measures to local conditions and give full play to their professional knowledge and skills, they can make full and long use of such resources. Biological resources are another example: such animals and plants as forests, pastureland, birds, beasts, fish, insects, fungi, etc., all have the ability of regeneration. With proper usage and scientifically managed and cultivated, they can not only grow ceaselessly, but also reproduce and expand at man's will according to plan. Mineral resources: coal, iron, petroleum and so on which have limited reserves and are basically non-regenerating must be used in a proper and planned manner. If they are exploited and wasted without plan, a crisis of mineral resources is bound to occur which will harm production and life, and give rise to no end of trouble for the future.

In short, the relationship between man and nature is twofold. On the one hand, mankind continuously conquers nature and reforms his geographical surroundings in the process of their development. On the other, mankind is always influenced and conditioned by natural surroundings in the process of conquering and reforming nature. The bridge between these is man's productive activity through which he continuously changes his geographical surroundings and marks nature with his own signs. Meanwhile, natural surroundings, through their influence on productive activity, control and restrict the development of human society and at times even accelerate or retard its development.

Since the beginning of human history, the great changes which have taken place on earth often have been caused by man rather than occurring naturally. Owing to human action nature has undergone enormous changes: this is the humanized or manmade nature we mentioned above. The history of the development of science and technology is the history of knowing and changing nature and of creating material civilization according to its own laws. Man opens vast fields; the forests and grasses grown by man cover the ground; canals and reservoirs are scattered everywhere. The surface of the earth is spotted by cities, towns, houses and roads. Rivers, seas and oceans are filled with boats and ships, large and small. All these greatly change the surroundings for human society. The earth changes with each passing day and these changes are increasingly difficult to limit. As Mao Ze-dong once said:

> In good health Goddess be,
> With the world's difference surprising her.

If we enter living rooms, factories and shops we find many things which are not only humanized, but man-made. Apart from their raw materials and laws, their appearances, contents, textures and functions are completely created by man. Humanized and man-made nature show man's ability to conquer nature; they are products of his practice, produced for the existence and development of human beings. In this way, man has been reforming the earth and making it more and more suitable to man's living. The more developed man's production, the greater his power to reform nature and the quicker the earth changes. According to this developmental trend the earth will become man's wonderland--a secular paradise--through the efforts of one generation after another.

The activity of every level of human society reforms nature directly or indirectly. Various revolutions and reforms change society, the result of which is the establishment and development of new productive relations and a new social and political system. The reforming of society is for the purpose of creating better conditions for reforming nature. Various spiritual activities are organized to promote the consciousness of reforming nature and society, to strengthen and stimulate man's will to do this, and to accelerate the process. True, there are many passive factors in social activities, such as wrong ideas and deeds, artificial hinderances, deliberate destruction and defects and loopholes in the systems. All these do harm to the cause of reforming the world and cause complications, hesitation, failure and retreat, but history proves that the general tendency is upward and progressive. Man's ability to reform nature and society is under continuous development, as are material and cultural civilization.

Once production, life and science develop to a modern level, a serious question is raised for human society: how to control the changes of nature so that they are profitable to human society rather than harming or even destroying it. At present, some signs indicate that the earth, which has generally been favorable to the development of human beings for thousands of years, may not push forward but, due to man himself, may hinder or even destroy the development of the whole of mankind if it is not able to control the changes of nature. Partial problems occurred not infrequently throughout history and even in modern times. Some areas in Asia Minor have become barren as a result of felling woods. It is said that the reason why Mayan civilization in Central America perished is simply that the Mayans destroyed the ecological balance. Some areas in China suffer from drought and flood due to the felling of woods. As Engels pointed out,

> we should not be intoxicated with our triumph against nature. Nature revenges itself on us for each of these triumphs. At its first stage, every triumph brings the results expected, but at the second or third stage, there usually follows a totally different and unpredictable influence which often abolishes the results of the first step.[1]

In history, global problems have not yet been central, but since man's ability to reform nature has reached a global level, such problems have begun to emerge. The recently frequently mentioned greenhouse effect caused by the augmentation of carbon dioxide, the increasing reduction of forests and the constant expansion of deserts, increasingly severe pollution of air, river and ocean are international and even global problems. Nuclear war not only would cause unprecedented death and destruction, but could bring on a nuclear winter and a drop in temperature throughout the earth. This would deal a devastating blow to human civilization. It is not impossible for man to kill himself, and the greater the ability to reform nature, the more possible it becomes to do so. But is it possible for man to control nature and avoid such global misfortunes?

Insofar as intellect and the level of science and production are concerned, man has the ability to control the changes of nature. Some objects are completely made by him, such as nuclear weapons, which therefore man must be able to control. Some things are just by-products of activities undertaken by man, for example, pollution of the environment and destruction of the ecological balance. These by-products might not have been known at first, but in modern times they must not be allowed to develop to such an extent that they could cause devastating and irretrievable results. Not only do we have historical lessons, but many contemporary problems have been recognized. Mankind always has the ability to solve the problems it has discovered, but that is not to say that man is sure to solve these problems without many obstructions. He has the preconditions for solving these external problems only after he solves the interior problems of human society. Fundamentally, only by liberating themselves from class exploitation and oppression and becoming masters of society can people become masters of nature.

The development of modern economy, politics and culture has united people from all corners of the world. There is no nation, no race, similar to the Qing people of ancient China in Taohuayuan who lived an isolated life and adopted a closed door policy. In the world-wide human society which has emerged in modern times misfortunes are unavoidable. Because of the difference of social systems and ideologies, the monopolies and strife by capitalist cliques, and the different religious beliefs and interests among countries and races, human society has been divided into various groups. Just as there are alliances and co-operations between them, there are also struggles and wars.

Of course, nuclear war is possible and hence the entire human society, especially those countries possessing nuclear weapons and their leaders, must be fully conscious of the dangers of nuclear war and its serious outcome. They must also know that in nuclear warfare there are no winners, but only losers. This is true, not only of people in the area where the nuclear weapons are used and whose civilization will be damaged at the first blow, but of the entire world which will suffer tremendous misfortune: human civilization will suffer immeasurable damage. The ghost of nuclear weapons produced by man now in turn threatens human existence and development. Since man has produced it, he can certainly abolish it if the proper solution can be found for the contradictions existing between nations and peoples. In our opinion, if we keep in view the global interests of all mankind, it will not be difficult to solve the contradictions between nations and peoples.

Global or universal human interests require first of all acknowledgement of the existence of human interests. If in the previous century global human interests remained abstract, in the present century after the appearance of nuclear weapons and under the conditions of highly developed industry they have become objective. Secondly, we must place global human interests above all others. That is to say, when other interests conflict we must first of all take the global human interests into consideration, and subject other interests to them. One view sees today's world in pluralistic terms according to which every country is a center of interests; all problems are then understood and evolved in these terms. This view contains only a part of the truth. Undoubtedly, every country is a sovereign state and an equal member of the international family; every country has its own right to deal with internal affairs independently, and no other nations have the right to interfere. No nation should bully, oppress or conquer other nations. But in handling international, and especially universal, human problems, we must take into account other nations' interests, and particularly universal human interests.

Placing universal human interests in the first place is in line with Marxism. The ultimate goal of communism is: to liberate the whole of mankind, to fight against class and racial oppression, and to oppose wars of aggression; to safeguard for everyone his right freely and richly to develop his abilities, and to fight against the control, oppression and enslavement of peoples. To realize this goal, we must not think first of the interests of an individual, a nation or a country. We must not think only of ourselves without paying attention to others' interests, benefit ourselves at the expense of others, or take our neighbor's land. In considering international or global problems, we must start from the common interests of mankind, and make joint efforts to realize these. The socialist system is most favorable for developing this idea, but the existence of two different systems does not exclude practicing it. Why can this not be done?

As is known to all, respect for other nation's sovereignty and not to interfere in their internal affairs has become an internationally acknowledged requirement. This has laid the basis for the peaceful solution of disputes among nations. Marxism is against exporting revolution; it advocates the peaceful coexistence of countries of different social systems--which is in line also with the international requirement. As long as every country really admits and seriously carries out this requirement, no international dispute is impervious to solution through negotiation.

Especially when the changes of nature caused by man himself threaten human existence, and when people realize that there is a crushing danger hidden in humanized and man-made nature, people of all nations should unite all the more to fight against the terrible monster man has created. A friend when under control, it becomes an enemy when uncontrolled. In history, when the country was invaded, all classes readjusted their inner relations and united to face their common enemy. Why should we not unite when we face the challenge put forward by nature against mankind?

The Book of Poems (Shijing) says:

Altercate within among brothers,
But unite without against enemies.

Since every nation and race lives on the earth, we are all friends in contrast to nature. Owing to differences in history, systems, interests and ideology, we dispute and struggle against each other, or even use weapons. Now it is time for us to forget the past and deal with nature's threat with united strength. If we let man-made nature lose control and cause disastrous outcomes, our generation will stand condemned through the ages. Problems between countries should be solved through negotiation; problems of each country must be solved by the people of the country themselves.

Peking University
 Beijing, People's Republic of China

NOTES

1. *Selected Works of Marx and Engels* (Beijing), III, 517.

CHAPTER IX

SLAVE - MASTER - FRIEND PHILOSOPHICAL REFLECTIONS UPON MAN AND NATURE

LI ZHEN

Ever since mankind emerged from its primitive animal state and entered upon human society,[1] it has come to realize the relations of unity and opposition between man and nature. With the evolution and progress of human society, mankind has progressively deepened its understanding of this relationship. To observe this process is an important and basic aspect of the philosophical reflection of mankind; this chapter is an attempt at analysis and interpretation.

THE NAIVE UNDERSTANDING OF RELATIONS BETWEEN MAN AND NATURE: ANCIENT GREEK AND CHINESE PHILOSOPHIES

Roughly speaking, before mankind entered civilized society, it was in an extremely weak position in relation to nature, like an infant in the arms of a harsh mother who knew neither mercy nor care for her children. At the beginning, foraging was the only means for survival; fishing and hunting came later; fire gave humans a primitive and meaningful weapon in their struggle against outside surroundings. During this long barbaric period when mankind was under the oppression of nature it was forced into a state of subordination, subjection and control. Even when animal husbandry and agriculture developed, mankind was not strong enough even to challenge nature's control. In this state of subordination to strong natural powers the varied alienated and terrifying forces of nature gradually developed into totism and worship of natural gods and spirits: mankind felt itself surrounded by miraculous forces. With the later emergence of the concept of life after death (the concept of soul), this primitive idea of being surrounded by miraculous forces affected not only everyday life, but the life of the soul which could be separated from the body, and hence have a "next life" after death. At this time, the concept of polytheistic worship gradually emerged, whose description and record constituted the primitive myths which in essence were naive, simple and absurd.

From this kind of cultural background mankind entered upon civilized society. The following essay, in analyzing the relations between man and nature at the beginning of civilization, takes as two typical examples ancient Greek Society for the culture of the West and the ancient Chinese society for the culture of the East.

Greek Society

Man made great advancements during the ancient Greek era. Marked progress was achieved not only in agriculture, animal husbandry and handicraft, but also in metallurgy (iron tools were already in use in ancient Greece), navigation and commerce. The development of the productive forces of society reflected and promoted the stunning achievements by the ancient Greeks in mathematics, astronomy, medicine, geography, wine brewing, navigation, etc. All this attests to the fact that mankind had developed a much deeper understanding of nature. Some basic, yet wonderful, achievements were made in the conquest and use of nature so that mankind somewhat freed itself from the oppression and bondage of natural forces. The ideological tendency to scientism and rationalism in ancient Greek philosophy expressed this theoretical progress and was the first great victory of man over nature.

What is most important about ancient Greek philosophy was that it began to realize for itself the strength of human reason. Mankind was able to understand the secrets of nature (the laws of nature or "logos") and apply what it had already known in its productive and social endeavors so as to achieve its predetermined goals. One interesting phenomenon was the group of so-called "physicists" who engaged in the study of nature. As most of their works were entitled "On Nature," it can be said that before the concept of "philosophy" appeared "physics" was another name for philosophy. What is common to this group of physicists is that they attempted to interpret the world in terms of natural causes instead of the supernatural forces and miracles which mythologists had used to explain worldly matters. Thus the science of philosophy and myth were separated.

To regard nature as a reality which could be effected by mankind instead of something that carried with it mysterious forces which could not be controlled by man is the essence of scientism and rationalism in ancient Greek philosophy. What really matters is not how many concrete results these early physicists achieved, but rather that they set a new direction for thought. Mankind was beginning to free itself from the state of slavery, to emphasize that man is the center of the universe and to proclaim itself master of nature. Plato (427-347 B.C.) made this point in one of his stories. He pointed out that human beings were endowed with the wisdom of a god and thus possessed some of the qualities of a god. Among living creatures mankind alone had learned to use the fire stolen by Prometheus, the mechanical techniques of Athena and the "dignity and justice" given by Hermes on behalf of Zeus. Protagoras' (481-411 B.C.) famous saying that "Man is the measure of all things on earth" strongly affirmed the central position of man. Aristotle (384-322 B.C.) made the following definitions based upon his observation of the essence of man: (1) "Man is a two-legged hairless animal." (2) "Man is a rational animal." (3) "Man is a social being," or a political being, etc. That is to say, man is a natural being (Definition 1). Man is higher than other natural beings (Definition 2). What is of particular importance is that Aristotle already made clear the social character of man (Definition 3). Of course, how to look at the social and political characters of man is a debatable issue, but this is, after all, a new subject with substantial content.

Of course, the older traditional powers are not to be neglected. The concept of a supernatural god derived from deifying natural forces was still strong and stubborn in the social life of ancient Greece. That is due partly to the force of law of inertia and also to a new social factor, i.e., the backward and reactionary classes "who" took advantage of, and supported, this concept. Since humankind split into the different classes and entered upon civilized society, traditional conservative ideas, concepts and systems always have safeguarded the interests of the reactionary classes and their own social strata. It is not surprising then that concept of deified natural forces above all and of man crawling as a slave under the feet of the gods was still deeply rooted in ancient Greece. Nor is it difficult to understand how rampant these stubborn forces ran if one recalls that one of the reasons for Socrates (469-399 B.C.) being sentenced to death was that he did not believe in the traditional god of the city-state of Athens.

However, in ancient Greece, the strength of man was greatly improved even as reflected in their mythology. The gods and goddesses in Greek mythology were different from the primitive ones in that they were personified. Their intelligence, strengths and beauty were modelled after man rather than being an image of some strange supernatural being.

The constant social turmoil and wars in the latter period of ancient Greece paved the way for Neo-Platonism and allowed the mysticism and fatalism advocated by Stoics to become rampant. Man again lost confidence in his own strength and was relegated to a plaything in the hands of "god" and "destiny." In fact, man was once again thrown into the position of being enslaved by nature. However, in contrast to their enslaved situation in the barbaric period of mankind's early existence, the new tendency was to mingle man and nature. Man held that he could be promoted to a point at which he could be combined with nature, that is, since man emanates from god he could return to god. In this sense, man and god enjoy an equal or identical relationship. This idea was coated with mysticism and illusion, and eventually led to the ruling of Christian theology in the Middle Ages in Europe. But it is worth noting that it put forth the idea of combining man and god in an illusory and distorted fashion. Actually, this idea was an expression of the desire to establish an harmonious relationship between nature and mankind.

It can be concluded that there has been a further and richer understanding of the relationship between man and nature in the ancient Greek period, the first stage of human civilization. This realization included the concept left over from the barbaric period that man is the slave of nature, the germ and development of the concept that man is the master of nature, and also the illusion and desire that man and nature should be regarded as one entity. The naivete of these thoughts was determined by their understanding of the relationship between man and nature. Just as the variety and richness of the ancient Greek philosophy demonstrated the pioneering spirit of the intelligent Greek people, their understanding and observation of the relationship between man and nature was also varied and filled with a pioneering spirit. Thus, it contributed an invaluable cultural heritage for mankind.

Chinese Society

Reflection upon the relationship between man and nature in ancient Chinese philosophy was on a par with ancient Greek philosophy in terms of richness and variety. But at the same time had its own characteristics.

The situation of the ancient Chinese people before recorded history can be understood in the traditional ideas that existed in the Sang Dynasty (C. 16th cen.--1066 B.C.). Strong natural forces were embodied in the concept of "Heaven." An all powerful god, "emperor of heaven," controls the luck, the ill omen, misfortune and happiness of man in the mortal world. Since this time the concept of ancient China that man is the slave of nature has merged with the ideas of an undying soul and worship of one's ancestors. The souls of the ancestors seem to have been injected with the will of "Heaven," thus becoming the conveyer and representative of the will of "Heaven." The souls of the ancestors, together with "Heaven," become the opponent of man, even his enslaver. The so-called "Shang people worship ghosts" showed this state of mind.

The period ranging from the Western Zhou (c. 1066-771 B.C.) to the Warring States (403-221 B.C.) was equivalent to the ancient Greek period and its subsequent "Hellenistic" era (about 8th cen. - 2nd cen B.C.). The ancient Chinese and Greek cultures flourished at the same time in their respective hemispheres. Agriculture, handicrafts and commerce were highly developed in ancient China. Marked progress was made in wine brewing, metallurgy (coating of copper and iron), textiles (especially the silk products), water irrigation and architecture.

The fierce class struggle and social turbulence during these periods of Spring and Autumn (722-481 B.C.) and of Warring States opened the way for spectacular development in the cultural field called "the contention of one hundred schools of thought." On the whole the Confucians were advocating the authority of heaven: "Man proposes, heaven disposes," "Fearing the orders of Heaven," and "Worshipping the ancestors"; "Following the laws of the former kings," "Managing the country like Yao and Shun," and "Elaborating King Wen, King Wu, and Duke Zhou's Orthodox Way." But, Confucius (551-479 B.C.) also proposed such ideas as "universal love" and "a kind person should love others," which have strong humanistic characteristics. He advised, "do not say eccentric forces and mysterious gods." He also took a cautious attitude toward ghosts, god and superstition, saying "If you pray, it seems god is just in front of you." Xun Zi (C. 289-238 B.C.) had more progressive and valuable ideas such as "enforcing the laws of the present kings" and "controlling the laws of Heaven and making use of it." As for the Legalists, they held that we should carry out the "Reform and Renovation" and should make way for the initiative of manful play.

Of course, the scope of "man" in the eyes of Confucius, Xun Zi and the Legalists covers only the "big men": "gentlemen" and the "bright and good kings and emperors" who had "high moral standards." Only they were thought capable of "conquering and making use of Heaven," of "ruling on earth and under heaven and controlling all things on earth." As for the "small men" and "women," they should kneel in front of "Heaven" and of the "big men." These ideas are identical with those of Aristotle, who regarded slaves as "tools that can speak": slaves do not belong to the category of "man." Also in Athens women had no right to join the political life. Thus, the emancipation of man at this time was partial and incomplete.

Similar to the conservative idea of obeying "god's will" and "destiny" advocated by Neo-Platonism and Stoicism as a result of the social turmoil in the Helleninstic era, Lao Zi (C. 6-5 cen. B.C.) and Zhuang Zi (C. 369-286 B.C.) in ancient China spread the philosophy of escapism. They upheld that to realize the "perfect state" of making man and nature one entity, man should "abandon wisdom and intelligence" and "go back to nature" so as to overcome its control and achieve the position of "Real Man." They cherished the hope of cancelling the contradiction between man and nature by destroying man's instinctive characteristics, i.e., to abolish the contradiction subjectively from a relativist point of view. This idea that "all things are the same" which is colored by an illusionary asceticism, and the neo-Platonic idea of "merging with god" which is coated by mysticism are both subjective hopes which lead to the same end.

It can be seen from these philosophical reflections on the relationship between man and nature in ancient Greece and ancient China that, after escaping from subordination to nature in primitive society and on the basis of its basic understanding and conquest of nature, mankind foresaw that it could gradually control nature and become its master; it also envisaged combining with nature and forming one entity. These brilliant and creative ideas of mankind in ancient times promised a rich and continuing development of the relations between man and nature.

MAN ENSLAVED BY NATURE IN THE MIDDLE AGES

Mankind has traversed a tortuous road in its development. Speaking generally, man was again enslaved by nature in the Middle Ages (this period being equivalent in China to the long feudal autocracy beginning from the Qin and Han Dynasties).

One of the obvious characteristics of the relationship between man and nature in this period is that apart from worshipping the awesome power of nature, as was done in primitive society or in ancient times, mankind was now also under another strong and rapidly developing social force, that is, the political, economic, military and cultural forces possessed by the ruling classes. It controlled the destiny of society, thus becoming an alienated and seemingly super-social force--a "second natural force." The so-called "first natural force," when combined with the "second natural factor," constituted a more terrifying oppressive power threatening mankind.

Europe

This situation is fully exemplified by the theological rule of Christianity in Medieval Europe. The lives of men were filled with tears and pain, for they had to make up for their sins since man was regarded as sinful. Everything about man was decided by God's either choosing or abandoning one (the so-called "chosen ones" and "abandoned ones"), by God's will and grace or by their predestined "fate." "Looking down upon mortal life and looking up to God" became the highest article of faith and the rule of life.

The entire life of man thus became a world of tears. Men were regarded as poor lambs at the mercy of God in an endless sea of pain and sufferings. Their only way out was to expect God to show charity and kindness. In this way man's life from the cradle to the grave was enveloped in the seamless dark net of destiny.

Human stupidity was thus fully exposed. Progress in social production had freed a group of slaves economically and politically who had not originally belonged to the category of "man," thus expanding the scope of the meaning of man. But, on the other hand, by supporting and manipulating Christian theology, the exploiting classes once again put man--to some extent, man itself is included in the ruling and exploiting classes--at the mercy of God by weaving a bigger net of God's will. That is to say, man is under the duel control of natural forces and social oppression. Consequently, he lost that tiny bit of dignity gained in ancient society.

China

In the East, the Chinese went through a feudal period marked by some distinctive features. The traditional humanism and rationalism which long had existed in ancient Chinese culture had undermined any possibility of a religious group or theology gaining dominance, as did the Christian Church and its theology in Europe. The outstanding characteristics of this culture manifested the vitality of Chinese civilization and the profound strength of rationalism.

If we say that in medieval Europe the subordination of man to nature and to alienated social forces were manifest in the strict rule of the Christian religion and theology, then in China the subordination to nature and to the social forces was manifest in the absolute autocracy of the emperors and by the autocratic ethics of feudalism. In Europe, the representative of almighty God was the Christian Church set up by those, like St. Peter, who proclaimed himself to be the servant of God. Mortal power was only a tool given by God, via the Church, to rule the people.

In China, the feudal emporers considered themselves to have the qualities of both Jesus and the Christian Church. The emperor regarded himself as the "Son of Heaven" entrusted by Heaven to represent it in the mortal world. The life of the Chinese people under the rule of the emperor, who gathered in himself the powers of Jesus, the Apostles, the Church, Pope and King, was no easier than that of their counterparts in Europe.

If the Europeans were regarded as the sons, daughters and subjects of God (though entrusted by God to select the mortal heads to rule the people), then the Chinese at this time were sons and subjects of feudal emperors who "receive instructions from Heaven." The average Chinese at this time called their local magistrates "parent official" or "state herdsman." This concept indicated that the officials were entrusted by the "Son of Heaven" to supervise over his children and subjects. Or to put it more bluntly, they were like herdsmen told to look after this group of sheep, cattle and horses.

The Chinese in the Middle Ages threw away the pedantic overcoat of theology, regarded as unimportant, and resorted to an effective feudal ethics regarded as in compliance with the "ethics of Heaven." The so-called "three cardinal guidances" and "five constant virtues" put heaven and earth above man. The ideas that "ruler guides subject, father guides son, and husband guides wife" ran through the concept of the power of God, ruler, father and husband and the worship of ancestors. The medieval Chinese initiated a social hierarchy based upon this political ethics. In principle, under this kind of social order man was reduced to nothing because this terrible social order stipulated that the altars of Heaven and the Emperor are unlimited and the rights of man are infinitely small--which equals nothing.

Both in Europe or in China, the social order of feudal society showed the brutality, benightedness and hypocracy of the feudal ruling classes. Meanwhile, the dignity, pride and the rights of man were ruthlessly violated and destroyed. Of course, this does not mean that no progress had been made in the field of sciences and production. But the progress made did not save people from a state of subordination.

THE EMANCIPATION OF MAN IN MODERN TIMES: CONSOLIDATION OF THE CONCEPT OF MAN AS MASTER OF NATURE

Europe

As Europe moved gradually into the modern society from the time of the Renaissance, capitalist political and economic systems replaced those of the feudal Middle Ages.

Alongside this progress, mankind gradually restored its awareness and confidence in its own strength through a better understanding, and even conquering, of nature in its scientific and productive endeavors. Once again man developed the idea that he should control nature and be its master. This is a great breakthrough for mankind in modern intellectual history.

To overthrow feudalism in modern Europe, the first step was to destroy Christian theology which served it and provided its foundation. In particular, the submissive position of man to God and to nature should be demolished so as to restore the dignity and confidence of man in himself. A large group of outstanding and courageous poets, scientists, philosophers and thinkers have made great contributions in this respect. They developed such slogans as: "I am man and hope only for mortal happiness in this world"; "Our happiness is in this life, not in life after death." At the same time they attacked the Christian Church as the embodiment of benightedness. They strongly held that humans are all-powerful and possess enough wisdom to do everything for themselves. The strong wave of humanism in the Renaissance swept away the suffocating rule of theology. Men raise their heads high to face nature squarely. To some extent we can say that man was emancipated once again from nature and from theology, and restored to his true image.

The theoretical idea that man is able to understand and control nature, and thus become its master, was initiated by Bacon and Descartes, and later consolidated by Kant and Hegel in modern European philosophy.

Francis Bacon (1561-1626) demonstrated that man is capable of understanding the secrets of nature, i.e., the laws of nature, through summing up his experiences. Consequently, man is able to make use of, and conquer, nature. He pointed out: "Man . . . is the servant and explainer of nature";[2] "The only way to conquer nature is by obeying it."[3] This is what his phrase "Knowledge is power" actually meant, as do his statements: "The road to attain man's strength and his knowledge are next to each other"[4] and "Man's knowledge and power is consistent."[5] The direction pointed out by Bacon paved the way for the rapid development of the natural sciences and demonstrated the strength of Bacon's philosophy.

Descartes (1596-1650) proved a similar principle from another angle, by strongly emphasizing the importance of man's reasoning power. The earlier sacred, inviolable "authority" and "belief" are now subject to the "universal doubt" of human reason. Such slogans of the Middle Ages as "Believe and then understand" are cast away and everything has to be reestablished on the basis of the "Cogito, ergo sum" through the examination of reason. This shows that man occupies the central and dominant place in relation to god and the deified natural forces: Only "reason" is real and all-powerful. Hence, Descartes said with pride, "By way of practical philosophy, we can . . . enable ourselves to become the master and ruler of nature."[6] Talking about physics, he produced the famous saying, "Give me matter and motion, and I will make the world for you."[7] (It is interesting to note that a century later Kant repeated this sentence almost word for word). This led to setting up the "court of reason" established by the French enlightenment and materialist thinkers of the 18th century.

The two schools of empiricism and rationalism represented by Bacon and Descartes have some major differences as to the source, process and capability of understanding. But they both agree on the fundamental point, namely, that man is able to understand and control nature. This consensus was later proven by the philosophy of Kant (1724-1804) which contain strong elements of humanism. He proclaimed such famous dicta as "Man is the end, not only the means," man has absolute value and objective goals are regarded as the highest moral standard. This allows everyone to enjoy the same right and freedom in the "republic" (or in "the kingdom of ends"). A strong feature of Kant's philosophy, moreover, is his stress upon esteem for man not merely in a broad sense, but with particular regard to subjective initiative. This is what is meant by "Man is the legislator of nature."

He stated that "the highest legislation of nature must lie in our heart, i.e., in our understanding" and that "the understanding does not derive its laws (*a priori*) from nature, but prescribes them to nature."[8] According to Kant, man "goes back to nature and learns lessons from it; . . . he must not, however, do so in the character of a pupil who listens to everything that the teacher chooses to say, but of an appointed judge who compels the witnesses to answer questions which he has himself formulated."[9] That is, he approaches nature in terms of his own principle. This idealist theory has grave weaknesses and contradictions because he concluded that nature is the aggregate of all phenomena put together through the process of cognition, and not through "matter itself." By holding that the "thing-in-itself" belongs to an objective world over which man has no control, Kant restricted man's reason and left room for "belief."

Hegel (1770-1831) occupied this area under the name of "absolute spirit," which he put under the jurisdiction of reason. He regarded reason as the master of the whole of nature. Even nature is the outgrowth and alienation of "spirit" in his strange absolute idealism. In this way, "reason" and "spirit" are promoted to the highest, dominating position.

China

Compared with this modern development in Europe, the struggle against feudalism in China developed very late (after the Opium War in 1840) because of such special circumstances as the long continuation of the feudalistic society, the slow development of capitalism, the disasters brought about by imperialist invasions, etc. This struggle was interwoven with that against imperialism and national oppression at home, rendering comparatively weak the content of the movement for democracy and freedom in the intellectual history in China.

The peasant uprising known as the "Heavenly Kingdom of Peace" (1851-1865) led by Hong Xiuquan (1814-1864) was a search for a super combination of the Chinese feudalistic hierarchy and the free and equal relationship between Christianity's children of God. This strange combination of the hierarchy of the Catholic Church and Munzer's "Kingdom of one thousand years" is obviously very incomplete and contains grave internal contradictions. But it is a great breakthrough in the history of modern Chinese thinking, in that it fiercely attacked feudalistic ethics and Confucianism, advocated the ideal of the Great Harmony and praised free and equal relations between men.

Later Kang Youwei (1858-1927) and Tan Sitong (1865-1898) stated the weaknesses of the Chinese bourgeois classes and their illusion of compromise with feudalistic forces by following the road of reform known in history as the Constitutional Reform and Modernization. But Kang, in terms of explaining the ancient Chinese ideal of the Great Harmony, justified his advocacy of "seeking happiness and getting rid of pain," and expounded the despotism and ruthlessness of Confucian ethics.

Tan's "Theory of Charity" attacked harshly the cruelty and irrationality of the three cardinal guidances and the five constant virtues which plagued Chinese history for several thousand years. He advocated that this "net" should be torn up in order to set up a "free" and "equal" relationship of fraternity. This theory manifested a desire for the emancipation of man. Zhang Binglin (1869-1836) and Dr. Sun Yat-sen (1866-1925) were two great democratic thinkers in modern Chinese history. They held that the only way to achieve freedom and equality is through revolutionary means, i.e., to get rid of feudalistic bondage and set up a democratic republic. Sun elaborated the traditional ideal of the Great Harmony in terms of a strong belief in, and search for, man's emancipation and happiness.

CONTEMPORARY IDEAL: THE CONSCIOUS CONSTRUCTION OF AN HARMONIOUS RELATIONSHIP WITH NATURE-- MAN BEFRIENDING NATURE

A new ideal, namely, that man should have an harmonious relationship with nature has formed gradually along with the evolution of the idea that man should be the master of nature.

The new concept developed from the doctrine of 18th century French materialism and Feuerbach's anthropological materialism: Man is one entity with nature. The French materialists proved in particular that the unity of the world lies in its materiality. As La Mettrie (1709-1751) said humorously, "Man is not made of mere precious things; man is made of the same flour by Nature, but it used various yeasts and in a variety of ways."[10] They expanded Descartes' idea that "An animal is a machine" so much that they held that "Man is a machine," even "Man is a plant." Of course, La Mettrie's doctrine is wrong in that it underestimated and neglected the qualitative difference between man and other animals and plants. This erroneous trend was partially overcome when Diderot (1713-1784) put forward the idea that man's consciousness is a product of matter developed over a long period on the basis of the "sensibility" common to all matter. He concluded that this sensibility is a product of the special matter which makes up man's brain. When Holbach (1723-1789) and Helvetius (1715-1771) emphasized that "Man is a product of education," they touched upon the question of the social nature of man.

However, they did not fundamentally overcome their rigid naturalistic understanding of man and nature as a simple whole. That is, "Nature is the aggregation of all things on earth,"[11] "Man is the product of nature in which he exists; he is subject to its laws and can not transcend it."[12] Marx (1818-1883) and Engels (1820-1895) pointed out this crucial point when analyzing subordination to nature in the ideas of Feuerbach (1804-1872): "Being a materialist, history is beyond his vision; when he explores history, he is by no means a materialist."[13]

Production in capitalist societies developed at a stunning rate and paved the way for the rapid development of science and technology, while conversely, the contributions made by science and technology accelerated production. Successful transformation of nature by mankind appears to have demonstrated man's unlimited capabilities. The expectations cherished by the early philosophers that man should be the master of nature is being made a reality. By the 1980s mankind not only has conquered the earth, sea and sky, and utilized the natural resources that lie deep in the ground, but also is now extending its "magic stick" into space. It has landed on the moon, is exploring the space of the universe, and is approaching the other stars in the solar system. No doubt, all these achievements made by mankind in its struggle against nature have attested to the fact that mankind is not only identical with nature, but also its master.

But there is another side to the matter. The development of capitalist production and science has shown not only utilization and control of nature by man, but also how natural forces could control and "take revenge" upon mankind. The history of capitalist development has proven that the system of machine production has turned man into an auxiliary part, destroyed his health, happiness and instinctive nature, and made him into a distorted, impoverished and enslaved being. The focus of the present question is not that some part of mankind is being jointly enslaved by nature and society (the big hand that controls the destiny of the masses); but rather that the natural forces, like the evils released from a "Pandora's Box" are aiming the sword of revenge at the whole of mankind. In two world wars advanced military technology has destroyed tens of millions of lives. Mankind is now faced with nuclear power like the "sword of Damocles" hanging over its head. Rapid disappearance of forests, desertization of the land, ecological imbalance, disappearance and extinction of various animal species and plants, acid rain, pollution of air and environment, waste of water resources, plundering of mineral and aquatic resources, unplanned growth in population and explosive expansion of cities: all this shows that nature is not a submissive slave of mankind, but is capable of striking deadly blows at its cruel master.

When these phenomena began to emerge early in the 19th century a group of far-sighted socialists stressed the importance of adjusting human relations and their relationship with nature, and of converting the exploitation of man and nature into a harmonious relationship so as to realize the goal of turning nature into a human paradise; the communist doctrine of Marx reflected this insight. Ever since the 1950s, in light of the potential threat of nuclear weapons to mankind, scientists have issued a solemn call that "Science should be used for peaceful purposes." The Green Party which has sprung up in Europe in recent years and is now growing has taken upon itself the protection of the environment as an urgent humanistic and political task.

All this shows that there is a reawakening that man should be united with nature as one entity in this new historical period. Man and nature should have a harmonious relationship of dependence upon each other and of peaceful coexistence. Human history so far has proved that only through continuous efforts has man escaped from being enslaved by nature; thus he should not in turn simply enslave nature. Man should handle his relations with nature by enhancing its rational level. In dealing with this relationship of unity with its opposite, man should strive to push it to a higher stage--that of harmonious and interdependent unity with its opposite. That is, he should build a friendly relationship between man and nature--or befriend nature.

CONCLUSION: TURNING IDEALS INTO REALITY

Mankind has been through hundreds of thousands of years of evolution since it emerged from the animal world. It has witnessed additional thousands of years of development since it formed human society. The history of mankind, on the one hand, is one of tears and slavery, of conquering and being conquered, of killing and of man "eating man": human beings have suffered countless hardships. On the other hand, it is a history of mankind's constant search for a kingdom of reason and freedom through its endless efforts to rid itself of subordination to natural necessity and animality. Human reason, through its own efforts, has been building a kingdom--called by Kant the "Kingdom of Ends," in which human dignity and pride is respected. Countless martyrs, revolutionaries, sages, philosophers, great masters and scientists, together with the rank and file, have opened this road to further development for mankind through their constant and consistent groping and struggles toward this end.

Our era calls for the institution of a cordial relationship between man and nature through conscious human efforts. This is a grave historical task in which everyone is called to help. The least that one can do is to improve his or her level of consciousness by achieving a better understanding of the problem. Of course, the road of human development still will be accompanied with fire and sword, blood and tears; but mankind will, no doubt, pursue the course leading to the ideal and harmonious free kingdom.

Hegel has a famous saying: "What is reality is reasonable, and what is reasonable is reality."[14] "Reality" today, including the relationship among men and man's relations with nature, has a basis on which to exist: it is "reasonable." Further, it is a "reasonable" ideal to build an harmonious relationship between man and nature in accord with the law of historical development. This ideal should be turned into reality; it is the brilliant future sought by mankind.

Peking University
Beijing, People's Republic of China

NOTES

1. When this period began is a very difficult but interesting scientific problem of the pre-history of humankind, but will not be discussed here.

2. F. Bacon: *Novum Organum* (Indianapolis: Bobbs Merrill, 1960), I. 1. 3. 3.

3. *Ibid.*, II, 4.
4. *Ibid.*
5. *Ibid.*, I, 1. 3. 3.
6. R. Descartes, *Principles of Philosophy* in *Philosophical Works*, eds. E.S. Haldane and G.R. Ross (Cambridge: Cambridge Univ. Press, 1967), Vol. II.
7. *Ibid.*
8. I. Kant, *Prolegomena to Any Future Metaphysics* (Indianapolis: Bobbs Merrill, 1950), p. 36.
9. I. Kant, *Critique of Pure Reason* (New York: St. Martin, 1969), pp. xiii–xiv.
10. La Mettrie, *Man a Machine* (La Salle, Ill.: Open Court).
11. Holbach, *System of Nature or Laws of the Moral and Physical World* (New York: B. Franklin, 1971).
12. *Ibid.*
13. *The German Ideology* in Marx and Engels, *Complete Works*, Chinese ed., Vol. 3, p. 51.
14. Hegel, *The Principle of Philosophy of Law* (Oxford: Oxford Univ. Press, 1942).

PART IV

SUBJECTIVITY AND PERSON

CHAPTER X

MAN VS NATURE AND NATURAL MAN ONE ASPECT OF THE CONCEPT OF NATURE IN CHINA AND THE WEST

CHEN KUIDE

It is becoming more and more widely accepted that many important differences between relatively independent cultures of mankind may, in reality, be traced back to earlier, especially to so-called "Classical times" (about 500 B.C.). The basic hypotheses, value systems and modes of thinking which extensively dominate the various cultures were established at that time. This is especially true in philosophy. It raises the problem of identifying the essential factors which confront people in different cultures and exert a great influence in generating the above-mentioned hypotheses, value systems, etc.

Undoubtedly, people in every culture must first deal with their natural environment; their basic problem must be that of the relationship between "Man and Nature." True, a problem such as how people should form a community or a society must be important, but even problems of this kind arise from man's primary need to cope with nature so as to protect and develop himself. Therefore, the relation between men as well as social ethics are derivative of the relation of "Man and Nature." We can move a step further and suggest that reflection upon, and behavioral response to the essential problem of "Man and Nature" greatly influence the features of particular cultures, especially their basic philosophical hypotheses, modes of thinking and value systems.

Despite apparent differences, theoretical research about early features of cultures all touch upon the cause-effect relation between the natural environment of a certain culture and its reflection on the problem of "Man and Nature." This paper is concerned with the basic differences between the philosophical reactions to the relation of "Man and Nature" in Chinese and Western cultures, the elements related to this difference and present developments in this respect.

MAN'S NATURE AND NATURAL MAN

A correlation between the natural environment and culture seems undeniable. Ancient Greek civilization, one of the sources of Western culture, supports this point of view, for the Greeks attached great importance to the natural environment and its influence. Hippocrates, father of medicine and Greek scholar, suggested a theory of difference with regard to geography, soil, and climate: "human physiognomies may be divided between: a mountain type resulting from rich forests and water; a scarcity of water type on barren marshland; and a marshland type where there is wide low land that drains well. . . . Human body and character depend largely upon the natural circumstances."

The modern Irish writer G. Bernard Shaw agreed. A. J. Toynbee, the famous historian, disagreed, adding the untestable physical and behavioral reaction of human response. Nevertheless, his reciprocal behavioral model of "challenge and response" does consider the challenge from natural circumstances to be one of the prerequisites of civilization, and in the final analysis he still includes human reaction to the relation between "Man and Nature" among the essential elements that form early civilization.

In detailed research, however, this emphasis upon the hostility of natural circumstances seems insufficient to explain the birth of all cultures and only potentially reflects the natural circumstances in which ancient Greek civilization came into being. For example, as the islands in the Aegean Sea had poor soil three fifths of the land was unfit for cultivation, while commerce and fishing often suffered from storms. Therefore life in this area was challenging. This kind of seashore and hilly land is a typical non-agriculture area. Though nature provided scant food, the beautiful sea and landscapes compensated for this loss. Meanwhile, for the sake of commerce, it was necessary to predict storms. All this helped form basic visual-centered hypotheses for knowledge of nature. The rise of commerce that made possible communication among states and resulted in the exchange of cultural outlooks also helped to create an open, even aggressive, culture. In view of this, it is not difficult to understand why the basic Greek hypothesis was one of separation between the subject and the object. Given this contrast between man and nature, the basic aim of Greeks was to know the laws of nature so as to conquer and reform it.

Thus, early (Pre-Socratic) Greek philosophy was focused upon nature or "nature-centered." Contrary to man by whom it is to be known and conquered, this nature will be termed "Man's nature" in this paper. This rational, analytic and logicized outlook sets man and nature as opponents. It is characterized by a separation between subject and object, and by a dualism that counterpoises the two in mutual confrontation.

Another main element, the Hebrew element, in the formation of Western culture contributes a transcendent dimension. In some respect this has something to do with the natural environment which surrounded the Jews, their national characteristic and their unfortunate historical experiences.

The barren environment, the bitter racial surroundings, and the misfortune of being conquered by other countries exerted great influence upon the Hebrew psyche and the essential features of Hebrew civilization. As "the chosen of God," they imputed all their suffering to their betrayal of God. That is, they believed that worldly seeking and satisfaction were evils against God; man should regard worldly life as a punishment from God, as a hell or degradation. The only way to save oneself was to be converted to God, to regard worldly life as a pilgrimage to heaven and thus transcend the real world. This led to a highly transcendent cultural psychology and to philosophical hypotheses contrasting God and man, heaven and the world. In this philosophical horizon, God and heaven are transcendent, outside of man and beyond his reach. The combination of Hebrew transcendence caused by religion and the Greek separation of subject and object based upon reason formed Christian civilization or Western culture.

But this "challenge-response" model cannot be applied without limit, especially in meeting other cultures. In fact, hostility to nature represents only the basic feature of seaside environment or of hubs of communication; it cannot be a feature of all cultures. For example, it is quite alien to the Far Eastern continental and agricultural milieus.

Clearly, the cultural formation of ancient China is typically continental and agricultural. For this vast land--with the Pacific ocean to the East, the Gobi desert to the Northwest, Qingzhuang Plateau to the West and Siberia and Mongolia to the North--contact with the outer world was difficult. China was seen as "the center of the world" and the people living here for generations developed a corresponding illusion that influenced their cultural psychology. This continent did not experience the drastic climatic changes of ancient Greece or Europe; here, the climate is mild, plants prosper and agriculture is the backbone of life. Since nature provides man with what he needs, and good will surpasses hostility, man cultivated a kind feeling toward the land, even combining himself with it. As nature did not present a serious challenge to man or threaten his life, philosophical hypotheses did not separate man and nature, or regard nature as something dead opposed to man, or an object to be known and conquered. On the contrary, these hypotheses emphasized agreement between man and nature. They held that the former was the product of the latter, and that the two were one: "Knowing all one's nature and finally knowing the laws of nature (*Tian*)," said Mencius. (Note that *Tian* in Chinese means: 1. nature, 2.

heaven, 3. laws of nature.) Therefore, in Chinese culture the study of nature retreated from primary to secondary place. Ancient Chinese philosophy focused upon moral, human and social relations, upon shaping an image of man, and finally elaborated a "human-centered" culture.

In this culture what is the best example for man, what principle should one follow in order to be a man? The answer is nothing other than nature, or *Tian-Di* (Heaven and Earth). The so-called "*Tian-Di*, ruler, parents, teacher" means that nature (*Tian-Di*) is above teacher, even parents and ruler. The various schools in Pre-Ch'in (Dynasty), though differing in particulars, agreed upon the following of nature, belief in an intimate relation between man and nature. This can be seen in the following quotations:

  - Lao Tzu's basic hypothesis was that man should follow nature: "Man follows *Di* (Earth), *Di* follows *Tian* (Heaven), *Tian* follows *Tao* (Way), *Tao* follows nature" (*Tao Te Ching*; Heaven Chap. 25).
  - Confucius took nature as man's bosom friend by saying: "Who knows me but Tian?" (*Xian Wen*, 14, Chap. 35).
  - *Yi Zhuan* illustrates the Tao of man by means of the Tao of Tian: "Tang Wu revolution followed Tian, and therefore applied to man" (*Yi Zhuan*, p. 341-342).
  - Mencius declared: "Everything is bestowed on me" (*Jin Xin* I, Chap. 4).
  - Chuang Tzu followed nature in a calm manner and without intensive efforts: "You are perfect when you know nature and man" (*Da Zhong Shi*).

In these quotations, most ancient Chinese thinkers believed that the "little cosmos" of man and the "great cosmos" of Tian-Di share the same natural feature: the two are correlative and correspond one to the other, as is expressed by the term: "interaction of man and nature." Once we know this we can thoroughly understand the fact that people predicted their fate by examining the movements of the sun, the moon and the stars, and could call someone "a star descending to the world." This, of course, does not mean that everyone is the "true man" following nature. It is only a model of the Chinese cultural ideal: the perfect or true man is the one who "knows fate," who is the disciple of nature, who follows nature, who performs the will of nature and who himself is part of nature. His character is in accordance with laws of nature (*Way of Heaven*); immanently he actually contains these laws. This is the essential hypothesis, quite characteristic in Chinese philosophy: the unity of Nature and Man. In this paper the man with ideal personality is called "natural man". This manifests that Chinese philosophy is essentially monistic and immanent. Monism here indicates that "Nature" and "Man" are not different objects independent of, and separate from, each other, but form an inseparable unity.

Chuang Tzu sought to "go along with the law of nature and adapt to changes of the six kinds of air, ("*Xiao Yao You*" thus minimizing individuality and excluding self-centeredness and other elements contrary to nature. This is what Chuang Tzu meant by "Xiao Yao," free and unfettered in nature: "*Tian-Di* (Heaven and Earth) with me, everything with me" (*Qi Wu Lun*). This, finally, is the "true man."

In brief, few ancient Chinese thinkers advocated that man should be separated from nature; it is only a minor current of thought. Moreover, we should not ignore the fact that for man to be separated from nature implied the latent prerequisite that man and nature were united and unseparated in origin. If nature and man were independent substances, there would be no need to divide them.

In sharp contrast to western philosophy, Chinese pre-Ch'in (Dynasty) philosophical schools did not think of *Tian-Di* and nature as transcendental objects, independent of man and in another world, nor did they believe that there was another deified *Tian* (heaven) or creator beyond everything in the world. There was no such concept as two absolutely separated and independent cosmos. Their cosmos was naturally formed, monistic and immanent. There was no room for exterior transcendence in Chinese philosophical hypotheses. There was no place in the hypotheses of Chinese philosophy for a dualistic contrast between man and nature, for the concept that it was man's duty to know and conquer nature, or for a separation of subject and object.

In sum, the emphasis upon "natural man" in Chinese philosophy and upon "man's nature" in western philosophy are drastically different from the beginning. The features are natural for Chinese culture originating in an agricultural society located in the environment of the Central Plains at that time.

DUALISM AND ITS CRITIQUE: THE WESTERN APPROACH TO CHINESE PRINCIPLES

As has been illustrated, Western civilization with Greek and Hebrew elements as its main components is basically dualistic. In Greek civilization this has its source in the hypothesis of a separation of subject and object. From the outset, nature appeared as something outside man. This hypothesis constituted the basis for a naturalistic, logicized and epistemological civilization.

Note that the definition of dualism in this paper is based on an absolute separation of subject and object. If this separation is the prerequisite of human epistemological activities, the basic spiritual orientation of civilization is dualistic. Thus, many so-called doctrines of monism in history, for example Hobbes' monistic materialism and Hegel's monistic absolute idealism, were more basically dualistic in the sense that only on the ground of the separation of subject and object could they develop ther ontological systems.

The impassable gulf between man and God in Hebrew civilization gradually became more apparent and deeper in Christian culture. These two factors were unchangeably independent and unrelated, not two poles of a unity.

The basic dualism in western culture gave rise to various dualistic oppositions in Western philosophy and religion: nature and super-nature, God and man, the creator and the created, subject and object, cause and effect, soul and body, spiritual and material, general and particular, phenomenon and essence, form and matter, knowledge and opinion, idea and action, theory and praxis, reason and experience, and so forth.

This fundamental opposition within culture formed a certain dynamic tension, tendency and immanent dynamic that made the dualistic powers and Greek and Hebrew elements grow or decline, rise or fall, conflict or combine; it brought about historic revolutions and development in the culture which it thereby rendered dynamic.

In their primary principles, the fundamental contrast between Chinese and Western cultures is that of "monism" and "dualism," "combination" and "separation," "immanence" and "transcendence." The rest of the differences are attached to these primary ones.

Anyone who studies Western culture will soon feel two different or even contrary fields--two different worlds: the objective and the subjective, nature and man. The former, submitting to the iron scientific law, with objectivity as its basic feature, is a dead, quantitative, geological and physical world in which everything except man has its own place. The latter, with subjectivity as its basic feature, is the live, qualitative, psychological world full of feeling, reason and free will. The two are absolutely separate and independent. The cosmos is divided into two quite different parts. The latter is only the audience for the former which it observes, recognizes, studies and conquers, whereas the former is basically passive, analyzed and discovered. From this there develops a culture oriented toward strict logic, analysis, preciseness and science. At the same time, it should noted that this logicized culture is closely linked with the dualistic hypotheses above. Indeed, it is when this culture focuses its attention upon nature as dead and opposite to man that the logical, geological, scientific and objective cultural patterns emerge.

This logicized and dualistic pattern is further strengthened by the "subject-predicate" pattern in Western language systems. The main Western language systems (Greek, Latin, English, German, French, etc.) belong to the Indo-European linguistic family. All use the basically dualistic "subject-predicate" pattern. This is potentially influential for such philosophical prerequisites as the dichotomy of substance and attribute. As the English mathematician, logician and philosopher A. N. Whitehead noted:

> Here the reaction between his (Aristotle's) philosophy and his logic worked very unfortunately. In his logic, the fundamental type of affirmative proposition is the attribution of a predicate to a subject. . . . The unquestioned acceptance of the Aristotelian logic has led to an ingrained tendency to postulate a substratum for whatever is disclosed in sense-awareness, namely, to look below what we are aware of for the substance in the sense of the concrete thing. . . . Accordingly 'substance', . . . is a correlative term to 'predication'.

It is not clearly known which--language or philosophical hypotheses--was the cause and which the effect. However, the fact that they are related through positive feedback and that both have contributed to each other is unquestionable. We cannot ignore the positive impact of Western language systems upon its dualistic cultural formation.

In Western dualistic, logicized and analytic culture, the cosmos is divided into two separate parts. This separation became all the greater with the emergence of Cartesianism. Descartes defined spirit and matter as two independent substances that could not be linked. His theory, carrying the tension within Western philosophy to the extreme, became the origin of a series of arguments and prejudices which extended until the end of the last century. Two worlds, two sets of truth, yet without truth: this became the tragedy of Western culture when dualism was carried to its extremes. But when things become extreme the develop in the opposite direction. Thus, since the end of the 19th century a new spiritual tendency directed toward the Oriental has developed.

In the Twentieth century, in the fields of philosophy and science there arose a critical introspective trend that reexamined these cultural hypotheses, especially the dualistic opposition. The philosophers by their insight, and the scientists by their achievements met in a general tendency to emphasize cosmic organicism, systematization, wholeness and unity. Their stress upon the concept that man is product and part of nature, upon the philosophical connotation of the harmony and agreement between the two, had something in common with the basic hypotheses of Chinese philosophy.

H. Bergson was the first to criticize the belief in traditional logicized Western modes of thought. Whereas the traditional concept regarding nature was still and lifeless, he emphasized the creative flow of life in nature.

In William James's theory the subject-object and soul-material dualisms and the epistemological orientation came under ever greater challenge. John Dewey questioned dualism in every form: nature and life, mind and body, material and form, feeling and reason, action and standard. Further, he pointed out that experience should be, not a wall separating man and nature, but a link between the two as fundamentally continuous and united.

A. N. Whitehead sharply attacked "The bifurcation of nature" and tried to build a bridge between man and nature, between what was spiritual and what material. "We require that the deficiencies in our concept of physical nature should be supplied by its fusion with life. And we require that, on the other hand, the notion of life should involve the notion of physical nature" (Whitehead, *Modes of Thought*, p. 205).

M. Heidegger opposed especially the so-called idea of an "objective world" which regards the world as an epistemological object for the subject. He pointed out that in German the term "object" had the etymological meaning of "opposite," whereas it was the concept of "opposite" that Heidegger tried hard to eliminate. In his later philosophical works, he regarded Lao Tzu's Tao and his own philosophy to be similar in tone. In *The Way to Language* he had arrived at an interfusion of nature and man.

A similar rebellion was taking place among natural scientists. N. Bohr argued that modern science, especially quantum physics had shown that "Man is both the audience and the actor on the stage of nature." This emphasized man's involvement in nature as caused by modern science.

"The Principle of Uncertainty" in quantum mechanics discovered by W. Heisenburg tells us that there is no "pure objective reality" because of the uncontrollable interaction between observation and phenomena. The Greek subject-object dualistic "pure observation" is gone forever: the distinction between subject and object, man and nature, self and universe, once limited by the principle of uncertainty was no longer absolute. The development of science has led to what Bohr calls "the principle of integrality" and "the principle of complementarity." To illustrate these principles, Bohr quotes time and again from Buddha and Lao Tzu. We can easily find in Bohr's works statements similar to such propositions as "correspondence between man and nature," and "interfusion of nature and man."

I. Prigogine, founder of the theory of dissipative structures, claims that the separation of man and nature hypothesized by Western philosophy and science has, through the development of science itself, come nearly to an end. The theory of dissipative structures about self-organization in non-equilibrium systems has probed into the laws shared both by the inorganic and organic worlds, built a bridge between live and dead things, and introduced unity between man and nature on the bases of scientific achievement. Prigogine also mentioned his admiration for ancient Chinese philosophy.

A CRITIQUE OF UNITY IN CHINESE THOUGHT: A SEARCH FOR SOME FACTORS IN WESTERN THOUGHT

The direction of this new trend in Western culture is quite clear. However, we should avoid being misled by it and blindly contented. This paper does not intend to over-emphasize a trend toward, or an admiration for, oriental culture: just the contrary. Hence, it will attempt to illustrate briefly the following three points.

First, the comparison of the historical richness of the two. True, some Western philosophers and scientists over a long period of time have established a concept of integral nature with such anti-dualistic features as the unity of subject and object and of man and nature. This must be seen in the context of the basically dualistic Western cultural background and moves from "man as contrary to nature" to "natural man." The words which explain this concept of unity are undoubtedly similar to the ancient Chinese philosophical hypothesis of the Interfusion of Nature and Man, but they carry a quite different meaning. The former is the result of overcoming obstacles and proceeds through a spiral development, while the latter is primary, continuous and without negation. One is dynamic, the other is static. As far as richness and concreteness are concerned there is a difference also in the range and depth of the historical connotation, and at present in the main historical trend and challenge confronting the two. In brief, the inert primary hypotheses of Chinese culture are by no means advantageous.

Secondly, there is a difference in basic methodological principles. Though the critical reexamination by Western philosophers and scientists of some primitive hypotheses in their culture has reached radical conclusions, it must be pointed out that philosophical criticism is still the product of logical deduction. This "logos-centered" doctrine is the inherent prerequisite of Western culture: scientists reach their conclusions through the natural sciences which are "logos-centered". It should be noted that the dualistic subject-object principle, which holds that the laws of nature have nothing to do with man, is the basic hypothesis in science. In a logically paradoxical movement the conclusion drawn from this methodological prerequisite has now arrived at its opposite in a logically paradoxical movement. Thus, the Western philosophers and scientists who look critically into their own culture still regard their culture's logic as their basic method.

Though there is a trend toward the primary features of Chinese culture, the foundations of these, that is, the methodological starting points, are essentially quite different. At the same time it should be kept in mind that the conclusions achieved by logical thinking and science may also change according to the same logical deduction or future scientific achievements. That is to say, as change is the character of Western culture, we have no reason to suppose that its basic feature will remain directed toward the concept of unity as some scholars hold now. Nor can we rule out other possible features that may be quite different from those of Chinese culture. We should be clear about this.

Thirdly, let us consider the strengths and weaknesses of the hypotheses in Chinese culture. There are many excellent propositions in the works of Pre-Ch'in (Dynasty) philosophers. As the ancient Chinese language is highly inclusive and condensed, it is rich in meaning and deep in thought; but as it lacks complete logical form it is often polysemous and metaphoric, and thus relatively ambiguous in meaning. The merit of this concise language lies in its self-protection from questioning and negation by logical argument. On the other hand, the lack of logical forms makes it difficult to establish the objective criterion of its truth and falsehood, its truth or error, and to certify this by facts and deductive reasoning.

On further study, we find also that the early linguistic expression of this culture is aesthetic in its essence. It can enlighten varied kinds of images, and has a strong poetic quality; it is full of genial intuition, cleverness and enlightennment. But it is short of Platonic, Aristotelian and Euclidian logical deduction; it is not "logos-centered." Therefore, it is very hard for Chinese culture totally to falsify or reject any proposition, for lack of an acknowledged criterium to judge a theory or a school. We can say whether a poem is beautiful, but not whether it is right. The process of break-up and falsification needed for historical development and revolution can hardly happen. For reasons mentioned above, deepening ancient Chinese philosophical propositions and theories, as well as new and creative achievements, are nearly impossible; vitality shrinks. Due to their linguistic features ancient Chinese philosophical propositions are over-broad, over-inclusive, too unspecified, ambiguous and polysemous; their aesthetic intent is more important than their logical intent, and their significance is greater in enlightening than for knowledge. They aquire tenacity against refutation and falsification, and hence are conducive to stagnation and conservatism.

In one sense, during the last hundred years one of the important tasks for the Chinese cultural reform has been to solve the above problems, namely, in this new age when different cultures meet, how to create within the Chinese culture or assimilate from without the dynamic elements needed for its development. As is known, because of the historical stagnation of the ancient forms, this reform often has changed course, advancing and retreating with great spiritual suffering, social divisions, and upheavals.

In contrast, contemporary western culture has been carrying out a self-examination of its own perduring logos-centered doctrine at unprecedented depth. We cannot say if it is able to escape this position because, in spite of some novel and creative critical texts, at its deepest levels it continues to emphasize logic. Perhaps this is the ineluctable fate of the West.

In general, both China and the West are facing up to their own history. Clearly these are different and even take contrary directions. The question remains: is there any point of convergence of the two cultures? The answer to that question must be left to history.

Fudan University
Shanghai, People's Republic of China

CHAPTER XI

WESTERN AND CHINESE PHILOSOPHY ON MAN AND NATURE

RICHARD T. DE GEORGE

Western philosophy differs significantly from traditional Chinese Philosophy and Professor Chen Kuide's paper perceptively notes a number of the differences. Western philosophy, with its roots in both Greek philosophy and the Hebraic tradition developed a dualistic approach to reality, distinguishing man from nature, subject from object, mind from matter. The Hebraic-Christian tradition added the notion of transcendence, completing the ultimate separation--that of God from this creation.

Chinese philosophy, by contrast, has from the start emphasized immanence and unity. Where Western dualism led to an opposition of man and nature, Chinese monism led to a harmony between the two.

The Western division led to considering nature as an object and its study as science; whereas the study of the human subject or spirit led to logic, to epistemology, and to the study of human psychology and freedom. By contrast the Chinese emphasis on monism and harmony led to aesthetics more than to logic, to a search for deeper meanings rather than for falsification or verification of propositions. As a result Chinese philosophy has less tension in it then Western philosophy. Where the contrasts present in the West were a source of dynamism, the harmony of the Chinese view, the respect for tradition and the search for wisdom led historically to a more static worldview.

These generalizations based on Professor Chen Kuide's paper are acute, plausible and suggestive. His paper does more than just note them. He attempts to account for the differences and argues that a number of important contemporary philosophers and scientists find the insights of Chinese monism more compatible than Western dualism and transcendence with the theories to which they are being led by the internal logic of their research and thought.

Suggestive though they be, Professor Chen Kuide's paper and his explanatory hypothesis are not convincing as they stand. To criticize them is to exemplify the concern with logical argument, analysis, and the truth and falsity of propositions that he correctly notes are typical of Western philosophy.

Professor Chen Kuide traces Western philosophy back to its Greek and Hebraic roots. He explains the Greek contrast between man and nature, subject and object as resulting from

Greek environmental conditions, and the Hebrew notion of transcendence as resulting from the difficulties of the Israelites. Although there may be some link between a country's physical environment and the thought developed there, any serious attempt to demonstrate that link must show how the thought comes from the environment. We cannot simply take what we know of Greek, Israeli, and Chinese environmental and historical conditions and claim that these determined what we know their thought to have been. Explanations require that the causal links be found and demonstrated.

Nevertheless, suppose that together with Professor Chen Kuide we believe that conditions determine (in some sense of that term) the thought or world view of a society. A difficulty then arises in explaining why and how the Greek and Hebraic traditions were successfully transported out of Greece and Israel and why they were accepted and developed in Europe, Great Britain, and the New World. The many Western societies that are so greatly influenced by Greek and Hebraic thought are very different environmentally from the conditions of Greece and Israel. Agriculture was the backbone of Western Europe, just as it was the backbone of China. Why did the Greco-Hebraic tradition, rather than something like the Chinese view, take root and survive in these lands?

It is clear that natural environmental conditions are insufficient by themselves to determine thought. It is also clear that origins are different from validity and the one is not sufficient to explain the other.

If the environmental thesis were accurate, we would expect different philosophies to have developed originally in what is now France, Germany, Great Britain and America than that in Greece. Since Greek thought influenced and to some extent was adopted by the Romans, it must have had something to recommend it over the indigenous philosophical counterpart. Similarly, for Christianity to have triumphed in the Roman Empire requires more of an explanation than can be provided by environment and the hardships of the Israelites. Chinese thought may be traced to its original roots and the influence of tradition may there be used to explain later Chinese thought. Original roots might help explain later Greek thought in Greece. But it does not easily explain why Greek thought was adopted by the countries to which it was transported, where it was partially lost and then rediscovered.

Moreover, Greece gave rise to both Plato's rationalism and to his pupil's, Aristotle's, empiricism. They do not share a similar view of the relation of man and nature although they grew from the same society, the same geographical environment. Both exerted a strong impact on Western thought.

Why they dominated Western European thought arguably has to do with their comprehensiveness, logical consistency, coherence, and their power in making sense of human experience in comparison to the other available worldviews. Neither environmental nor historical conditions by themselves are adequate to explain either the specific views or their continuing power. If worldviews as a whole are not true or false, they are more or less adequate to experience, more or less fruitful. They can be and are evaluated, changed, discarded or exchanged for other views, as the history of Western thought demonstrates.

The development and power of Christianity and of the Judeo-Christian traditions is also difficult to explain only in terms of environment and socio-cultural conditions. The rapid rise of Christianity in the Roman Empire from the status of a slave religion to the religion of the Empire requires more than geographical and cultural causes. The Judeo-Christian notion of transcendence was joined to an ethic that had, and continues to have, strong human appeal, both logically and emotionally.

Professor Chen Kuide's paper, as well as a common view of comparative East-West philosophy, presents a picture of a dynamic West and a static East. But the picture is not entirely accurate. China developed many inventions before the West. At least until the 16th Century China was more inventive than the West. If the traditions were the same in China for 2,500 years and in the West for 2,500 years, how do we explain the change as of 500 years ago when the West started to develop science and technology in a way China did not? There may be something in the claim that Western thought with its subject-object dichotomy lent itself more easily to the scientific study of nature than did the Chinese view of harmony with nature. But that is not even plausibly the whole story.

The Chinese inventions discovered and borrowed by the West were made by Chinese who viewed man and nature in harmony. That harmony did not in itself preclude inventiveness and in some sense for a time fostered it. Why and how it did, and why it failed to continue to do so are questions that deserve investigation. But the historical facts indicate that the answer cannot be obtained by looking only at a society's view of the relation of nature and man. Western culture for many centuries did not produce as much in the way of inventions as did Chinese culture. Western Europe experienced "dark ages" that China did not. The rediscovery of Greek thought in the West in the late Middle Ages helped bring about the Renaissance and the rise of modern science, which the Greeks had not themselves developed. Clearly the story of the development of science is a complicated one and we should not place too much weight on oversimplifications.

Professor Chen Kuide notes that advanced Western philosophers and scientists are learning from Chinese thought and that they quote Chinese monistic views favorably. What we are to make of this is not clear. If it is that Chinese monism is more favorable to the findings of contemporary science than Western philosophical views, it is puzzling why the Western rather than the Chinese views have led to the developments of contemporary science. There is, of course, a monistic line of thought in the West--the Greek atomists, Spinoza, the materialists of modern European philosophy from Hobbes to Marx. Did modern science in fact develop from Western monism rather than from Western dualism? Is the source of Western dynamism less monism or dualism than the tension between different views, e.g., between monism and dualism, idealism and materialism? What is the attraction of some contemporary philosophers and scientists to Chinese thought? These are questions that call for detailed examination and explanation. Whether in fact the best--whatever that may be--of both Eastern and Western thought can be combined is yet to be decided.

If the claim that Western thought is built on dualism and transcendence is correct, are they compatible with Chinese monism and immanence? If the dynamism of the West is due to dualism (of many sorts) and transcendence, should they be given up? If monism and dualism, transcendence and immanence are opposites, then they cannot be held simultaneously. If Western dualism and transcendence are really at the base of Western scientific development, then the argument from the success of the West in developing science and technology is a reason for not giving up dualism and transcendence. If one places dualism and transcendence at the heart of Western thought and then claims them false or mistaken or misleading, one is forced to hold that error is more fruitful than truth or that misleading notions are better than correct ones--views that seem both to be implausible and to be contradicted by the advances of science.

We are thus lead to reconsider the accuracy of the claim both that dualism and transcendence are at the heart of Western thought and that they are the reasons for the dynamism of the West, especially since the Renaissance. No doubt it helps to study nature if it is seen as an object, as Western science views it. Transcendence, it might be argued, led to Western philosophers placing emphasis on subjectivity, spirit, and freedom. A combination of human freedom, of intellectual curiosity, logical thought, and an approach to nature as an object to be investigated are probably necessary to the development of science as we find it in the West.

The rise of modern science went hand in hand with the rise of modern economics, which required a degree of political freedom. It is not clear that we can separate science from economics from politics. The development of science may well require not only a view of nature as object but also a degree of human freedom which requires a view of man as subject. The latter, in turn, has developed together with the notion of human beings as moral persons with human rights. Whether the pieces can be separated, whether science can develop without freedom, and intellectual freedom flourish without political freedom are empirical, as well as logical questions. Historically we find them together; logically we can distinguish them. Whether Western and Chinese views of nature and man can be combined, and if so how, are questions of both logic and experience.

The introduction of Marxism into China, which might be seen as an attempt at integrating Western and Chinese thought, also poses a special puzzle. Marxism is thoroughly Western in its origin and in its original development. It had no Chinese roots, yet it has been widely adopted in China. Ironically, Marxism has long been criticized in the West for its inability to explain Asiatic development as clearly as Western development and for its Western bias. Marx studied primarily Western bourgeois capitalist society and its development. He saw industrialization and the development of productive forces necessary for the development of the post-capitalist phase, which he called socialism. Yet we find a version of Marxism strong in China, which is still heavily agricultural, while Marxism does not flourish in the Western industrial countries about which Marx wrote.

This paradox raises the question of the compatibility of Marxism and traditional Chinese thought. Marxism claims to be monistic and lacks the notion of transcendence, yet it is Western and claims to be scientific. Its monism is not Chinese monism and it emphasizes contradiction as the heart of reality rather than harmony. Despite its claims to being scientific, the natural sciences arguably continue to develop more fruitfully in the West than in countries that have adopted Marxism as their ideology.

All this implies that although Chen Kuide's paper is suggestive, it may be more fruitful to ask where it is incomplete, misleading, or incorrect than in simply agreeing with its undoubted insights. This is, in fact, an essential part of Western method. Popper has argued that in physical science we look for falsifications. The same is true in Western philosophy: we are clearer and surer about what is false than we are about what is true. A pragmatic stream of Western science and philosophy seeks for fruitfulness. In the approach to the relation of man and nature Western philosophers seek fruitfulness as well. Some Western thinkers are attracted by the traditional Chinese view of the harmony of man and nature. Whether it can be integrated fruitfully with Western views we can determine only by trying. So far the attempts have been few and the fruits minimal.

In the East the attempt is to learn the science of the West while avoiding the many pitfalls of Western development. The practical Chinese adoption of Western science is further advanced than either the reconciliation of the Western scientific view with the traditional Chinese views of nature and man, or the intellectual task of attempting to combine the best of the Chinese and Western views. The hope of many is that the best of Chinese thought can be preserved and that it can assimilate Western science. The success so far is also minimal.

Nonetheless there is reason to believe that both China and the West can learn from each other's traditions in rethinking a relation of man and nature that is appropriate and that will be fruitful for our respective societies. Such rethinking need not lead to identical views, unless one believes there is only one proper relation between man and nature. History provides a basis for arguing that this is not the case.

Although physical, social, and economic conditions are not the sole determining factors of thought, they undoubtedly exert an influence. The present growing interdependence and interconnection of East and West thus provide both the impetus and the general ambience for seeking new, fruitful, and mutually compatible views of the relation of man and nature. The growing interrelation of peoples demands a reconciliation of differing views as the interaction of one society with nature impacts on other societies, e.g., through failure to control the pollution it generates. Yet here, too, practice demands compatibility, not identity of views. Mutual learning is the ideal, rather than dominance by any view or forced conversion, both of which would lead to the loss of the best in each tradition. The intellectual task of combining the best of Chinese and Western thought on the relation of man and nature, is a task still to be done. It is clearly one worth attempting.

University of Kansas
  Lawrence, Kansas, U.S.A.

CHAPTER XII

THE DEVELOPMENT OF THE PRINCIPLE OF SUBJECTIVITY IN WESTERN PHILOSOPHY AND OF THE THEORY OF MAN IN CHINESE PHILOSOPHY

ZHANG SHI-YING

The philosophical ideology of various countries and peoples constitutes an organic whole; the historical development of human thought is the historical development of this organic whole. It resembles a giant tree which will live forever; the philosophical schools of various countries and peoples are the branches, leaves, flowers and fruits of this tree. We can make either a horizontal or vertical comparison of the philosophical ideologies of various countries and peoples. A horizontal comparison refers mainly to a study made of the characteristics, similarities and differences between philosophical schools in various countries taken statically. By vertical comparison we mean the study of the development of different schools with regard to their philosophical ideologies as found among various countries and peoples, their historical role, stages of development, contributions and inadequacies on this giant tree.

Our comparative research should not be limited to a simple horizontal comparison, but should include a deeper vertical comparison which has great significance for comparative research. Only a vertical comparison can find the basic rules for the development of philosophical ideology. Also, only if we place the philosophical ideology of each nationality and country in the context of the historical development of ideology can we see whether it is advanced or backward, good or bad. On the contrary, an abstract or static comparison can hardly claim which school of philosophical ideology is good and which is bad, which has value and which does not have value.

Thirdly, a comparative study is not made for the sake of making comparisons, but in order to discover what kind of effort the countries of the world should make in the future in the fields of culture and ideology. Only by making a vertical comparison will it be possible for us to do this.

What then is the basic principle and orientation of the ideological development of the whole of mankind? This is a question which can be answered only when we have looked at a considerable amount of historical material and, on that basis, make a careful study of the history of ideological development. No subjective assumptions can be made. Judging by the level of our present research, the history of the development of human ideology is largely the history of an integrated subject and object as they first become separated and opposed to each other, and then demand unity once again. This basic trend conforms to the process of the development of individual ideology.

The German word *subjektivität* and the English word *subjectivity* are translated into *zhutixing*, or sometimes, *zhuguanxing*. *Zhugunaxing* often appears to be a term which means arbitrary, willful and one-sided in Chinese. In fact, in Western or German philosophy, and in particular in classical German philosophy, *subjektivitat* refers mainly to independence, self-decision, freedom, initiative, self, self-awareness, the particularity of the individual, the display of the wisdom and ability of the individual, with the free will and ability of the individual as a basis, etc. To be controlled or ruled by the others, to take orders from God, to believe in superstition and fate, to be at the mercy of nature and other forces, to be lacking in self-awareness, to speak generally to the neglect of the individual, to judge or evaluate a person by his family background and for one's marriage to be arranged by parents or match-makers--all these are expressions of a lack of subjectivity.

The history of the development of human ideology is first and foremost a history of the separation of man from the ranks of the animals--a history of development from lack of subjectivity to the attainment of subjectivity. The difference between man and animal is, in a sense, that animals cannot tell the difference between the subject and the object but man can. To animals, the subject and object are one and the same; for this reason animals do not have an awareness of "self." The subject will exist only when the subject and object are separated and set against each other; only man is able to do this. The existence of self-awareness and a concept of the subject is a watershed between man and animals.

Of course, once man has acquired self-awareness and become conscious of the subject after having differentiated subject and object, the subject of the self-awareness still has to go through a process of development from a low to a high level, as well as a process of constantly overcoming the antithesis between the subject and object and seeking unity. Once the concept of subject and self-awareness has been established it is not unalterable. Therefore the process of separation of man from animals or the process of the development of subjectivity is long and tortuous. The development of an individual from birth to old age in fact takes place within a short and limited space of time. From the history of the development of human ideology and the history of the ideological development of a people or a state one is able more clearly to perceive the tortuous and eternal nature of the course. The time needed for the development of an individual until he acquires self-awareness can be calculated in terms of years or months, but the development of human ideology or the development of the ideology of a people or a state--from lack of self-awareness to attainment of self-awareness--should be calculated in terms of hundreds or thousands of years.

There follow some examples from Western philosophy which can be used to explain the above process.

THE DEVELOPMENT OF THE PRINCIPLE OF SUBJECTIVITY IN THE HISTORY OF WESTERN PHILOSOPHY

In ancient Greek philosophy (the infant stage of the development of human ideology) people were merely surprised by the external environment and nature; they had no time for self-examination. Therefore, the naivety of ancient Greek philosophy found its expression first and foremost in its failure to perceive the antithesis between subject and object. The doctrine of hylozoism which was in vogue at the time regarded the subject and object, man and nature, as a united whole. The theory of Parmenides on thinking and existence cannot be explained according to modern theories. One view held that this is merely an expression of the above-mentioned doctrine (hylozoism) which regarded the subject and object as a united whole.

However, Plato's "theory of ideas" set the world of ideas and the world of senses against each other. In a sense, this theory separated thinking from existence, but both worlds were external environments outside man. Plato took the world of ideas to be the universal and unified aspects of the outside world and the world of senses to be its specific and diversified aspects. He failed to take them as relationships between the subject, man, and the object, the external environment and nature. Like most ancient Greek philosophers, Plato studied philosophical questions mainly with regard to nature itself. In other words, they were questions concerning ontology. Man was not regarded as a subject with an independent nature and subjective initiative to be opposed to, or associated with, the object. Ancient Greeks in the infant stage of philosophy would not have raised such a question. No ancient Greek philosopher had as yet regarded man as a subject who was at liberty to make independent actions. They merely contemplated the world.

The sophists, however, were somewhat unusual. From research into nature itself, they moved on to the study of man.

The proposition that "man is the measure of all things" was the earliest source of the ideology of contemporary humanism. They held that man was able to understand early phenomena, but in their eyes phenomena meant everything. Unlike some modern philosophers, they did not believe in the existence of an unknowable world behind phenomena. Although these people were wiser than others, they were still naive and had not managed to understand, as do their modern counterparts, that the subject and object are opposed to each other. If we call them agnostics, this is different from modern agnosticism. They were content with understanding phenomena and did not appreciate the world behind the phenomena. Such an idea is an expression of the separation of the subject from the object, it cannot be understood by people with a naive mind. Primitive religion differs from later developed religions in that the former belongs to a naive way of thinking which fails to differentiate the subject from the object. Besides the sophists, ancient Greek philosophy also contained the philosophy of Socrates and the philosophy of skepticism. Although to a small extent they all had a vague perception of self-awareness, we cannot say they contained the principle of subjectivity as does modern philosophy.

The lack of the principle of subjectivity in ancient Greece is shown not only by the fact that state affairs were decided by natural phenomena, but especially by its political ideas. In his utopia Plato advocated that if one was made of gold his posterity would also be made of gold; if one was made of silver his posterity would also be made of silver, and likewise for steel. His theory of a rigidly stratified hierarchy based upon blood relationships was in conflict with the principle of subjectivity which would be developed in modern Western philosophy.

The question of the relation between subject and object is found in the philosophy of the Middle Ages in theories regarding whether the world was created by God or existed originally and by itself. At that time the subject referred to the soul, God and Heaven, and the object to the body and this world. People lived in the next world in order to rescue their souls. Hence, the conflict between the subject and the object in the philosophy of the Middle Ages appeared as an opposition between Heaven (God) and man, the soul and the body, spirit and nature and religious and secular life. The spirit and soul of man which existed in Heaven and in religious life and were in accord with God, constituted the subject; on the other hand, human nature, the human body and the external environment constituted the object and were in opposition to God. The dominance of God not only made the world, nature and the human body obstacles to be overcome, but also stifled the spirit and subjectivity of man. In other words, the theocracy of the Middle Ages ruled human rights and nature, suppressed the subjectivity of man and thereby natural science.

Nonetheless, the separation of subject and object and the supreme authority of God in the philosophy of the Middle Ages gave rise to the idea that all men are equal before God. This is an important stage in the history of the development of the idea of subjectivity; it is much more advanced than the hierarchy of Plato in ancient Greece.

The question of the relation between subject and object truly emerged and achieved its full significance only after the Europeans "awoke" from their religious Middle Ages. One of the basic principles or characteristics of modern philosophy is its principle of subjectivity; gradually the thinking subject, man, was understood to be a subject possessing subject and independent initiative. The relationship between thinking and being in modern philosophy is precisely the relationship between subject and object. Only this kind of relationship can penetratingly and completely represent the relationship between thinking and being. Therefore, unlike the philosophy of ancient Greece, the outstanding question in modern philosophy is not that of ontology but of epistemology.

If we agree that man's approach to the natural environment in the philosophy of ancient Greece was one of contemplation (quiet observation) and that man's approach to the natural environment in the philosophy in the Middle Ages was one of reclusiveness, we must also agree that the basic approach of man to the natural environment in modern philosophy is one of initiative, or to be more exact, of subjectivity. Here, the word "subjectivity" is used with the meaning of the German word *subjektivität* which means independence and initiative. In the first paragraph of *Thesen uber Feuerbach*, Marx said that the so-called old materialism "does not look at anything *subjectively*." The original word used by Marx was *subjektiv* which means also initiative.

However, the development of the subjectivity of man in modern philosophy also has gone through several stages. Man was discovered during the Renaissance: human rights were emancipated from the yoke of theocracy and the subjectivity of man was developed to some extent. The other achievement of the Renaissance was the discovery of nature. The Renaissance encouraged people to attach importance to the study of nature, not only to the applied science directly useful to man, but also to pure science and pure knowledge. During the 17th and 18th centuries modern science was in its early stages, and so was metaphysical. Therefore, the philosophy of the 17th and 18th centuries observed man as a being completely in the power of the inevitability of causality. Descartes, for example, regarded animals as machines; La Mettrie even regarded man as a machine. Thus the subjectivity of man was again oppressed: before the Renaissance the subjectivity of man had been stifled by theocracy, now it was stifled by the inevitability of the causality of nature.

Great achievements were made in all fields of historical dialectics during the 18th century French Revolution and in natural science during the period from the late 18th to the early 19th centuries, especially in the theory of evolution. These achievements enabled modern Western philosophy to reach its highest stage. The theory of development and evolution now replaced the mathematical method of Galileo Galilei and the metaphysical method of Newton which had prevailed until then. To different extents and in different ways the German idealist philosophers summed up the ideas of their predecessors in their dialectics and established classical German idealist philosophy as represented by Kant, Fichte, Schelling and Hegel. They were not satisfied with the state of affairs in which the mechanical causality of the 17th and 18th centuries decisively trammeled the subjectivity and free will of man. Standing on the side of idealism they struggled to protect once more the subjectivity of man in the field of abstract philosophy. The former struggle had been aimed at theocracy; this time it was aimed mainly at mechanical causality, while at the same time struggling against theocracy in different forms.

The classical German idealist philosophers agreed that the nature of the world was spiritual: spirit, self, self-awareness and the subject constituted the central focus of their philosophy. They wanted to destroy the opposition between subject and object and integrate the two, with the subject in the dominant position. Kant was the first philosopher to prove the subjectivity of man systematically from the heights of philosophical theory. He confined the scope of knowledge and actuality in order to leave room for the free nature of man, namely man's subjectivity. As the creator of this philosophy, Kant could not help but over-emphasize man's freedom and self-determination and the separation of freedom and necessity. Hegel, who epitomized the thinking of classical German idealist philosophy, also talked systematically about the free nature and subjectivity of man, but he stressed the unity between individual freedom and the whole society.

Since Hegel over-emphasized the subordination of the individual to the whole society, many contemporary philosophers after Hegel stressed the value of the individual in order to oppose Hegel or to correct his deviation. The philosophies of Schopenhauer, Nietzsche and the existentialists all placed emphasis on the value of the individual. Connected to this is the fact that, whereas the basic philosophical principle of classical German idealist philosophy from Kant to Hegel was unity and integrity, the leading principle of contemporary philosophy is multiplicity or plurality--the principle of unity having been criticized by many philosophers.

In recent years, however, there has been a tendency in Western Europe to return to classical German idealist philosophy, especially in West Germany. This return is not simple repetition, but a study of the principle of unity in classical German idealist philosophy from a new angle and under new historical conditions. Its goal is to find a new form of unity to explain the various social phenomena of our time. The main reason for the emergence of this new trend is that the principle of multiplicity is unable to satisfy the need for subjectivity. People have realized that the subject cannot be separated from unity and that the subjectivity of man cannot develop without unity.

Whether to use the principles of multiplicity and individuality or unity and integrity to develop the subjectivity of man may be one of the central issues for present and future philosophy, especially in the comparison between Western and Chinese philosophies.

Generally speaking, the process of the development of subjectivity in Western philosophy is a process from the unity of subject and object, through the separation of the two, to the demand for the unity of the opposed subject and object. Not until contemporary Western philosophy was subjectivity used as a principle, but the unity of opposites has not yet been achieved and the principle of subjectivity has not yet been properly established.

The process of development of subjectivity in the history of Western philosophy illustrates the following:

1. To separate and distinguish between subject and object is the most important step for the realization of self-awareness; when subject and object are a united whole, the subject disappears.

2. The discovery of man is the discovery of subject, and the discovery of nature (including the natural aspect of man) is the discovery of object; each helps and strengthens the other. Only if nature is regarded as important can the subjectivity of man develop. If importance is attached only to man, but not to nature and natural science, the development of the subjectivity of man will be hindered. The man who separates himself from nature and from body is without substance, just as the subject

which separates itself from the object is not a true subject. On the other hand, only the real discovery of man and the true consideration of his subjectivity as important can promote the development of natural science.

3. To value pure knowledge and theoretical knowledge is the result of discovering the object and regarding it as important. Only by doing so will the substance of man be enriched and the subjectivity of man developed. On the contrary, to underrate pure and theoretical knowledge and to value technology and the application of technology alone is the result of a one-sided stress upon man alone. By doing so, the substance of man becomes monotonous and the subjectivity of man cannot develop.

SUBJECTIVITY IN CHINESE PHILOSOPHY: PHILOSOPHY IN THE SLAVE SOCIETY AND RELATED FEUDAL TIMES

According to the oracle descriptions of the Shang Dynasty (c. 1500-1000 B.C.), the rulers at that time would consult oracle bones on military matters, hunting, harvesting and diseases. This undoubtedly indicates that there was no recognition of the subjectivity of man.

"The *Tao* (also translated as 'way') of Heaven is remote while the *Tao* of man is near" is a statement by Zi Chan (Tzu Ch'an, ?-522 B.C.), a statesman and thinker of the Spring and Autumn Period (770-476 B.C.). It expresses the inclination to go against Heaven and superstitions. His idea, though simple and crude, can be regarded as the ideological seed of man's attachment of importance to himself.

Confucius (551-479 B.C.), however, seldom spoke of the *Tao* of Heaven, but was more concerned with the *Tao* of man. He said: "Who can go out but by the door? How is it that men will not walk according to these ways"?[1] It is argued by some that this is precisely an expression of Confucius' idea of man's subjectivity and that Confucius had discovered man. This is an over-estimation, for Confucius talked solely of man and overlooked nature. His ideas show a lack of differentiation between man and Heaven and a lack of opposition between subject and object. His philosophy did not attain self-awareness or the subjective principle of man's freedom, self-decision and self-awakening. When speaking concretely of what man is, Confucius said: "When a man is not virtuous (*ren*) of what account are his ceremonial manners (*li*)"? He also said: "To subdue one's self and return to propriety is perfect virtue. . . . Look not at what is contrary to propriety; listen not to what is contrary to propriety; speak not what is contrary to propriety; make no movement which is contrary to propriety."[2] When asked about the meaning of *ren*, Confucius replied: "To be able wherever one goes to put five things into practice constitutes *ren*." When asked what they were, he replied:

> "They are respect, magnanimity, sincerity, earnestness and kindness. With respect you will avoid insult; with nagnanimity you will win over people; with sincerity men will trust you; with earnestness you will make achievements; and with kindness you will be well fitted to command others.[3]

Thereby Confucius asked people to restrain their speech and behavior so as to become true men. His philosophy of life was to observe the *Li* of the Zhou Dynasty (c. 1000-771 B.C.).

Confucius was "the first great thinker in the history of Chinese philosophy to establish the system of life discipline which later became the core of Chinese philosophy."[4] Indeed, Confucius' philosophy of life, "To subdue one's self and return to propriety," became the mainstream of philosophy in feudal China and seriously hampered the establishment of the principle of subjectivity in the history of Chinese philosophy. Although Confucius said that one should "leave all men" and "not do to others what one would not like to have done to oneself," his words cannot be viewed abstractly, for he also said: "Superior men, and yet not always virtuous, there have been, alas! But there has never been a humble man who is at the same time virtuous."[5] That is, there is no way of talking about the virtue of benevolence among the ruled, for they are just small men.

There were two major philosophers during this period whose views differed radically from those of Confucius. One was Lao Zi (Lao Tzu) who placed emphasis on nature, and the other was Yang Zhu (Yang Chu, or Yang Sheng) who was well-known for his principle of "Each for himself."

Lao Zi raised the issue of the origin of Heaven and Earth by saying that the *Tao* was the "beginning of Heaven and Earth" and "the mother of all things." Unlike Confucius who was interested only in the study of man's life, Lao Zi emphasized the study of the origin of the universe. His major contribution lay in his cosmology, centered on the *Tao*. Yet Lao Zi was also the first among the Chinese philosophers to give a prominent place to man. He said: "Therefore Tao is great, Heaven is great, earth is great and man is great. These are the Great Four in the universe, and man is one of them." (*Lao Zi*) This means that man is as great as Heaven and Earth and is even above all other ordinary things.

Lao Zi's philosophy shows that the study of nature will not reduce the importance of man, but on the contrary will make us place more emphasis on man's importance. It also shows that he put man and nature on an equal plane. Compared with that of Confucius, Lao Zi's philosophy shows a slight recognition of the concept of subjectivity. In connection with this, Lao Zi did not consider benevolence (*ren*) to be the loftiest virtue. In contrast to the philosophy of life: "To subdue oneself and return to propriety," it contains an element of subjectivity, although we cannot say that Lao Zi's philosophy had reached the stage of taking subjectivity as a principle. There are, in fact, many negative points in his philosophy which should be done away with, and his idea of subjectivity was not at all systematically expounded.

Yang Zhu did not leave any works behind and his ideas were recorded in the writings of others. Mencius said: "Though he (Yang Zhu) might have benefited the whole world by plucking out a single hair, he would not have done it."[6] Mencius remarked on another occasion: "Yang's principle of 'each one for himself' is to be without (the allegiance due to) a sovereign."[7] Mencius' account of Yang Zhu is obviously analogous to the *Lushi Chunqiu's* (third century B.C. XVII) statement that Yang Shen "valued self," and also to the *Huai Nan Zi* (second century B.C.) when it says that "the completeness of living, the preservation of what is genuine, and not allowing external things to entangle one's person, is what Yang Zhu established."[8]

However, a close observation of the overall statements about Yang Zhu shows that Yang's "each for himself" is by no means simple selfishness. Rather he means that people should not get engaged in outside things and thus become tools of the rulers.[9] Zhang is correct in saying that Yang Zhu was the first Chinese philosopher to stress "self."[10] In fact, Yang was also the foremost figure in the early history of Chinese philosophy to have the concept of subjectivity. Unfortunately, under the heavy pressure of the Confucian tradition as represented by the *dictum*: "To subdue one's self and return to propriety," Yang Zhu who stressed the subjectivity of the individual was unable to elaborate and develop his idea.

Xun Zi (Hsun Tzu, c. 298-c. 230 B.C.) stressed the distinction between Heaven and Earth and man, as well as man's ability to tame nature. He said:

> To understand the distinction between Heaven and man, that is to be a great man. . . . Instead of exalting Heaven and contemplating it, why not pile up wealth and use it advantageously? Instead of obeying Heaven and praising it, why not adapt the decree of Heaven (*Tianming*) and make use of it"? (*Xun Zi: Tianming*)

However, although Xun Zi's meaning was to make use of man's subjectivity, he did not ask people to understand Heaven, nor did he stress the study of nature. Therefore, his philosophy did not attain the principle of subjectivity--to overcome and to use nature, as is the idea in modern Western philosophy. This idea of taming nature, as advocated by modern Western philosophers such as Francis Bacon, is inseparable from the idea of understanding and knowing nature and from their stress on knowledge of Heaven. To control Heaven one has to know Heaven, and to give full rein to man's subjectivity one has first to distinguish subject from object and pay due attention to epistemology and methodology.

PHILOSOPHY IN FEUDAL CHINA

In his theological idealism concerning the "interaction of Heaven and man" Dong Zhongshu (Tung Chung-shu, c. 179-c. 104 B.C.) in the Han Dynasty (206 B.C.-A.D. 24) held that Heaven and man were identical. The physical form of man, in Dong Zhongshu's words, was this: "His head is large and round, like Heaven's countenance. His ears and eyes, with their brilliance, are like the sun and moon. His nostrils and mouth, with their breath, are like the wind." The theory of the "interaction of Heaven and man" is, in effect, one version of the theory of "the oneness of Heaven and man," which makes no distinction between subject and object. Moreover, on this basis, Dong Zhongshu explicitly put forward a theory that suppressed the rights of man. He thought that the Three Cardinal Principles of the Kingly Way could be sought in Heaven, so he advocated that people should obey the emperor, who in turn should obey the will of Heaven. In other words, to use the divine and sovereign powers to suppress the rights and subjectivity of man. This idea was identical in some respects with medieval philosophy in Europe, except that Dong's idea lacked the idea of the immortality of the soul because he did not make a distinction between subject and object. At the same time, his philosophy did not contain the idea of all men being equal before God. So Dong's idea was, in fact, typically Chinese.

An important issue discussed by the metaphysical school (*xuanxue*, also known as the mysterious or black studies) in the Wei and Jen dynasties (220-420) concerned the differentiation between the Confucian ethical code and nature. Wang Bi (Wang Pi, 226-249) held that nature is the root while the morals and institutions (*mingjiao*, Confucian ethical code) are the branches, and that they do not contradict each other. This is, in effect, a positive view of the morals and institutions which formed the classical tradition of Confucianism. Contrary to Wang Bi, Ji Kang

(Chi Kang, 223-262) and Ruan Ji (Ruan Chi, 210-263) believed that Confucian morals and institutions contradict each other, that they do not conform to nature but constitute a human bondage. They advocated that one should conform to nature in disregard of the classical Confucian tradition. Ruan Ji held that "if a man does not have a house, Heaven and Earth will contain him; if a man does not have a master, Heaven and Earth will own him; if a man does not have things to do, he is free to walk under Heaven and on the Earth."[11] Ji Kang and Ruan Ji believed that the most ridiculous thing in this world is to be tied up by fame and wealth. Apparently then, Ji Kang and Ruan Ji were not only contemptuous of the ethical code, but actually opposed to it. This was a charge against the Confucian doctrine "To subdue one's self and to restore propriety"; to a certain extent it was an expression of subjectivity.

Guo Xiang (Kuo Hsiang, d. A.D. 312) disagreed with Ji Kang and Ruan Ji. In his view, the Confucian ethical code was in accord with nature: to follow the code was to conform to nature. In addition, he considered the social hierarchy and the sovereign authority to be in conformity with both nature and Heaven. Guo's philosophy was behind that of Ji Kang and Ruan Ji in the evolution of the principle of subjectivity.

During the Sui and Tang dynasties (581-907) Buddhism and Taoism were both encouraged, although Confucianism remained the orthodox philosophy. Confucianism's opposition to Buddhism lay in the latter's view of the distinction between spirit and body. Taoism advocated the training of the body to nurture the spirit so that immortality could be attained. There was here no distinction between spirit and physical body. Confucianism was opposed to Taoism not for that, but for the latter's stress on nature at the expense of the Confucian morals and institutions. This gives us a glimpse of Confucianism's opposition to man's subjectivity during the Sui and Tang dynasties. Han Yu (768-928), the famous Tang Dynasty writer, was against Buddhism because "Being sons, they (Buddhist followers) do not treat their father like a father; and being subjects, they do not treat their ruler like a ruler." The "King" and "prince" principle as advocated by Confucianism really does fetter man's subjectivity.

In the view of Liu Yuxi (772-842) of the Tang Dynasty, heaven and man restrain each other. Liu made a distinction between the *li* (principle) of Heaven and that of man, and held that the *li* of man was superior to that of Heaven. However, Liu's view was too unsophisticated to have any significant influence on the development of Chinese philosophy.

The contention between *li* (principle or reason) and *qi* (material force) in the Song, Yuan, Ming and Qing dynasties

(960-1911) is somewhat like the contention between thinking and being in the history of Western philosophy. It differs, however, from the latter in that the critical point of contention in Western philosophy is the relationship between subject and object, and man, as an independent, free, self-deciding and self-initiating subject, is both opposed and related to the object. The ancient Greek philosophers did not realize the principle of subjectivity, nor did Plato's idealism. The distinction between *li* and *qi* resembles the distinction between Plato's world of ideas and the perceptual world, which cannot be regarded as having realized the principle of subjectivity.

The philosophers of the Song, Yuan, Ming and Qing dynasties also talked about the relationship between man and Heaven, yet they held a negative view of man's subjectivity. The theory of unity of man with Heaven created by Mencius was epitomized by the Neo-Confucianists of the Song Dynasty. Zhang Zai (Chang Tsai, 1020-1077) said: "A state of functioning in which differentiation is made between Heaven and man cannot be said to be 'sincerity.' A state of Knowledge in which differentiation is made between Heaven and man cannot be considered as the ultimate 'enlightenment.'"[12] Nevertheless, Zhang also attached great importance to man's action. He also differentiated between visual and auditory knowledge and the knowledge of the nature of virtue. This reminds one of Kant's distinction between "theoretical" and "experimental reason."

Both Cheng Mingdao (Cheng Hao, 1032-1085) and Cheng Yichuan (Cheng Yi, 1033-1108) were proponents of the unity between man and Heaven. Cheng Mingdao held that it was entirely unnecessary to discuss the integration of man with Heaven for the two were one from the beginning. He also thought that man should not seek knowledge from Heaven or nature. Therefore his philosophy contained nothing like an opposition between subject and object or between spirit and nature, or the subject overcoming the object. Cheng Yichuan said: "Heaven, Earth and man are of one *Tao*. . . . Is there anyone who knows the way of man yet does not know the Way of Heaven?"[13] His idea of seeking knowledge from man himself and not from Heaven or nature, of the knowledge of man himself being equal to one's knowledge of Heaven, and of closing one's eyes and ears to the outside and being isolated from nature is, of course, a denial of man's subjectivity.

According to the *li* (principle) expounded by the Cheng-Zhu (the Cheng brothers and Zhu Xi), philosophy in fact constituted the moral principle of feudal society. The theory of unity between man and Heaven meant the obedience of the people to the

Tianli (the principle of Heaven) which fettered man's subjectivity.

Lu Xiangshan (Lu Chiu-yuan, 1139-1193) believed that man should be independent and should be his own master. However, although he stressed self-awareness in the acquisition of knowledge, his main emphasis was on moral training.

Contrary to the philosophy of the Neo-Confucianists and the School of Mind during the Song and Ming dynasties, the philosophy of Yang Chuanshan, Yan Yuan and Dai in the late Ming and early Qing dynasties attached importance to man's deeds, physical form and achievements.

Wang Chuanshan (Wang Fu-chih, 1619-1693) not only generally advocated that the Way of man should lead the Way of Heaven through life (*Siwenlu, Nanpian*), and thus that one should not wait for opportunities to come; he believed that man can control Heaven and Earth and be creator of all things. He was also opposed to sole vacuity and quiescence in spiritual cultivation as advocated by the Song philosophers. He stressed physical form without which he thought that man could not exist. Unlike Xun Zi, Wang thought it important to have knowledge of things, as without knowledge one cannot use things. We can say that Wang did have the idea of subjectivity and humanism as in Western philosophy, though his idea was not sufficiently systematic, nor his deductions so meticulous.

Yan Yuan (Yen Yuan, 1635-1704) placed emphasis on utility and material things, an idea similar to that in modern Western philosophy. He advocated "the importance of the unrefined" which meant utility and material things, and considered that the lives of many people were wasted merely because of their love of subtlety and their dislike of the unrefined.

Dai (Tai Chen, 1723-1777) held that people should give vent to their emotions or feelings and do things according to their wishes, as opposed to the idea of freeing oneself from emotions and desires. In his understanding, when desire is not selfish the individual's desire is the common desire and the individual's feelings are the common feelings.

Wang Chuanshan, Yan Yuan and Dai all hoped to shake off the yoke of old feudal ideas and to be released from the empty, vacuous and quiescent Neo-Confucianism which belittled utility and man's desires. Although in some ways their ideas were identical to the humanism of the Renaissance in Europe, they still could not help being governed by the idea of the unity of man with Heaven and the idea of being in accord with nature. It is therefore hard to say that they discovered nature and man as was the case during the Renaissance in Europe.

CONCLUSIONS

From the above analysis of philosophy during the Slave Society and in the period from the Slave to the Feudal societies, we can make the following observations:

1. The history of Chinese philosophy as compared with Western philosophy lacked the stage at which the subject was separated from the object and the opposition between subject and object made systematic; it lacked also a concept of the next life.

By saying this, we do not mean that no Chinese philosopher stressed the difference between subject and object. In fact, the idea of a distinction between man and Heaven embodies the idea of the difference between subject and object, for even among those who upheld the idea of unity between man and Heaven there were those who observed the difference between the two. However, the idea of unity between man and Heaven was predominant in the history of Chinese philosophy, while the idea of separation and opposition between subject and object never dominated. Nor did any philosopher establish a complete system of basic principles based on the separation and opposition between subject and object. Xun Zi placed emphasis on a distinction between man and Heaven, but he was not very influential or important in the history of Chinese philosophy. Liu Yuxi's idea of "mutual restraint" between Heaven and man was too unsophisticated to have any significant influence on later philosophers.

In addition, Chinese philosophy lacked the concept of other worldliness. Confucianism regarded the attainment of virtue to be of primary importance, the achievement of fame to be of second importance, and the writing of books as of third importance. All these three were considered to be immortal achievements in this world. Taoism taught people to become immortal in this world, rather than in the next. These concepts of immortality all reflected that subject and object were not regarded as separate and opposed to each other.

In the West however, the philosophy of the Middle Ages which continued for about one-thousand years was primarily a philosophy which differentiated subject and object and which attached importance to the next world. Modern Western philosophy advocated the separation of, and opposition between, subject and object; it then went further to demand the unity of opposites, although so far this has not been achieved. The completeness of the theory of separation and opposition between subject and object and the long period of time during which it dominated the history of Western philosophy are missing in the history of Chinese philosophy.

2. The history of Chinese philosophy lacked a relatively systematic philosophy based on the principle of subjectivity.

This does not mean that the philosophers as individuals failed to attain self-awareness or self-awakening, which develops gradually in any individual after birth. However, the fact that an individual or philosopher has self-awareness does not mean that he or she can establish a philosophy with self-awareness or subjectivity as the basic principle. The philosophers in ancient Greece had self-awareness as did other peoples, yet generally speaking they did not attain the level of taking self-awareness or subjectivity as a basic philosophical principle and attended mostly to ontology.

By saying that Chinese philosophy lacked a philosophy based primarily on subjectivity, we do not mean that there was no philosopher in China who attached importance to individual self-awareness and subjectivity. On the contrary, even among those who upheld the idea of the unity of man with Heaven, there were those who stressed man's free will. Phrases like "The will of man cannot be taken away" are familiar to the Chinese. Individual phrases show that the philosophers did see man's subjectivity, but again, this does not mean that subjectivity was the primary principle on which they based their philosophy, nor does it mean that they had made a systematic theoretical deduction. If one disregards a philosopher's whole philosophical system one will find it difficult to make an analysis and comparison since the same word often appears with completely different meanings in the writings of different philosophers.

Without going through the opposition of subject and object one cannot attain self-awareness or subjectivity. Only through the separation of subject and object can one advance the object as well as the subject. This is true not only of the growth of the individual, but also of the development of the ideas of a nation and state. The chief reason for the absence of the system of philosophy based on the principle of subjectivity in the history of Chinese philosophy is the lack of an historic stage of separation and opposition between subject and object, as well as the lack of differentiation between this world and the next. Here I have only stated the fact. I do not intend to advocate the separation and opposition between subject and object or to ask people to believe in religion: even less would I wish China to follow in the wake of Western philosophy. When we say that the Napoleonic invasions of Prussia brought about capitalism in Prussia, we do not mean that the underdeveloped nations should welcome invasions by the developed countries so as to develop capitalism.

3. Stress on man alone is not the same as stress on the principle of subjectivity or the attainment of a level of a philosophy based on the principles of self-awareness and subjectivity.

We must be aware, not only of man, but of nature's opposition to the self apart from man so that we can pay due attention to nature. Only this is the true consciousness of self and of man as is proven by the history of Western philosophy. (In the Middle Ages, the underestimation of nature and the natural side of man resulted in the suppression of human subjectivity; during the Renaissance period focusing attention upon nature and the natural side of man led to upholding human subjectivity). This had also been proven by the history of Chinese philosophy. Confucius' stress on man alone to the neglect of nature resulted in the suppression of human subjectivity. In the Song Dynasty the Neo-Confucian stress on morality, vacuity and quiescence to the neglect of nature also suppressed human subjectivity. On the other hand, the emphasis upon utility and human desires as advocated by Wang Chuanshan, Yan Yuan and Dai are close to a philosophy based on subjectivity.

In addition, as the history of Chinese philosophy was dominated by the stress on man alone, the emphasis on technology and applied science also prevailed over the theoretical knowledge of the natural sciences. Closely connected with this, epistemology, methodology and its understanding of thinking were all neglected. This also manifests the lack of a philosophy based upon the principle of subjectivity.

4. In the history of Chinese philosophy, the impediment to the development of the principle of subjectivity came not from the theocracy of the next world as in the West, but rather from the monarchical power in this world, from the feudal ethical code, the feudal patriarchal clan system and the hierarchial system. In the West, the religious authority was supreme, and provided a spiritual buttress to the secular feudal system: men were all equal before God. Thus, the overthrow and weakening of religious power brought about a relatively high development of the rights and subjectivity of man. In China, however, the idea that men are equal before God never existed. In the Slave and Feudal societies the prevailing idea was that the monarch was the supreme power and that the ethical code, feudal patriarchal clan system and hierarchical system all served the purpose of the monarch. Therefore, man's subjectivity could not be established unless the monarchical power was overthrown. Yan Zhu's idea of "no sovereign" and Ji Kang and Ruan Ji's idea of following nature in disregard of the Confucian morals and institutions and the like are all bold attempts at an advancement of man's subjectivity in the history of Chinese philosophy.

EPILOGUE

In China there was no movement resembling the Renaissance in Europe until the May Fourth movement. The slogans for "Mr. Science" and "Mr. Democracy" were rather similar to the discovery of man and nature in Europe. Only after the discovery of nature could people begin to pay attention to science, and only after the discovery of man could people start to respect democracy. The May Fourth movement was the beginning of self-awareness and self-awakening and of a philosophy based on subjectivity (as historic stages) in the history of Chinese philosophy.

The "Renaissance" (if it can be called that) in China differed from that in Europe in three ways:

A. Although the Chinese Renaissance had the shoots of capitalism from the Ming Dynasty as its internal cause, it was propelled mainly by external forces and was the result of the Chinese people's search for truth from the West since the Opium War.

B. The aim of the Chinese Renaissance, in addition to rejecting imperialism, was to liberate China from the yoke of the feudal ethical code, hierarchical system and patriarchal clan system, instead of from religious authority as was the case in the West.

C. The road China took after the May Fourth movement was different from that of the West. In the West the anti-feudal force had been strong, its development was much smoother and lasted for a longer period; therefore, the development of subjectivity was fairly complete. In China, the May Fourth movement was followed by the wars between the warlords and then the reactionary rule of Ching Kai-shek. The combined force of imperialism, feudalism and capitalism caused the development of subjectivity to be even more arduous. In addition, there were less than thirty years between the May Fourth movement and the founding of New China, all of which account for the slower development of subjectivity in China compared with the West.

The objective of Communism to liberate mankind is, in the words of Western philosophy, truly and fully to develop man's subjectivity. Our present task is to carry on the tradition of the May Fourth movement and to develop man's subjectivity under the guidance of Marxism-Leninism. It is thought unnecessary to follow the path of the West step-by-step because in history China lacked the stage of a distinction between, and the opposition of, subject and object, and lacked a philosophical system based on the principle of subjectivity. However, on the basis of the development of our own history, we should learn from the West.

There are some advantages to the emphasis on the unity of man with Heaven and on integration in the history of Chinese philosophy. Contemporary Western philosophy is dominated by the principle of plurality (separation and isolation of everything). In recent years, however, people in the West have come to realize that the principle of plurality cannot fully develop man's subjectivity, and thus have begun to think of returning to the principle of unity and oneness. China should not, and cannot follow the path of the West without making alterations now that the shortcomings of the West have been exposed. Yet the history of Chinese philosophy attached too much importance to the unity of man and Heaven and integration, while neglecting the distinction between, and opposition of, subject and object, plurality and individuality, nature and natural science, pure theoretical knowledge, epistemology and methodology. It is very important for the advancement of thinking and culture to overcome the elements which bar the growth and development of the subjectivity of the Chinese people. We should still safeguard the principle of unity, but now make a greater effort to learn from the idea of placing emphasis on plurality and individuality as expressed in Western philosophy. This is a key to the development of Chinese culture and philosophy.

Peking University
 Beijing, People's Republic of China

NOTES

1. *Analects*: IV.
2. *Ibid.*, XII.
3. *Ibid.*, XVII.
4. Zhang Dainian, *An Outline of Chinese Philosophy* (China Social Science Publishing House, 1982), p. 165.
5. *Analects*: XIV.
6. *Mencius*, VII.
7. *Ibid.*, III.
8. Ch. 13.
9. Zhang Dainian, p. 282.
10. *Ibid.*
11. *Daren Xiansheng Zhuang*
12. *Correct Discipline for Beginners*, Chengming
13. *Yulu*, XVIII.

CHAPTER XIII

THE FATE OF METAPHYSICS

ZHU DESHENG

At one stage in history the study of metaphysics enjoyed such high esteem that it seemed a symbol of wisdom. Later, it became so disparaged as to be treated synonymously with unscientific thought. Even now, scholars are divided in their assessments. What is more, some are still arguing over whether such a subject has actually been established and whether it is necessary. The controversy has lasted for hundreds of years and will very probably last for hundreds of years more. This is bizarre because since the beginning of human civilization no other subject has encountered such problematic treatment.

What is the reason for this and what lesson can be drawn?

THE SEARCH TO ESTABLISH METAPHYSICS

The term metaphysics did not appear until the post-Aristotelian period, but the real inauguration of the subject came with Aristotle's statement that there is a subject which studies being as being.

Greek philosophy had made inquiries into essentially metaphysical problems before Aristotle and this pre-Aristotelian philosophy was the embryo of metaphysics. The earliest Greek philosophers focused their discussion mainly upon principles. As Aristotle explained, a principle is something out of which everything takes its origin and into which it finally returns. This problem, in effect, proved to be the same as the subsequent problem of substance. Questions of principle or basic stuff are attempts to arrive at a unity or basic principle underlying the surface of directly perceivable and ever-changing phenomena. Such attempts gave rise to Aristotle's question: What is being? This is what is meant by the question of being as being.

There was historical necessity to the raising of this question. The difference between man and animals lies in man's ability to alter nature consciously. To do this it is, of course, necessary to know why nature is the way it is. If every individual thing, changeable as it is, has its own origin, what of the whole world? This is an inevitable question for experiential perception. However, at that time people were not yet capable of offering a correct answer. Directly perceived experience tells people that as you sow, so will you reap. As such, the whole world must have a principle or essence. Thales believed it was water, Anaximenes that it was gas, etc. A great advance was achieved in the history of human knowledge when people came to explain the unity of the cosmos by a perceptual entity. The effort to elucidate the existence and development of nature by drawing on causes within nature proper shows that the human view of the world had broken away from the worldview of legend and religion and embarked on an independent road, thereby signifying the birth of philosophy.

Of all the philosophers of this time, the most noteworthy was Heraclitus. Like thinkers of the Milesian school, he ascribed the principle or essence of the world to another perceptual entity--fire. For him, as Diogenes Laertius relates, fire produces everything and everything returns to fire, everything obeys fate and is subject to its opposite process, and everything is filled with spirit and soul. He not only questioned the principle of the world, but also tried to reach the way and method of knowing about the principle. Unlike Anaximander, he did not comprehend production as the separation of opposites, but as their collaboration. This was a quite provocative conjecture.

At least one thing is clear. It is impossible to go deeply into knowledge of an object if people confine their cognition within the scope of a directly qualitative approach. John is a man; Morris is man. . . . Such knowledge is too sweeping. Clear knowledge of an object required not only consideration of its qualitative, but also of its quantitative determinations. Generally speaking, people begin their understanding of an object with qualitative determination; inevitably they will come to quantitative determination as their cognition deepens. This is also the view of Pythagoras and his school.

When the Pythagoreans took numbers as a basic principle, they did not actually liken numbers to substances such as water, gas or fire, for they defined number as a determining principle inherent in any entity. Aristotle says of the Pythagoreans in *Metaphysics* I, 5 that they thought that the principles of mathematics were the principles of all things.

> Since of these principles numbers are by nature the first and in numbers they seemed to see many resemblances to the things that exist and come into being-- more than fire and earth and water (such and such a modification of numbers being justice, another being soul and reason, another being opportunity--and similarly almost all other things being numerically expressible).[1]

But a one-sided view pertaining to quantity is no more satisfactory than that pertaining to quality, for it cannot explain movement, as Aristotle observed, nor how a perceivable substance comes into being.

Of course, in that era it was still too early to understand the relationship between direct and indirect means of knowledge, for the scope of knowledge was placed almost wholly within the scope of direct experience, and indirect knowledge was accepted as direct. Thus thinkers of that time usually started with the question of the relationship between one and many. No way, however, could be found to unite one and many within the scope of direct perception, though practice required it.

This problem led to the first examination of the notion of "being" by the Eleatics. Since everything has being, they posed the question of what "being" itself is. In my opinion, a great step was made with this question in the development of a philosophical view of the world, because with it the philosophical view of the world, which had freed itself from the mythic worldview, began to gain further independence from natural philosophy.

The following was the Eleatics' understanding of "being."

1. Thought is identical with being, which means, according to Parmenides, that what can be thought and what can be are identical. Their interpretation is trustworthy because Parmenides once commented: "thinking and the thing for the sake of which we think are the same; for without that which is, in regard to which it is uttered, you will not find yourself able to think."[2] This judgment tells us that entities exist, while non-existence does not.

2. Being cannot possibly be produced and therefore cannot be eliminated: it must be eternal and infinite. Parmenides agreed to this, but he also stated that it is not infinite, for if it were, it would become imperfect. "It is finite on all sides, like the bulk of a well-rounded sphere, equally balanced from the center in every direction."[3]

3. For existence, "destruction is inconceivable. Nor is it divisible, since it is all alike."[4] Besides, "it is all inviolate."[5]

4. "Being the same and remaining in the same place, it likewise lies within itself and so remains locked in the same position,"[6]--i.e., it is static and motionless.

These were Parmenides' fundamental views of "being." From these we can come to the rough conclusion that for Parmenides, "being" and existence were more or less the same thing. He discovered "being" in the place of existence, and all his judgments were based on directly perceivable experience.

If Parmenides is considered to be like the natural philosophers who preceded him in discussing "being" by way of the relationship of one and many--i.e., if his thinking did not go beyond the scope of direct experience--Gorgias achieved a breakthrough in this respect. He is known for his three propositions: first, nothing exists; second, assuming that a thing were to exist, it could not be known; and third, were it to exist and be knowable, no communication of what is known would be possible.

It is not necessary here to go over his over-elaborate dialectic, since we are all familiar with it. But it should be stressed that he was able to advance these propositions because he had arrived at the fundamental contradiction for knowledge--that between the general and the individual--but did not know how to resolve it. In other words, he discussed "being" by way of the relationship of the general and the individual, which means that "being" in general for him is not confused with the existence of individual objects.

Socrates' dialogues made the general-individual relationship even more explicit. On beauty, for instance, what Socrates was after was not which things are beautiful, but what beauty is; not manifold examples of beauty, but their universal character: that is, beauty in general or beauty itself.

Thus, the discussion of the world's principle or basic stuff, following an initial examination of the idea of being, became a problem of substance. This is the view which Plato takes of this change. He says in his *Cratylus* that all things "have their own proper and permanent essence; they are not in relation to us or influenced by us, fluctuating according to our fancy, but are independent, and maintain in their own essence in accordance with the relation prescribed by nature."[7]

Plato absolutized the universal essence into an ultimate actuality or idea. Idea is a truly independent substance, whereas the changeable perceptual world is relative and not actual. An object in the perceivable world is an object because it partakes in (or initiates) idea. This is Plato's idealism.

Idealism, however, is theoretically self-contradictory. Even Plato himself was unable to tell how many ideas there are, how the perceivable object partakes in ideas or how ideas are known. Thus, in his later period, he was obliged to posit the "theory of types."

Aristotle's criticism of Plato's idealism was quite to the point, though not acute. He pointed out that whenever Plato tried to probe the causes of matters around us, he always resorted to adding on a number of ideas equal in number to the names of perceptual objects. But this leads us nowhere; still worse, it increases our difficulty. Aristotle was quite clear that Plato's error lay in the separation of the general and the individual, and the isolation of the general. He argued that a doctor may see a patient named Garcia or Socrates, but he cannot see "man" in general. "Man" cannot exist independently of Garcia,

Socrates and so on. Plato erroneously isolated idea as a result of his lack of understanding of the general-individual relationship.

In Aristotle's opinion, a new overall study needed to be made of this relationship. He was also explicitly conscious that science always aims at the general, despite the fact that different sciences belong to different realms. He reasoned that since medicine as an exclusive science is devoted to studying health and the like, there ought to be an independent science dealing with all being--being as being. It should be on the very top of the pyramid of science: "first philosophy" as he called it. This branch of learning inquires about what "being" is and how it is to be known (*Metaphysics* IV, 1 and 2).

In fact, Aristotle did not come up with a definite answer to his own question. The root cause again goes back to the general-individual relationship, regarding which his knowledge was very limited. He was clear-minded when criticizing Plato's idealism, pointing out definitely that general categories (whether species or genus) is unable to exist independently. Thus he felt that the basic feature of essence (or substance) is that it neither accounts for subjective entities nor exists in them. But obviously such an interpretation is unable to elaborate what "being" is.

In *Metaphysics* VI, 1 Aristotle, restating his opinion from Book IV, says that although all subjects of science require principles and causes of being,

> all these sciences mark off some particular being--some genus--and inquire into this, but not into being simply nor *qua* being, nor do they offer any discussion of the essence of the things of which they treat; but starting from the essence--some making it plain to the senses, others assuming it as an hypothesis--they then demonstrate, more or less cogently, the essential attributes of the genus with which they deal. It is obvious, therefore, that such an induction yields no demonstration of substance or of the essence, but some other way of exhibiting it. And similarly the sciences omit the question whether the genus with which they deal exists or does not exist, because it belongs to the same kind of thinking to show what it is and that it is (i.e., philosophical thinking).[8]

Seemingly, it is made quite clear that each specific scientific discipline proceeds with hypothetical premises or objects except for philosophy, which presses the question of whether its object of inquiry exists because it studies being as being. He continues, however, to say that the paramount object which philosophy studies, the highest "type," is eternal, static and independent of all else, though it is "general" and not "particular." This is to say that, like the "particular," the "general" can have independent existence. "A man as entity" or "man as entity," he goes on, "a man" and "man," are the same thing.

In the third century A.D., the neoplatonist Porphyry (233-304) worked through the philosophical confusions of Aristotle and came up with the following questions: a. whether "species" and "genus" are "independent or reside only in pure reason; b. supposing they are, whether they take form or are formless; whether they are separate entities and are in unity with them. This conception facilitated the argument between nominalism and realism, thus promoting the rapid development of metaphysics. On the other hand, it was this argument and its development that pushed metaphysics onto a road of self-negation.

THE CRITIQUE OF METAPHYSICS AND ANTI-METAPHYSICS

What conclusion was reached after almost a thousand years of controversy, from Boethius' (480-525) *Porphyry's "Isagoge"* to William of Ockham (1300-1350), regarding the existence of "species" and "genus"? During that protracted debate, a remarkable change took place on the part both of the nominalists and of the realists, though it would be hasty to judge who won: both sides changed their positions from extreme to moderate.

Thomas Aquinas, for example, the most important realist thinker and the official philosopher of the Church in the Middle Ages, was a moderate realist. He claimed that the "general" has three forms of being: a. as the prototype of everything that God creates, which exists in advance of anything created; b. as the form of the individual, residing in the latter; and c. as concept, existing in human reason. But the medieval realists no longer insisted that only the general is real.

Another example is William of Ockham, a known nominalist of the fourteenth century who claimed that it is wasteful to accomplish with much what could be done with little and that entities are not to be multiplied beyond necessity. This is because it only makes the problem more complicated to explain matters with "secret substance" and "objectified form." He therefore held that they should all be shaved away--the so-called "principle of economy" or the well-known "Occam's Razor." He could not deny that universals are objects of thought when placed in an appropriate context (ie., appropriate to an object of rational thought); but they are not primary objects at the source of cognition. That is to say, the universal or the general is of objective significance in cognition.

What do these changes from extreme to moderate nominalism and from the extreme to moderate realism suggest? The relationship between the general and the individual is not a problem of two kinds of substance, but of the relationship between perception and rationality. That is, both realists and nominalists agreed that perception takes the individual as its object whereas rationality takes the general, and that perception and rationality represent only two stages of one cognitive process. Hence, the relationship between the general and the individual is actually that of perception and rationality.

Changes occurring in social and economic systems of that age accelerated the clarification of this problem. "We come across the first beginnings of capitalist production as early as the 14th or 15th century, sporadically, in certain towns of the Mediterranean," noted Marx.[9] The appearance of a capitalist economic system produced two immediate results. First, anti-theological ideas were strengthened, which inevitably promoted the development of anti-metaphysical thought, since Scholastic philosophy had treated being as being as a synonym for God. Second, experimental science developed; this took shape in the trend toward empiricism, holding that nothing is in thought before it has been experienced. As experience grasps the individual entity, the individual alone is real, while concepts and names are only abbreviated forms of experience. This, in turn, intensified anti-metaphysical thought.

For this reason, the task of philosophy was seen to be knowledge of the concrete and of various phenomena of manifold nature, instead of studying the infinite essence or substance behind these natural phenomena or, to be concrete, providing a method for understanding these phenomena. It could also be defined as approaching what experience can grasp, instead of pursuing a sort of transcendental substance. At this point, the inquiry into "existence" takes the place of the inquiry into "being." As Hobbes put it: "whatsoever we imagine is finite. Therefore there is no idea, or conception of anything we call infinite."[10] Thus philosophy moved from the stage of metaphysics, which has ontology at its center, to an anti-metaphysical period centered upon epistemology.

The beginning of the new stage was marked by the advent of two opposite philosophical trends, empiricism and rationalism, for both empiricism and rationalism study mainly epistemology and cognitive method. When epistemology took the place of ontology as the focus of philosophical study, the controversy over the two types of entities (the general and the individual) shifted to that over the relative dependability of perception and reason. Those who stressed the content of cognition when ana-

176 *The Fate of Metaphysics*

lyzing its origin, process and truthfulness were empiricists; whereas those who stressed the form of cognition when doing the analysis were rationalists.

However, the two sides took different anti-metaphysical attitudes. Empiricists chose a stand of open opposition, whereas rationalists still allowed a place for metaphysics. The reason is that empiricism developed from nominalism and thus easily came to oppose substance in general; rationalism, initiated by Descartes, was, however, a later development of scepticism. As Descartes intended to find something which was beyond doubt and self-justifying, he preserved an ultimate substance as first principle. At that time, France was backward politically and economically compared with England, and the Roman Catholic Church was much more powerful in France than in England. This also contributed to the difference between the two trends. For instance, Descartes explicitly declared in his *Discourse on the Method* that he is to abide by the current law and customs and believe in God, and that he tries "always to conquer myself rather than fortune, and alter my desires rather than change the order of the world."[11]

In spite of all that, the enthusiasm of both empiricists and rationalists centered on understanding the actuality of nature and the methods for understanding it. The two camps' agreement on major issues, e.g., on opposing Scholastic philosophy and demanding direct inquiry into nature, out-weighed their heatedly argued differences. Besides, both sides emphasized the applicability of theory. No remark is more apt than Francis Bacon's "Knowledge is power" as an embodiment of their common spirit.

It seems that mankind has a very rich treasury of knowledge, but Bacon claimed that a close examination exposes its actual poverty, for it is rich merely in controversy and lacks actual content. He even held that the study of metaphysics since Aristotle "has done more to establish and perpetuate error than to open the way to truth."[12] Therefore, he advanced an inductive method as opposed to the traditional deduction prevalent since Aristotle, in order to establish a legitimate tie between the perceptual and the rational, and between mind and nature.

Descartes' views were largely similar. He remarked that philosophy as a scientific subject, being the crystalization of the most brilliant thought through hundreds of years, leaves nothing in itself undebated. As a result, "I entirely quitted the study of letters, and resolved to seek no other science than that which could be found in myself, or at least in the great book of the world."[13] Like Bacon, he was determined to work out a method independently, unlike all previous ones, so as to assure that the human intellect could attain correct knowledge. His method was deductive in a manner which, he insisted, was different from any in history. The ancients merely concentrated on some very abstract and useless problems which were good for nothing but causing confusion; he, however, aimed at offering reliable help for the intellect, such that our knowledge could be enhanced by way of his method.

An amusing change took place with the argument between empiricism and rationalism in the early eighteenth century. Originally empiricism seemed more reasonable than rationalism in terms of its overall thrust, since empiricists believed that knowledge comes from the experience of natural objects, while rationalists held that such experience is unreliable and that reliable knowledge must be obtained by proceeding from clear-cut concepts extended from the rational faculty proper. But is not knowledge from such origins like water without a source or a tree without roots? So Spinoza, Leibnitz and others successively revised Descartes' principle. Leibnitz, especially, claimed in no uncertain terms that truth can be divided into two kinds: the rational and the factual. The latter was to some extent an acquiescence to the principles of empiricism. But Bacon's successors, such as Thomas Hobbes and Locke, led empiricist principles in a more and more one-sided direction. Especially with Locke experience became the entire scope as well as the sole source of knowledge. As a result, what should have been the more correct theory turned out, in the early eighteenth century, to be even more absurd. This was the stage at which George Berkeley equated being with perception.

In fact, this absurd conclusion was an inevitable result of the anti-metaphysical one-sidedness of empiricism going to extremes. But thinkers of that age had no grasp of this and kept trying to resolve the contradiction within the scope of empiricism; this was distinctly reflected in the theory of French materialists of the eighteenth century. These materialists realized that the philosophical core of Berkeley was subjective-idealism and that in this regard he coincided with a number of Locke's principles. Accordingly, Denis Diderot remarked that this absurd system, though a humiliation for mankind, is the most difficult to refute.

This did not, however, lead the French thinkers to realize the need to revise fundamentally the empiricist stand. On the contrary, they still threw in their lot with empiricism, relying only on what could be proven by experience and denying that which transcends experience. In metaphysics, says Claude Adrien Helvetius, the argument over such terms as matter, space and time has been protracted and empty. But substance is not a thing; we have in nature only some individual objects which we call objects with form.

Matter can be defined as only a collection of those characteristics which are common to all objects having form. Metaphysical substance, agrees Paul Henrich Dietrich d'Holbach, is but a bunch of meaningless, confused and conflicting concepts. Even the most striking genius will not be able to comprehend the essence and the real nature of matter; what we do comprehend is merely certain determined characteristics and properties in accord with the modes in which matter acts upon us. Accordingly, matter for us is something that, generally speaking, stimulates our sense organs in any number of ways. Hence, matter should have been regarded as a great number of things. All the different individual objects, in spite of certain characteristics they hold in common, such as extension, divisibility and pattern, should not generally be lined up under one category and named 'matter'.

When the French materialists tried to answer Berkeley's challenge in conformity with this view, their efforts proceeded on two fronts: they strove firstly to prove that sensation and thinking are but a capability of a physical body and therefore that the metaphysical problem of the relationship between physical and spiritual substances becomes the relationship between body and mind. Secondly, we obtain our perceptual experience through our sense organs acted on by an external source; these organs are not a "crazy piano," and will not function when left alone.

Despite their great contributions to the development of materialism, these thinkers left the vital point of Berkeley's challenge unimpaired in their criticism, for they failed to disclose the epistemological root cause of Berkeley's subjective idealism. Hume restated this issue in an intensified way. Since all our knowledge comes from experience, says he, the question of whether there is anything independent of experience and existing beyond the scope of experience can be answered only by experience; but experience keeps silent on this score, for it has nothing more to offer. This is Hume's scepticism.

This scepticism shows more than anything else that if man's knowledge cannot transcend experience, empiricism carried to its logical conclusion will run counter to its original intention and reach a dead end. Its original intention was to oppose the metaphysical teaching on "substance" and to stress that the reality of the external world does not lie with a "substance" which lies behind the ever-changing phenomena, but with the phenomena proper. These phenomena are approachable by experience, and what can be experienced directly is real. But how can we state abruptly that there is something independent of experience if the real is nothing more than what can be experienced? Thus, Hume says of this anti-metaphysical system of empiricism that we shall not be able to explain the action of external objects with this system, but rather, we shall eliminate them.

Though in coming to his conclusion he reflected Berkeley's premise of a radically narrow empiricism, Hume differed greatly from Berkeley, who was satisfied with the conclusion deduced from that premise. Hume attempts to uncover the fact that the premise and conclusion, so consistent in appearance, in effect conceal insurmountable conflicts. In this way, his sceptical conclusion had positive theoretical significance, for the trend toward anti-metaphysical thought and ancient metaphysics were proved to be alike in their one-sidedness. The development of philosophy was once again approaching a pivotal juncture.

It was not by chance that Hume came to make this exposition. It resulted from his summing up both historical and contemporary experience, including that of metaphysics and anti-metaphysics and that of the empiricist-rationalist controversy.

He resented the ancient metaphysics, especially that represented by Scholastic philosophy. He refuted "substance," "substantial form," "contingency," "hidden substance," etc., as fabrications unreasoned and random. This is why he admired Berkeley's anti-abstract thought and hailed it as one of the most outstanding discoveries of that age. He also detected difficulty for the modern anti-metaphysical trend, especially empirical ideology. On the one hand, empiricists declared that the external world is approached through perceptual experience; on the other, they believed that the external world exists independently of perceptual experience. This is a direct and overall antithesis. It is a pity that Hume refused to give up the anti-metaphysical stand in which his narrow empiricism fixed him. Thus he says that when viewing the world from his philosophical system he has to reject materialism which attributes all thoughts to actuality, but he realizes that materialists can refute their opponents for similar reasons after a little reexamination. This means that spiritual entity as well as material entity is groundless. In a word, he is dubious of everything.

METAPHYSICS AND ANTI-METAPHYSICS

The old metaphysics failed, since the search to reveal "substance" behind various perceivable qualities reached a dead end; anti-metaphysics also failed is as shown by Hume's scepticism. So where was the open road along which philosophy could develop?

Kant

The first important philosopher who meditated with some success on this dilemma is Kant. He saw that the old metaphysics could not make a tenable argument in theory, and that the negation of metaphysics would also encounter trouble, so he was determined to initiate a new metaphysics. He refers to this as the question of the future of any metaphysics as a science. To answer this question, he set up the system of transcendental idealism.

Kant said,

> . . . since the Essays of Locke and Leibnitz, or rather since the origin of metaphysics so far as we know its history, nothing has ever happened which was more decisive to its fate than the attack made upon it by David Hume. He threw no light on this species of knowledge, but he certainly struck a spark from which light might have been obtained had it caught some inflammable substance and had its smoldering fire been carefully nursed and developed.[14]

He disagreed with Hume's conclusion, he added, but Hume inspired him to break out of his dogmatic illusion and pointed him in the direction of speculative philosophy.

Two points are clear in the preceding quotation: a. Kant disagreed with the old metaphysics, which he explicitly criticized in the "Transcendental Dialectics" of *The Critique of Pure Reason*; b. he did not agree completely with Hume's scepticism. Hence, it was necessary for him to inquire into a new metaphysics to relocate the foundation of objective reality and objective necessity.

The new problem was where to discover such a new metaphysics. As recognition of the new orientation was to result from the breaking of the "illusion of dogmatism," a fairly concentrated analysis of the content of the illusion would open the new path. "So far as one keeps to the ordinary concept of our reason with regard to the association between the thinking subject and the things outside us, we are dogmatical," said Kant.[15] This is also the point on which Hume focused his scepticism. By declaring an end to dogmatic illusion, Kant meant to do away with objective reality and objective necessity independent of all experience, for such independence is an unproved and unprovable hypothesis. He kept his word and characterized his work as another Copernican Revolution.

In the preface of the second edition of *The Critique of Pure Reason* Kant says:

> Hitherto it has been supposed that all our knowledge must conform to the objects: but, under that supposition, all attempts to establish anything about them *a priori*, by means of concepts, and thus to enlarge our knowledge, have come to nothing. The experiment therefore ought to be made, whether we should not succeed better with the problems of metaphysics by assuming that the objects must conform to our mode of cognition, for this would better agree with the demanded possibility of an *a priori* knowledge of them, which is to settle something about objects, before they are given us. We have here the same case as with the first thought of Copernicus, who, not being able to get on in the explanation of the movements of the heavenly bodies as long as he assumed that all the stars turned round the spectator, tried, whether he could not succeed better, by assuming the spectator to be turning round, and the stars to be at rest.[16]

Kant was opposed to infinite substance, both spiritual and material, due to the impossibility of its being the object of knowledge, and for this reason was opposed to the old metaphysics. In his own Copernican Revolution, Kant made an important discovery: the object of knowledge--which refers mainly to what is now called the thing--is not pre-determined, but hypothesized during the process of cognitive activities. This discovery brought the development of philosophy to a brand new stage--the convergence of metaphysics and anti-metaphysics and of ontology and epistemology.

Going a little further into the suggestion that the object of cognition is hypothesized, it can be seen that this is no exaggeration. As the object of cognition is not pre-determined *a priori*, neither is the opposition of subject and object (knower and known). It takes a knower and an object of knowledge independent of the knower to constitute cognition. Without an independent object of knowledge, cognitive activities become a process of self-examination or an interior monologue on the part of the knower. The independent object can only be discovered during cognition. At the same time, the assertion that the object of cognition is independent of cognition is itself part of the cognitive activity. This confirms that it is meaningless to talk about the object of cognition or about the subjective-objective relationship disengaged from cognition.

We still need to realize that although these independent "objects" appear individually as far as their direct mode of being-in-itself is concerned, they may become the object of knowledge only when the individual finds expression in the general. Out-and-out particularity is never an object of cognition, but remains something mysterious like the one and only God. In cognition, man always gets to the general through the particular, and to something infinite through the finite. It is wrong to think, as did the old metaphysicians, that the general and the infinite have independent existence parallel to that of the individual and the finite, or to deny like an anti-metaphysician the objective reality of the general and the infinite. The two sides must be in unity--a unity of metaphysics and anti-metaphysics and of ontology and epistemology. The actual unity is a process in which unlimited incremental advances are achieved through an endless recurrence of subject-object contradictions.

Kant, of course, did not draw this out distinctly, but he did make it clear that the object of cognition cannot be predetermined. To view the object of knowledge as something determined *a priori* is to predispose oneself to the inescapable scepticism indicated by Hume. But as Kant remarked, the conditions that bring forth knowledge bring forth its object. Consciously or not, ontology and epistemology are thus brought into unity. In strict terms, this is the new metaphysics that Kant sought.

What then are its conditions? They are not concocted out of the void by the human brain, but condensed from historical and current experience. Regardless of what Kant himself thought, this was in fact the route he followed. Kant's most direct experience of history and reality was of the controversy between empiricism and rationalism, including of course the experience of metaphysics and anti-metaphysics. From an epistemological stand, Kant pointed out conclusively that an instance of knowledge always takes the form of judgments which can be divided, according to their content, into the "a priori" and the "a posteriori." The former are statements of all impressions independent of experience and even of sense organs, e.g., 1+1=2. The latter, on the contrary, refers to any statement made on the basis of experience, e.g., "the flower is red."

Statements are divided into the "analytic" and the "synthetic" according to the connection of subject and predicate. A statement in which the concept of the subject term encompasses the concept of the predicate is analytic, e.g., "the blackboard is black." In this example, the subject stands clear of substantial augmentation or extension by the descriptive predicate. In a synthetic statement, also known as an "extensional statement," the predicate cannot be deduced by analysis of the subject and thus enhances and extends our available knowledge. Combination of the two types results in four new types of statements: *a posteriori* analytic, as Kant believed, is out of question because an analytic statement, with its strict universal necessity, must be independent of experience and therefore is contradictory to "a posteriori." Of the three remaining, only two were involved in the preceding debate between empiricism and rationalism: *a priori* analytic statements were upheld by rationalists and *a posteriori* synthetic statements by empiricists. Thus Kant accounted for the one-sidedness of both sides. *A priori* analytic statements, despite their strict universal necessity, are cut off from the supply of new knowledge; whereas *a posteriori* synthetic statements, despite all their new knowledge, lack strict universal necessity. Accordingly, he reasoned that real knowledge of science (either mathematics, the natural sciences or metaphysics) should possess both qualities. Hence, the question of a possible scientific metaphysics is replaced by the possibility of the *a priori* synthetic statements, i.e., the possibility of scientific knowledge (cognition).

How can we expound the possibility of the *a priori* synthetic statement? "A priori" is held by rationalists and "a posteriori" by the other side. Obviously, the possibility lies in the combination of the *a priori* universal necessity and the experiential understanding pursued respectively by the two schools, or with the compromise and mediation of both sides. To be brief and descriptive, we need to leave out anything but the pure form of the *a priori* universal necessity, render all experiential data into pure substance without any determination, and then apply the pure form to the pure substance. As a result, the substance with its new determination becomes the object and the form with new content becomes cognition. In this way, knowledge and its object go through a complete cycle of division and combination.

Though Kant seems to have succeeded in bringing about a unity of ontology and epistemology by his theory on the establishment of knowledge and its object out of identical conditions, actually he failed. In his *Critique of Pure Reason* he elaborated the possibilities for mathematics and the natural sciences, but he became vague concerning metaphysics. He criticized the old metaphysics but skipped over the possibility of a scientific metaphysics, except for a remark that a scientific metaphysics is necessary and abides necessarily by the principles of the innate comprehensive judgment. His failure was due to an antithesis of subject and object, which was axiomatic to his theory (though his knowledge of subject and object is much more advanced than that of his predecessors).

As mentioned above, both knowledge and its object are constituted of two parts, substance and form. The substance comes through sense organs from an external thing, which is called the "thing-in-itself." The faculty of perception is vested with certain innate (or *a priori*) and intuitively available forms, i.e., pure direct perceptibility (time and space), so as to be in position to be acted upon by the external object. But mere processing by means of transcendental time and space is not enough to attain its object and knowledge, for we still need to go through the pure *a priori* category of understanding.

Although pure direct perceptibility and pure category themselves lack the reality of experience (despite the way Descartes and some others understand it), and are only *a priori* and identical in nature, they are the conditions for the establishment of experience, and from this aspect possess the reality of experience. Both the experiential object and the cognition of the object are subject to subjective transcendental conditions. Consequently, what people understand has hardly anything in common with external matters, which are excluded from, and beyond, cognition. For this reason, he called such an external object the thing-in-itself, which means unknowable. By this he theoretically blocked any connection between the subjective and the objective.

At the starting point of his theory, Kant harbored the ambition to open up a new road for the development of philosophy. In the end, his theoretical conclusion led him away from this. However, an idea with actual significance that is so positive in its insightfulness will arrive at its proper destiny. The idea that Kant misread unfolded its brilliant possibilities in the thought of Hegel.

Hegel

Kant's error lay, as Hegel believed, in his axiomatic opposition of the subjective and the objective, which resulted in a series of difficulties and dilemmas. Axiomatic premises are not acceptable as far as philosophy is concerned, though they have been introduced into all sciences other than philosophy. The reason is that sciences other than philosophy take as the object of their study something finite obtainable from direct perception. Thus the opposition of the subject and the object can be accepted as a reasonable premise for all the other sciences. Philosophy, however, must extend its study into the objective foundation of the opposition. This was also the question of Hume.

Still, Hegel confirmed the explanatory power of Kant's insight into the subjective and objective. The common conception holds that the object is counterposed to the person but perceivable by his sense organs (like an animal or a star); it is being-in-itself and being-for-itself. Moreover, thinking is dependent on this material. Kant, however, held the contrary opinion: what is given by sense-perception is subjective, and what is in conformity with the principles of thought (having both universality and necessity) is objective. Thus, he contradicted the usual sense of the subjective and the objective by reversing their positions. Hegel approved this and said that the stiff antithesis of the subjective and the objective can be smoothed over and the unity of ontology and epistemology realized only if one persists with this idea. It was a pity that Kant gave it up half way, for he considered that, on the one hand, what is in conformity with the principles of thought is objective, and on the other, such principles of thought will remain a subjective form of absolute emptiness until perceptual material coming from the outside is applied.

Kant was caught up in a self-contradiction because he, like all the anti-metaphysical thinkers before him, went on to claim that what comes directly from experience is real, and all that comes directly from experience is finite. Thus only the finite is real, while universal and necessary thought is without reality. As Kant realized the importance of universal necessity, he treated it as a pure form with no content. Its real objectivity emerges when perceptual material comes to its rescue. But if the objective attaches to the quality of universal necessity, which in turn is determined by the subjective, is not objectivity something subjective?

In Hegel's opinion, the infinite is not beyond the finite but lies in it. For this reason, it is not contradictory to grasp infinite thought by grasping finite appearance, for thought infiltrates various appearances. However, appearances may be available to a person without that person being able to understand their significance for thinking, and without being able to understand the thoughts and concepts made explicit to these appearances. The task of philosophical thinking is none other than understanding the object conceptually, and upgrading from appearance to thought--i.e., performing a conceptual examination of the thing. This concept should not be something devoid of content. The content should not be externally given, but extend out of the concept itself. Hegel refuted the claim that this content is a groundless "arbitrary notion" unless it is externally given and feels that Kant's thing-in-itself is nothing but a useless hypothesis without actual content. In accord with Hegel's idealistic views the content of a concept is concept itself, for a concept is determination and the determination is the content. No concept is capable of being thought except for the concept of thought.

Hegel made into one the two starting points (thing-in-itself and pure form) of Kantian philosophy. As there is no longer an independent thing-in-itself, this leaves only conceptual thinking, and as such thinking has content, it is not pure form. Hegel's intention was to restudy the subject-object relationship on the basis of a more thorough-going idealism: to be brief, to solve the objectivity of thought (universal necessity) on the basis of idealistic monism. For this purpose, he summed up four characteristics of philosophical thinking.

1. Thought is universality in itself and for itself. He believed that what sense-perception grasps is mutually exclusive individuality and what thought grasps is universality. This universality refers not only to generality within individuality, but also to internal connection. "I think," for example, is an action in which I take "I" as my object (as if I am speaking soundlessly to myself). Hence thought is a self-realized universality in itself and for itself, and can be simplified as "I."

2. Thought is not satisfied with perceptual phenomena directly perceived and resorts to self-scrutiny of the phenomena through which it peeps to reach the essence. The essence is indirect, intrinsic, universal and directly unperceivable.

3. The essence obtained through self-scrutiny of what has been directly perceived is something real and objective as well as subjective idea.

4. In terms of its content, the essence or universality profoundly reveals the crux of the matter, for in terms of its form it is a product of the person's spirit and liberty.

Here, thinking is not a special state or action privately owned by the subject, but abstract Idea of oneself free of all particularity, character and situation. It keeps in motion only something universal, and during such motion it is in unison with everything individual. The conclusion Hegel reached through this analysis is that logic intermingles with metaphysics. Metaphysics is a science that studies what thought has grasped, and thought is capable of expressing the essence of matters. This amounts to Hegel's declaration that with his speculative logic he has successfully solved the contradictions between phenomenon and essence, the finite and the infinite, and the objective and the subjective, which Kant had left unsolved in his transcendental logic.

Was Hegel right in saying this? In a sense, he was. For he saw that one should not search for substance outside of cognition (for the search itself is a cognitive effort), nor should one try to establish an epistemology without reference to this search for substance (for the basic task of cognition is to press for the universal objective essence). Regarding the "attitude of thought to objectivity," he pointed out that it was the essential error of the old metaphysics to assume as a matter of course the direct determination of the universal objective essence and therefore to take the essence as an independent substance. Modern anti-metaphysical thinkers, to their credit, deny that the universal or substance can be directly determined. But as they still insist that what is dependable is what can be directly determined, eventually they fall into scepticism and deny knowledge as their position on the universal essence. Cognition is actually the contradictory unity of directness and indirectness. It always starts from directness, which by virtue of its task and essence is inevitably transcended. The fundamental contradiction of philosophy is neither the metaphysical problem of two substances nor the anti-metaphysical problem of body-mind relationship. It is the thinking-being relationship, which expresses itself as the question of the objectivity of universal thinking and its unity with objective being. Based on this thought, Hegel developed his theory on the contradictory unity of thinking and being, i.e., dialectics. His dialectics is the theory of the unison of ontology and epistemology. Therefore he brought into unison ontology, epistemology and methodology, which marks his greatest contribution to the development of philosophical thinking.

In effect, Hegel did not really solve the subjective-objective contradiction in his idealistic dialectics, because he mistook contradictions of the subjective and the objective and of essence and phenomenon as being within the scope of thinking. For him, being as being or general being, as that to which philosophy is devoted, is thinking as well. This is because general being without any specific determination is no more than some notion of being. His answer to the question of how this notion of being remains in unity with objective being is that this unity is based not outside the notion of being, but inside. Consequently, the motion of the thinking-being contradiction is mistaken as a motion within the scope of thinking, which is tantamount to nullifying the subjective-objective contradiction.

Feuerbach

Feuerbach was very clear about Hegel's idealistic error on this issue. The being in Hegel's logic, Feuerbach says, is the being of the old metaphysics. It is used to express everything without any differentiation. For the old metaphysics, the common point of all things is being. But this undifferentiated being is an abstract thought, without reality. To prove the being of matters in thinking, he thought, one should not be confined within the notion of being or thought; on the contrary, the reality of thought lies nowhere but in being more than thought and in becoming the perceptual object of non-thought.

Like the empiricists, Feuerbach went on to say that the real is what has been grasped by the experience of sense-perception. This is because sense-perception is a confirmation of the being of something beyond me. The premise of this judgment is that "I" proper is a sense-perception. If the subject is perceptual, so must be the object, and vice versa. Thus he agrees with the idealists that one has to begin cognition from the subject or oneself, because the essence of the world, what it is for man and what impact it has on man are subject only to the essence of the knower himself, his cognitive ability and his general attributes. Since the world is an object for man, it is his objectified self, and this does not undermine his independence. But one's self, he then adds, as the starting point for the idealists and for their negation of the being of perceivable matters, has no being. It is an alleged, rather than a real, self. One's real self is in opposition to "you" and the object of another self; so for another self it is "you." But since the idealists' self has no object at all, for them "you" has no being.

It is clear that Feuerbach agreed with the principle of subject-object and thinking-being unities. He tried, however, to explain this in line with materialism, for as a materialist he emphasized the independence of object or the object of cognition. While criticizing Hegel, he did not set the independence of the object absolutely in opposition to the subject; on the contrary, with Hegel he believed in a subject-object unity. To the same extent, he relates, object is object-subject, just as subject is essentially the inseparable subject-object, i.e., I am you and you are I, and man is man of the world or of nature.

Besides, Feuerbach also realized that the thinking-being relationship cannot be simply reduced to the man-nature relationship, because man needs a perceptual substance to be the subject of cognition. But he will not become a subject of cognition if he is but a perceptual substance (individual). He still needs to be upgraded from being a specific individual to being a universal object. A universal object is an object, perceptual being or individual as a category, the subject of which, however, is not somewhere outside it, but is itself. If the object (the object of cognition) outside the "I" (the subject of cognition) is none other than "I", then "I" is not a finite object but a universal one. Therefore, a universal object refers to an object with thinking capacity.

He explains that man thinks by talking and speaking to himself. Animals cannot perform their species-specific functions without another independent individual; but man does not need another in order to perform such functions as thinking or speech, which are the true functions of his species. Man himself is "I" as well as "thou"; he can imagine himself as somebody else because he takes as the object, not only his individuality, but also his species and his essence. From this Feuerbach defined man the species as an entity.

It is inappropriate, however, to ascribe only to a natural procedure the upgrading of a perceptual individual to a universal object. Although man cannot be isolated from nature, as directly produced from nature he is not yet a "man." For man is a product of man, of culture and of history. That is to say, the human power of thinking comes with intercourse between men. Just as two people give birth to a man physically, in the same way a man is born spiritually through people coming together. Empiricism believes, he commented, that our ideas initially come from sense-perception and that is correct. What it forgets is that the most important and primary perceptual object is man himself and that the brilliance of the human mind and intelligence shows only when his attention is on man. So idealists make sense by searching for the origin of Idea within man, but they miss it when they try to approach it by way of an isolated and pre-determined substance of independent being and of predetermined man as spirit, in other words, by way of the "self" of a "thou" that is not taken as a perceptual object. Idea grows out of communication, out of the conversation of men. That means that it is possible to obtain notions and general understanding, not by oneself, but only by way of mutual action.

An important hypothesis is contained in this thought of Feuerbach: the thinking-being relationship goes beyond the thought-matter relationship, i.e., the man-nature relationship, and extends to the relationship between men. Without the intercourse of men, man will not become the universal object or subject of cognition. No previous thinkers in classical philosophy, either materialists or idealists, correctly understood this relationship. Briefly, without exception they understood the activities of man and nature to be in opposition and had never been able to locate any common ground between man and matter and between thinking and being; subject and object had been in absolute opposition. Kant realized that this is a dead end; he did his best to do away with it and was able to present some new explanations. Nevertheless, as the axiomatic premise remained the antithesis of subject and object (thing-in-itself and pure form) in a new version, he had to conclude that the thing cannot be known. Hegel joined nature and history as an integrated process resulting in the conclusion that substance is subject, thus doing away with the axiomatic premise of the subject-object antithesis. But he only changed thinking itself into the domain of the antithesis.

It was Feuerbach who discovered the way in which the subject remains in unity with the object objectively as well as subjectively. This conjecture predicts a brand new orientation for the development of materialism. Once this development is fulfilled, ontology and epistemology would be truly unified on the basis of materialism, and dialectics would be developed and improved in materialist terms.

But Feuerbach was not able to realize this new orientation because he approached the relationship of men only in terms of direct perceptibility. On the one hand, he saw the importance of the thought of subject-object unity; on the other, he thought that it is materialistic (of course, he would not use the term himself) to understand this unity within the scope of direct perceptibility. Perceptual objects include more than "external" matters. Through sense-perception man becomes his own object of cognition as perceptual object. The identity of subject and object is only an abstract thought in self-consciousness; it becomes truth and entity only when it comes to the direct perception of man by man. Perception is the key to the secret of mutual influence and only perceptual substances can exert mutual influence. I am an "I" for me, and a "you" for others because the "I" is a perceptual substance. Here Feuerbach became self-contradictory: on the one hand, he believed that the subject is in unity with the object, a relation which revealed the objective and manifested essence of the subject; on the other, he considered thinking and being to be not interchangeable, but to remain absolutely in antithesis.

The reason for his error is that he did not understand man, though his philosophy placed obvious emphasis upon man. He felt that we can take philosophy from the skies and pull it down to earth, that we can promote materialism while suppressing idealism, as long as man is reduced to perceptual being. This is incorrect because what history records is man's perceptual activities, i.e., his material activities, instead of his perceptual being. Without such activities, man will never evolve from the animal world to become the universal object or the subject of cognition. Certainly, Feuerbach notes that the ability to think does not cover all the differences between man and animals, that the essence of man as a whole is different from that of animals. But is this the perceptual essence? If it is, what is the difference of man from other animals? His answer is that man is not a particular substance like animals, but a universal one, that is, a free substance, not restricted by any specific object. The sense organs of animals, for instance, are subject to the restriction of certain objects, whereas man's sense organs are not, but are free organic functions. If an organic function goes beyond the restriction of particularity and the bond of necessity, it will achieve independence and an overwhelming theoretical significance. A universal organic function is intellect, and universal perceptiveness is spirituality. Feuerbach does not ask himself why this freedom is obtainable for human sense organs, nor can he answer that question.

But here we come to the crux of the issue. Marx answered the question that Feuerbach missed. Perceptual activities (activities of material production) enable human sense organs to be free by exceeding what the physical body needs directly. That is to say, in such perceptual activities the difference can be found between man and animals. Feuerbach's perception, Marx remarked in his critique, is abstract, though he gives much stress to it. But the being of man, including his relationship with nature, must not be separated from his productive activities. This is the discovery of historical materialism. Thereupon the real unity of ontology and epistemology is realized on the solid ground of materialistic theory.

Now, I will not describe Marx's theory on the unity of ontology and epistemology. Instead, I will ask a question: what conclusion shall we come to from the overall history of the development of metaphysics, anti-metaphysics and then the intermingling of the two? History is an endless source of treasures from which man can draw a great deal for his own benefit. I will be bold enough to single out four primary points:

1. The fundamental contradiction of philosophy finds its expression in the relationship of two substances at the metaphysical stage; in the relationship of physical body and spirit or of body and mind at the anti-metaphysical stage; and in the relationship of thinking and being at the stage of the intermingling of metaphysics and anti-metaphysics. This is what we usually refer to as the cause of the fundamental issue of philosophy and the theoretical content of its historical development.

2. The thinking-being relationship is a problem concerned not only with man and nature, but also with the relationship between men. Both are abstract, as are the separation of history from nature or of nature from history.

3. The central issue of the thinking-being relationship is the unity of ontology and epistemology. Thinking deals with the general, but the general at issue is not what metaphysicians understand as independent being, nor is it the anti-metaphysical non-being. The general in thought is something grasped during cognition and it is objective. It is a great error to place objectivity in absolute opposition to subjective activity.

4. Dialectics is the theory and method of the unity of

thinking and being. Objectively the individual contains the general; subjectively the general contains the individual. The two sides achieve a contradictory unity (infinite instead of finite) in the dynamic historical activities of the subject.

Peking University
Beijing, People's Republic of China

NOTES

1. *Aristotle I (Great Books of the Western World*, Vol. 8; Encyclopaedia Britannica, 1984), p. 503.
2. John Burnet, *Early Greek Philosophy* (New York: Barnes and Noble, 1962), p. 94.
3. *Ibid.*
4. *Ibid.*, p. 93.
5. *Ibid.*, p. 94.
6. *Ibid.*, p. 4.
7. Plato, (*Great Books of the Western World*, Vol. 7, Encyclopaedia Britannica, 1984), p. 86.
8. *Ibid.*, Vol. 8, *Aristotle* I.
9. Karl Marx, *Capital*, Vol. I, Part VIII, ch. XXVI, para. 7.
10. Thomas Hobbes, *Leviathan*, Part I, chap. 3, last para.
11. *The Philosophical Works of Descartes*, trans. by Elizabeth S. Haldane and G.R.T. Ross (Cambrdige: Cambridge Univ. Press, 1979), vol. I, p. 96.
12. *The English Philosophers from Bacon to Mill*, Edwin A. Burtt, ed. (New York: The Modern Library, 1939), p. 10.
13. *The Philosophical Works of Descartes*, Vol. I, p. 86.
14. *Ten Great Works of Philosophy* (New York: Mentor, 1969), p. 299.
15. *Ibid.*, p. 273.
16. *Ibid.*, p. XXXIII.

PART V

ETHICS AND NATURE

CHAPTER XIV

HUMAN NATURE REFLECTED IN MORAL EXPERIENCE

JOHN FARRELLY

The theme of "Man and Nature" is a subject of critical importance to our countries and our world. Professor Schmitz has analyzed for us a number of paradigms of nature that have held sway in the West. Among them was a mechanistic paradigm that was built on science and rejected the classical Western paradigms of nature derived from Greece and from Judeo-Christian religion. He pointed also to a contemporary movement toward a broader paradigm liberated from certain reductionist tendencies derived by some philosophers from science.

In accord with Professor Schmitz's description of current tendencies in the West, I would like to point to ways in which interpretations of praxis, in the sense of man's moral experience, give rise to views on human nature. I will indicate briefly two contemporary views which substitute the moral experience that leads to a classical view of human nature by new interpretations of our moral experience and hence of human nature. These are derived from the kinds of reasoning found in much liberal democracy, technology and the market economy. They discount the reality of human nature in any classical sense as basic to our moral experience, for they associate such notions of human nature with a traditional and conservative ethos incapable of serving as a criterion for issues of human decision in our rapidly changing and enlarging world. To look to human nature in the traditional fashion, they think, would be to look to the past, indeed to the past of a particular people, rather than to the future. They associate such a perspective with cultures that deny human autonomy or limit human freedom.

The two views I will note are associated respectively with an interpretation of the democratic process and an interpretation of reasoning found in technology and a market economy. I will examine these as they are found in psychologists who study human moral development, namely in Lawrence Kohlberg, on the one hand, and in Israela Aaron, who depends on John Dewey for some philosophical assumptions, on the other.[1] I wish (1) to characterize these briefly, (2) to defend a more integral interpretation of the foundations of moral judgment than these positions offer (incorporating what is valuable in their positions, but arguing that for an adequate interpretation of our moral experience we must retrieve and develop a classical understanding of human nature), and (3) to answer an objection that may be posed to our position. This means that at present we need both a retrieval and development of our classical understandings of nature.

It should be noted that we are dealing here with only one aspect of morality, which is basically an attitude rather than a judgment, and is inculcated or learned by a whole process of education. Moreover, even this limited topic is presented in only a skeletal fashion, for the paper is a response to some specifically Western interpretations of moral experience and human nature which are based on contemporary forms of experience but seem defective in part. Nevertheless, the question treated can be an issue also for other countries where democracy and technology call into question traditional criteria for moral judgment.

CONTRAST BETWEEN TWO INTERPRETATIONS OF MORAL JUDGMENT

The two theories studied here to illustrate current interpretations of moral judgment are those of Lawrence Kohlberg and of Isrela Aron. They have been selected because they represent the basic division among influential normative ethicists today in the West into deontological and teleological theories, respectively.[2] We shall survey the general character of each and the contrast between them.

Lawrence Kohlberg begins from a certain philosophical understanding of morality. In continuity with Immanuel Kant, he thinks that morality consists primarily in a kind of judgment with certain formal characteristics; they are, namely, prescriptive (rather than, for example, descriptive) and universalizable. That is, they are prescriptions that we can in principle make universal about how people should structure their behavior. He says that:

> We make no direct claims about the ultimate aims of men, about the good life, or about other problems which a teleological theory must handle. These are problems beyond the scope of the sphere of morality or moral principles, which we define as principles of choice for resolving conflicts of obligations.[3]

Moral judgment is a particular way of structuring human behavior, distinct, for example, from that of aesthetics or prudence.

As a developmental psychologist, Kohlberg asks how universal prescriptive judgments structuring human behavior emerge in the child and adolescent. He finds that these are not innate to the child, but rather emerge through a continual restructuring of the way the child judges conflict situations. There are six stages in this process, and in this development the motives of the growing person become gradually more universal and adequate. For example, initially the child thinks that the physical consequences of action, particularly punishment and reward by others, determine the moral status of an act. Somewhat later the child thinks that moral goodness consists in carrying out what others expect of one in his or her role or position, and in the approval given by others. Only by going through these stages and learning that there are conflict situations which these ways of judging cannot resolve does the growing person come to a universalistic ethics or the view that moral standards are those which are self-chosen and universalizable.[4] These characteristics are found particularly in judgments about rights and duties, or about justice. "No principle other than justice has been shown to meet the formal conception of a universal prescriptive principle."[5] This restructuring occurs through an equilibration process due to the interaction between the growing person and the enlarging social context.

On the other hand, a teleological theory of morality is offered as a basis by some psychologists of moral development. Israela Aron can serve as an example of this position. She acknowledges that there are advantages to Kohlberg's formalist position in that he claims to be stimulating moral growth rather than indoctrinating or inculcating particular values. However, formalist philosophers restrict themselves largely to meta-ethics and so do not deal effectively with substantive issues. But in moral education the teacher is trying to help young people face complex experience and learn how to make creative moral decisions among the alternatives available. So the moral educator has to use an approach that deals primarily with the process of ethical decision making. Aron suggests that John Dewey's work is helpful here. For Dewey, it is the interaction of organism and environment that is the context both for experience and for decision making. In situations of conflicting desire, practical deliberation begins with the formulation of the issue. The person rehearses in imagination competing lines of action.

> The competing lines of action cannot, according to Dewey, be evaluated by an a priori or abstract standard (such as an ultimate principle), but must be assessed in terms of their consequences. These consequences must be construed broadly. . . [T]he consequences of an act include the effects it will have on the character of the deliberator as well as its effects on the physical and social environment.6

Principles of the past are important here, not as absolutes but as summaries of wisdom that are themselves subject to modification. There are some rational ways of evaluating values, namely, through consideration of their consequences. It is true that "Dewey's denial of the prescriptive power of moral judgment seems to be the most troublesome aspect of his ethical theory."[7] But if one presents the consequences of a line of action that a friend is considering and shows that these are harmful, what can be added by saying that the line of action is immoral? This may add persuasion, but it is essentially a rhetorical addition and not an additional argument.

Here then we see two quite divergent approaches to the interpretation of our experience of making moral judgments. One of these interpretations is closely tied to the democratic process of making equitable decisions in conflict situations; and the other to the process of reasoning found in technology and a market economy.[8] Both discount a more traditional form of moral reasoning based on human nature; or, we may say, they offer new interpretations of human nature based on contemporary experiences. The proponents of both recognize the limits in their own positions and the strengths in their opponents' position. Basically, however, they hold to their own approach as the primary one--though this may profit by being supplemented by the other in some undefined way.

A MORE INTEGRAL INTERPRETATION OF MORAL EXPERIENCE

Is it possible to transcend these viewpoints in a more integral moral theory? Each of the proponents of these moral theories is defending something of importance in moral judgments, but each defends one aspect of our moral experience in a way that excludes the other. Thus the strength of each lies largely in the weakness of the other; in a sense they feed off one another. Is this due to the nature of the case, or is it due to some position they have in common, some premise from which a dilemma arises that results in a parting of their ways?

I would like to defend the viewpoint that it is necessary to accept the reality of a good that fulfills our human nature if we are to explain adequately our experience of moral judgment of right and wrong. To do this, I will present: (1) an hypothesis about the basis of morality that helps to integrate the above views and account for the divergence between them, (2) a brief phenomenology that supports this interpretation of morality and the moral judgment, and (3) an objection to this position that is common today along with a suggested answer. All of this will be done in a schematic fashion.

Implied here is the position that we must agree on what

constitutes a moral experience before we are able to evaluate moral theory, since moral theory is not an antecedent stipulation of what will be accepted as moral experience, but rather an attempt to explain moral experience to the extent that philosophy claims to do so. Some may claim that my approach is guilty of the naturalistic fallacy, since I argue from experience to what we should and should not do. However, I would argue, as I have elsewhere, that those who make the accusation of a naturalistic fallacy accept an epistemology that is either Kantian or Humean, and that neither of these is an adequate explanation of human knowledge.[9]

An Hypothesis

How do we critically evaluate the good or value of our actions? We can present our hypothesis on this in three steps. First, we show in our actions and desires that as individuals and as societies we value other persons, certain objectives, relationships and goods, and we show great diversity in what we value. This is antecedent to moral judgment; it is the context in which moral judgments arise. Secondly, we reflect upon our action and our desires, or upon the values we are seeking in these, to ask whether what we are valuing is really valuable, whether there is some basis for our valuing it other than the mere fact that we do so. The answer that this is justified by the consequences is not adequate since it must be asked what justifies the values of these consequences. Nor is it sufficient to answer that we can universalize the judgment that we should act in a certain way, since we should ask what justifies this universalization. Thus, thirdly, our experience of acting for a value and our reflection upon this value may give us access to an insight that takes us beyond the simply factual character of this situation for ourselves or our particular society.

Thus, we have the insight that as human beings we orient our action to values and that we become more fully human if we value certain goods such as respect for another and reject others which appeared pre-reflectively as values to us. There is something constitutive of us as human beings which precedes us *as* experiencers and choosers of value and which is a criterion or norm for the self-definition of values that enhance our humanity. We can call this a *constitutive human good*, namely, both the human attitude (e.g. respect for truth, for others, for self) and the term of such an attitude. That is our norm or criterion as we define our values, because in view of the structure of being which is characteristic of humans, certain attitudes and goals fulfill us whereas certain attitudes and goals diminish us or are regressive.

There is, of course, a whole class of actions which are oriented primarily not to the development of the one who acts, but to some product outside the agent such as a house to be built by a carpenter. Here the immediate criterion of the value of the act is the product, rather than the development of the agent. However, considering the agent superior in value to such products of human activity would be one of the elements of a constitutive human good; hence, engagement in such action should itself redound to the development of the agent as well as of the society which he serves.

An example, which we will develop more fully later, is found in our treatment of other persons in a way that is just and respectful. From our viewpoint the value realized by this action and the judgment enjoining it is part of the constitutive human good. There is worth in all human beings and this has a claim upon our acknowledgement and upon our action and attitude toward them. The claim that anothers' worth as human has on me is not contradictory to my own basic inclination as a human being, since in part I am constituted as human through being a social being, that is, a being oriented not simply toward my own fulfillment but also that of others and toward a community that embraces us both.

Neither Kohlberg nor Aron acknowledges such a basis for the moral order. Kohlberg makes no claim to say anything substantive about what the goals of human living are or what constitutes the good life because he equates such statements with relativism and indoctrination. On the other hand, while Aron does make the fulfillment of the moral agent and even society the context of decisions in life, she denies anything in moral judgment like a categorical imperative. The good for this position ends up meaning only what individuals or societies judge good through an examination of consequences. The denial of a constitutive human good as the foundation of the moral order is common to these positions.

Their common rejection of such a basis leads to weaknesses in their positions. Since Kohlberg does not give a basis for the universalization of moral judgments toward which the developing person moves other than the process called "equilibration" itself, the prescriptiveness he attains in such judgments is only hypothetical. That is, all should act in such a way if they want such and such a kind of society. Only if it is a constitutive human good which provokes the equilibration process and if it is acknowledged to have such a significance can Kohlberg defend the universality and prescriptiveness of the moral judgment.

On the other hand, since Aron begins with the agent making creative life decisions in a way that is self-defined and calls only upon consequences to justify choice, the kind of necessity in the decisions this position reaches is only hypothetical. That is, if people value such and such a goal, then they should take certain kinds of action and avoid others. For such a position, "good" ends up meaning only what individuals or societies judge to be such or choose to value. Perhaps their valuing of the autonomy of the human agent--as well as the influence upon them of a liberal democratic society always choosing between interest groups, and of a technological society in a market economy choosing among goods on the basis of consequences--obscures for them the presence of a constitutive human good in moral judgment, choice and action. As we will argue later, their differences from one another could be overcome if they accepted the reality of such a good as presiding over the moral life.

A Phenomenology

In support of the hypothesis we presented, we may ask what is really happening when we acknowledge the rights of another person to be treated with respect and fairness and when such acknowledgement affects our attitudes and actions. This would be recognized by both Kohlberg and Aron as an occasion for moral judgment and decision. The question is whether their interpretations of what is happening here are adequate or whether they are to some extent reductionist. Kohlberg would, of course, rightly point out that different things are happening at different stages of the child's, adolescent's or adult's moral development. But as a moral philosopher he does recognize a mature stage in this development, and it is of that stage that we are asking our question. What actually happens when we acknowledge the rights of others at this point? A brief phenomenology can perhaps help us here toward insight into whether formalism, consequentialism or a view such as we offered above best interprets this experience.

We can take the instance of a white person in the Southern United States in the mid to late 1960's facing a decision whether to discriminate against blacks in hiring for a job or in supporting voting rights. Such a person could experience the movement toward offering blacks civil rights as against his tradition, as aesthetically repugnant, and as threatening the purity of his stock. Also, if he were to join the civil rights movement, he could be thought a traitor by his own people. In circumstances where he could discriminate, he may nevertheless decide not to do so because the law is now opposed to this, or because he would lose economically through such discrimination, or because he would be subject to violence in revenge for his action. On the other hand, he may decide not to discriminate because through role-taking, that is, putting himself imaginatively in the place of the other, and through universalizing the resultant judgment he may opt for a social order that treats all with equity when it comes to such matters. After all, he would not like to be on the receiving end of such discrimination. This latter approach is the result of an equilibration process which results in a moral judgment of certain formal characteristics (universalizable and prescriptive) whereas the former approach is a consequentialist one.

However, in addition to these reasons and even as his primary reason he may judge that he ought not to discriminate against others due to their race because he thinks that they have a *right* to be respected and treated equally with others simply by the fact that they are human beings, even though they are not of his own group. As persons they, like the one hiring, are masters of their own actions; they live with their own human dignity and the essential worth that goes with it; they are moving toward their own human fulfillment. This calls for respect that precludes subjecting them to discrimination with all the indignities that this involves.

The necessity or prescriptiveness present in a judgment to this effect is not simply physical, economic or aesthetic, conventional or civil, utilitarian or consequentialist, or the result of role-taking or universalization. It is properly a moral necessity, that is, one which comes from the recognition of the rights which the other has as a human person and a correlative duty the moral agent has to respect this. Unlike the other bases given above, it has more than a hypothetical prescriptive force, namely, that he should act in a certain way if he wants certain consequences or a certain kind of society.

Language supports this interpretation of what is happening. If a person so respecting another is challenged to justify his action, he speaks of the natural or the human rights of the other based on his human dignity or worth, thus indicating that the basis for the injunction is more than consequences, law and order, or role-taking and universalization. It is a constitutive human good of the other that must be acknowledged and respected, and it is a constitutive human good of the moral agent to accept the claims that others have upon him since he is a social being.

Of course, there can be other phenomenologies offered to interpret what is happening here, and presumably both Kohlberg and Aron would offer alternative interpretations. Kohlberg holds that his own view of the sixth stage of moral development finds support in the philosophical position of John Rawls in his book, *A Theory of Justice*.[10] Rawls seeks to defend a social order that is fair in the distribution both of civil and of socio-economic goods and rights. He does so through inviting people to assume an original position in which they would choose the basic principles which are to govern the distribution of goods in their society. If they did not know their own talents and where they would fit in the socio-economic scale, they would be concerned that the principles be in their favor through favoring the least advantaged.

Without following him further into the details of his proposal, we can acknowledge that this approach may be persuasive in encouraging people to take an impartial stance, but if it is presented as a phenomenology of what is actually happening when people acknowledge the rights of others it is rather unhistorical and artificial. It may represent the basis for such acknowledgement on the part of those who have not got beyond individual interests as a basis for social life; and in this way, as Edmund Sullivan writes, it defends the ideology of liberalism. "The essence of liberalism is a vision of society made up of independent autonomous units who cooperate only when the terms of cooperation are such as to make it further the ends of each of the parties."[11] Of course, a society built on this principle would entail no more than hypothetical necessity in its recognition of the rights of others. The same is true for a society based on consequentialism.

Another difficulty with consequentialism is the following.

> If consequences are good because they help one grow toward the human good, then action is good more because it relates one to the human good in accord with reason than because it has good consequences. Similarly, an action contrary to this human good is morally evil more because it is against the human good proper to man in his action than because it has bad consequences for him and society, immediate and remote. To divorce consequences from the human good (and this includes the common good as well as individual human good) as a moral norm is to leave us without criteria for discerning good from bad consequences. To give them priority over the human good as norms is intrinsically contradictory, since their value depends upon their relation to the human good.[12]

We suggest then that neither Kohlberg's nor Aron's moral theory is adequate as an interpretation of what is happening in our moral experience, and that the approach we presented, namely, one that makes use of our human orientation toward a constitutive human good, is more adequate in interpreting our moral experience. Moreover, it overcomes the dichotomy between a deontological moral theory such as that of Kohlberg and a teleological moral theory such as Aron's and Dewey's consequentialism. Thus we claim that what our moral experience reveals about human nature is contrary to the views of those who interpret our moral experience in a manner that rejects any continuity with a classical view of human nature, and yet that this is needed in order to overcome the inadequacy of their own interpretations of moral experience and human nature.

An Objection and an Answer

Many contemporary moralists would claim that the interpretation we have offered represents a premodern anthropology. For example, Paul Taylor would characterize this as an ethics based on an "essentialistic conception of happiness":

> because it presupposes that there is such a thing as an essential human nature. . . . Essentialist philosophers view the good for man as an ideal of human perfection, a perfection which is uniquely suitable to characteristically human capacities. When this conception of happiness is used as the standard of intrinsic value, that standard becomes identical with the essentialist's standard of human perfection or virtue.[13]

In our world we are much more aware than previously of the great diversity among cultures and peoples. This diversity comes from human self-making and creativity in different environments. To assert the existence of a constitutive human good may appear to many to be a rejection of the evidence that what is good for human beings depends upon this diversity and this self-making that characterize human existence.

In answer to this, we fully acknowledge that modern experience and physical and human sciences do support a great pluralism of interpretations of the good human life, and the dependence of this upon the creativity and self-making of human beings in differing environments. This has significance for philosophical anthropology and ethics, because it shows us something of what it means to be human, and these findings modify an earlier anthropology and moral theory. What is good for human beings is historically conditioned. We do not dispute this, but we contend that this pluralism is consistent with there being intrinsic standards of the human good. What is good for human beings is intrinsically differentiated according to different ages of the person, differences of sex, and differing circumstances, and there are even different opinions about the standards of the human good.

This, however, does not eliminate unity. Biology supports a unity to human nature within its diversity, because it shows us that the human zygote takes twenty-three chromosomes from each parent with the accompanying genes that are determinants of hereditary traits. The resulting diversity and commonality among human beings exists not only at the present time, but also among human beings living today and those living in the distant past. It is appropriate for human beings as well as for lower animals to interact with a specific environment and to do so with a spontaneity that reflects the interest of the agent. However, for this interaction to be beneficial, it is important that it be correlated with a distinctively human potential and not simply with a specific environment and spontaneity.

Developmental psychologists also support the view that the development of human beings is due to the interaction of the growing person with his or her environment in a way that leads to a progressive restructuring of the self, of knowledge and of moral judgment. With this, however, seems to go a presupposition of the reality of human nature that sets standards and criteria for what may be understood as development and what as regression or failure to develop. For example, Kohlberg recognizes that the subject develops through the active restructuring of his moral judgments, but he acknowledges that some forms of moral judgement are more adequately and maturely human than others. Jean Piaget finds that the individual cognitive subject restructures his mode of knowing the environment through interaction with that environment, but he presupposes that some cognitive structures are more advanced than others. Erik Erikson shows that the personality structure of the adult is the result of the growing person's restructuring of the self through stages of interaction with an expanding social environment and stages of unfolding inner potential, but he holds that some personality structures are more appropriate to the adult than others. For example, the mature person should be characterized by generativity, i.e., a sustained interest in the development of the next generation in spite of its costs. All of this supports the viewpoint that we offered.

The human being is a subject who not only does, but must restructure himself through interaction with the environment for the purpose of actualizing his being. This actualization of his being which as an intrinsic principle evokes the subject's activity. Human nature then is not simply that which precedes human action and explains what kinds of action will be characteristically human. Rather the actualization of one's humanity faces the subject as a possibility in need of actualization, a possibility that is distinctive but also demands variety according to the environment of nature and history, differences of age, sex and many other individuating circumstances. The human good is achieved only through an historical process that rightly involves great pluralism without relativism. Freedom should characterize the way the person should orient him or herself to the human good, but it does not offer a basis for the ultimate definition of what this fulfillment or good is. The fact that the life a person leads as an adult is due to his own free construction manifests the *manner* of his orientation toward his fulfillment as human rather than the disengagement of choice from a good that is proper for human beings. If there were not some ways of living humanly which had intrinsic value, which enhanced and actualized a person and contributed to his completion as human, there would be minimal meaning in our choices. In fact, nihilism would be the inevitable result.[14]

Most anthropologists today reject relativism. Cultural anthropologists such as Clifford Geertz recognize that culture is an important determination of the human career for the individual, for a society and for mankind as a whole. They hold that culture, in the sense of "a set of control mechanisms--plans, recipes, rules, instructions (what the computer engineers call 'programs')--for the governing of behavior,"[15] is an essential condition of human existence. Man's very physical evolution in part depends upon it, because such things as the anatomy of the thumb, the representation of the thumb on the cortex, and the size of the brain depend upon man's development and use of tools, which by a feedback process affected even the evolution of man's central nervous system. While we must acknowledge the dependence of values on culture as well as on man's intrinsic drives and potentials, and so the historically conditioned character of the human good and morality, this recognition contradicts neither the unity of human nature nor the reality of the human good as a criterion of moral choice. To deny this is to consider all cultural conditioning and all human behavior as morally equal, for it is to abdicate the criterion for judging morally which is beyond particular customs, cultures and conditions.

CONCLUSION

We have argued that interpretations of praxis in the sense of man's moral experience have in our time led to views of human nature which agree with one another in rejecting classical views of human nature but cannot agree on the proposals they make. We have also argued that for an adequate interpretation of moral experience, we need to acknowledge and understand human nature, particularly in the sense of a constitutive human good that is the goal and criterion of our moral activity and judgments. This view of the human good and human nature is not exclusively wedded to the customs of our differing cultures. It orients us to the future more than to the past. It calls for change, but for change which can be shown to favor a genuine human development, rather than simply acquisitiveness. It promotes harmony, not primarily with the cycles of physical nature, but with the development of the human community, indeed, a world-wide human community. Promotion of such a community has its own costs because, while the human good allows us to treasure our own cultures, it is counter to particularisms or exclusivisms. Perhaps it is in this sense that we one can say in our time that this harmony with nature is harmony with God at work in the world, that is, with the "way of the gods."

De Salles College
Washington, D.C., U.S.A.

NOTES

1. See L. Kohlberg, "From Is to Ought: How the Commit the Naturalistic Fallacy and Get Away with It in the Study of Moral Development," in Theodore Mischel, ed., *Cognitive Development and Epistemology* (New York: Academic Press, 1971), and L. Kohlberg, *The Philosophy of Moral Development: Essays on Moral Development* (San Francisco: Harper and Row, 1981), vol. I. See Israela Aron, "Moral Education: The Formalist Tradition and the Deweyan Alternative," in Brenda Munsey, ed., *Moral Development, Moral Education and Kohlberg* (Birmingham: Religious Education Press, 1980), pp. 401-426. For an evaluation of current views on moral education, see F. Ellrod, George McLean, D. Schindler and J. Mann, ed., *Act and Agent: Philosophical Foundations for Moral Education and Character Development* (Washington, D.C., University Press of America, 1986). The present chapter is an adaptation of my contribution to that book, with the permission of the editor.

2. See Wm. Frankena, *Ethics* (Englewood Cliffs, N.J.: Prentice-Hall, 1973).

3. L. Kohlberg, "From Is to Ought," p. 154.

4. For the stages, see, e.g., Kohlberg, "Moral Stages and Moralization: The Cognitive-Developmental Approach," in Thomas Lickona, ed., *Moral Development and Behavior: Theory, Research, and Social Issues* (New York: Holt, Rinehart & Winston,

1976), pp. 34-35.

5. "From Is to Ought," p. 221.

6. Aron, "Moral Education", p. 413.

7. *Ibid.*, p. 421.

8. See Alasdair MacIntyre, *After Virtue* (Notre Dame: University of Notre Dame Press, 1981) for a division of prominent current models for ethical decision making along these lines.

9. See "Developmental Psychology and Knowledge of Being," chapter 9 of my book, *God's Work in a Changing World* (Washington, D.C.: University Press of America, 1985), pp. 287-314. One thing I show there is that when we make a factual judgment about what is, we are already dependent upon human action (i.e. an equilibration process). Since our human action is for the human good, our judgments about facts are already dependent on our orientation to, and action for, values. For example, our judgment about what the fulfillment or flourishing of our humanity means reflects not only knowledge dependent upon perception, but knowledge dependent on our values and action for values. It follows that in being derived from our knowledge and judgment of what is, the prescriptivity present in moral judgments is in part derived from our value knowledge. Thus, the exigency that exists in the moral judgment is not without basis in our judgment about our humanity. There is no fact-value dichotomy, as much contemporary moral philosophy claims, unless one's epistemology is Kantian or empiricist.

10. See John Rawls, *A Theory of Justice* (Cambridge: Harvard University Press, 1973).

11. E. Sullivan, "A Study of Kohlberg's Structural Theory of Moral Development: A Critique of Liberal Social Science Ideology," *Human Development*, 20 (1977), 362.

12. *God's Work*, p. 102.

13. Paul Taylor, *Principles of Ethics. An Introduction* (Encino, Calif.: Dickenson Publ. Co., 1975), pp. 132-133.

14. See Johan Goudsblom, *Nihilism and Culture* (Totowa, N.J.: Rowman and Littlefield, 1980).

15. Clifford Geertz, "The Impact of the Concept of Culture on the Concept of Man," in his, *The Interpretation of Cultures. Selected Essays* (New York: Basic Books, 1973), p. 44.

CHAPTER XV

THE CONCEPT OF AN ECO-ETHICS AND THE DEVELOPMENT OF MORAL THOUGHT

TOMONOBU IMAMICHI

THE DEVELOPMENT OF THE NOTION OF VIRTUE

Semantic Transposition

The history of moral philosophy is the history of the development of virtue through a series of dramatic changes. "Virtue" derives from the Latin word "virtus," which means "to be strong". It suggests the ideal situation of the male as posssessing the strength to combat uncivilized enemies in defense of his family or society. This original sense of the word did not express a transexual moral quality or general human virtue. In the course of time, however, with the development of human culture and changes in the environment the daily physical struggle for which virile and even savage strength was needed become no longer necessary. Thus, the ideal situation of being human changed into today's transsexual notion of virtue.

This semantic transposition of the moral concept is clearly manifest regarding the Greek word *areté*, virtue in classical times meant virtue. In the text of Homer this meant only a military strength for battle. From the time of the tragic poets to that of the classical philosophers, however, the semantic sense of *areté* changed. In uncivilized times persons needed physical strength to fight for the protection of the community. Bodily strength was important, admired and aspired to as the ideal; physical force was an ethical virtue. By the time of Socrates, however, virtue no longer had a functional sense, but had developed a more spiritual or moral meaning.

The concept *andreía*, which long had meant courage or audacity, is an almost parallel case. This notion derived from the word *aner* in the sense of a virile male and had the same meaning as virtue. In the classical Platonic texts, however, it signified no longer only strength for battle against the enemy, but also human courage in general. *Andreia* as spiritual audacity or bravery thus became established in moral philosophy through the creativity of Socrates.

In Chinese culture, too, one finds a parallel phenomenon regarding the notion of audacity (bravery or boldness). In uncivilized times when men needed physical strength for battle this effort was considered a moral virtue. Emphasis upon being strong which was expressed by the addition of the sign (᭲) to the ideogram for man (男) to signify a developed strength so that the ideogram (勇) meant audacity as *andreía* or virtue. Through the creativity of Confucius (552-479 B.C.) that notion of virility was deepened morally to become an interior force correlative to the virtue of responsibility which appears in the *Lun-yu* (dialogue between Confucius and his disciples) 1.1.14, "when one sees his responsibility and does not act responsibly he lacks *andreía* (audacity)." Boldness as *andreía* or virtue in Confucius also changed from a masculine to a transexual or general human virtue in a manner parallel to that of Socrates. Both were sensitive to changes in the human social environment from a village situated in nature to a cultured city, and this provided the basic motivation for their projects of ethical renewal.

Objective Development

Beyond the semantic transposition of virtue, its sociological renovation was taking place on the phenomenal level. For example, loyalty as fidelity of the nation to the king and of the citizenry to the city differ in their objects, but are entirely identical in their moral essence as fidelity. This transposition in the object of the virtue of fidelity constitutes a new discovery in moral virtue. Cicero in antiquity or Mencius in the classical Chinese texts perhaps first presented civic virtue as a new form of the fundamental virtue of fidelity.

The above two types of changes, namely of virtue, namely of virtue from a physical to a spiratal meaning and of loyalty from allegiance to a king to concern for a city, are not identical. The first is a semantic universalization of moral meaning, whereas the second is a specific determination in the object of a fundamental virtue. In both cases the renewal of virtue was carried out by philosophers sensitive to an ethical change; the theoretical clarification of such changes always has been one of the duties of philosophers.

Ethical crises are signs of critical points in human history. In our epoch the environment is structured not solely by geography and human culture, but also by a universal scientific technology; this calls for a further development of moral philosophy for which the two above-mentioned factors, namely, semantic transposition and the objective modification, do not seem to suffice. A technological society so different from the past requires that we show that there is such a thing as the radical innovation of a virtue entirely unknown in the past.

Moral Innovation as Discovery of New Virtue

The history of humanity contains one not merely renewal

as semantic transposition and objective modification, but also the invention of radically new virtue absolutely unknown in the past. One example is the virtue of *tapeinophrosyné*, which literally is the attitude of the beggar or mendiant, namely, modesty. The word in question is not found in classical Greek, but was constructed by a Christian in the second part of the first century where it appears first of all in the *Didache* and the letter to the Ephesians. Totally unknown in Western antiquity, this virtue of modesty undoubtedly found its origin in the precept of Christ: "With perfect humility . . . bearing with one another lovingly" (Eph. 4:2).

The mendiant as symbol of virtue is an invention of Christ. As the truly poor mendiant extends his or her hands for alms and accepts modestly whatever is given, the one whose heart is poor, like the beggar, extends his or her hand to God in order modestly to accept whatever difficult destiny is given. For such a person there is no discontent, grief or dissatisfaction. As a lessening of one's personal demands, modesty was unknown as a moral virtue to classical Western philosophers. Indeed Socrates felt at home at the table of Plytaneion; according to Aristotle *megalopsychia* as self-aggrandizement, the antithesis of *tapeinophrosyne*, and the pride of self-love were the virtues of a citizen of the city. Thus, at least once in human history there has beem discovered a new virtue which contradicted earlier axiology; modesty as *tapeinophrosyne* symbolizes of the possibility of moral discovery. This third type of moral renewal, namely, the creative discovery of moral virtue, is our moral task in these difficult times.

But is it possible to invent a virtue in a modern intensively developed society? This can be answered affirmatively by showing the historical fact of the invention in modern times of the virtue of responsibility--a neologism in the context of 18th century social contact theories. As I have shown in *Betrachtungen über des Eine* (1968) and *Studia Comparata de Aesthetica* (1976), that term is not found in any classical Greek or Latin text of antiquity or the Middle Ages; but appears first in French in 1787 in places where the English word "responsibility" was used. Its content, however, was not always precise. In John Stuart Mill, for example, responsibility signified accountability understood as a justification or apology for one's self. In German the corresponding term, *Verantwortlichkeit*, appeared for the first time at the end of the 19th century. As the virtue of responsibility is essential to a contractual society it was invented only in modern times.

The historical fact of the invention of a new virtue in modern times can be established then, and the history of philosophic reflection in morals is the history of the three types of innovation of virtue: (1) the semantic transposition of traditional virtue, (2) the objective modification of traditional virtue, and (3) the invention of new virtue.

THE PRACTICAL SYLLOGISM: A SEMANTIC TRANSPOSITION OF TRADITIONAL VIRTUE

In response to the present crisis of morals it is necessary to develop an appropriate ethic for our technological society. This is not a sociological compromise with technology or a psychological accommodation to our situation as a modern society, but a development of the moral horizons of humanity. Sociological compromise and psychological accommodations remain on the animal level; ethics as the morals of humanity is the self-establishment of the human spirit as conscious of its duty before the moral dilemmas of a technological society. We shall consider this development of ethics in relation to the three types of innovation of virtue.

It is necessary to distinguish act from action: action is the physical movement of a person without regard to their human interiority; act is action in view of a personal decision made from within. For example: A runs towards a station at the speed of 13 seconds per one-hundred meters; B and C also run towards the same station at the rate of 13 seconds per hundred meters. Thus the action of A, B and C are the same. However, A is fleeing prison, B pursues A in order to arrest him, and C follows in order to impede B. In these circumstances although the actions are parallel, the acts differ entirely one from another: that of A is resistance against militarism, that of B is obedience to the system, while that of C is friendship for A. Despite the identity of the actions as physical movements, the human acts as personal decisions and interior practical thoughts differ one from another. Whether theoretical or practical, conscious or not, however, human thought must be structured logically because, as decisive, an act is not a mere reaction bereft of thought.

As the structure of human thought is a syllogism, there must be a practical syllogism for decisive practical thought. The classical formulation of this practical syllogism is found in Aristotle's *Nichomachean Ethics*:

A)   A is desirable

   But p, q, r and s realize the A desired.

   Therefore, for some reason, I choose p as the means to achieve the A desired.

In this practical syllogism the minor is the horizon of the freedom of choice, the object of which is a means to achieve the end or goal; thus, the end as ideal is prior to the choice of an effective means. This primacy of finality or goal orientation has made possible rapid progress of the technology of these means. Now, however, the effectiveness of the means, has taken a qualitative leap as the technical world has moved from heteronomous instruments to autonomous technology. As power now assumes an absolute primacy over the goal, and means over end, in the realm of all human acts the structure of the classical practical syllogism becomes problematic. Power in the form of systemic, atomic and electro-magnetic energy, or capital in the economic order, invert the order of premises of the practical syllogism in the following manner:

(B) We have means P.
But, P can realize a, b, c and d as goals.
Therefore we choose A, for some reason, as the goal of these acquired means.

The minor remains the horizon of our freedom of choice: its object, however, is not the means but the goal to be realized. Further, the goal in question is not a transcendent ideal--an end which the human spirit spontaneously desires--but only the natural outcome of technological power. Thus, the means controls the ends by determining which end will be realized. Technological power as means assumes priority over the end which becomes one of its consequences. Though the human spirit chooses one of the outcomes of that technological power, the choice no longer reflects spontaneous desire.

This control by technological power considerably influences the problems of modern ethics. First of all, there is a change of grammatical subject between Aristotle's practical syllogisms and that of our technological age which substitutes the subject "we" for Aristotle's "I." This reflects a transposition of the earlier ethics of the individual into one of committee. In our technological society there remains a moral dimension in which the Aristotelian practical syllogism of the individual is necessary, but at the level of public interaction the individual is only a small part of large technologically organized whole which only committees acting in terms of "we" can manage effectively.

Thus a semantic transposition of the virtue of responsibility takes place, from personal responsibility to that of a committee or of solidarity. Because responsibility is grounded ontologically in the person it should be especially individual, but in technical interaction responsible decisions are made by committees because technical power has become a public or common good. Hence, there is need to develop an ethic of solidarity or of committee for the virtue of responsibility. For example, when a person resigns from a committee which does not work well he or she may be psychologically purified, but such a solution remains on the level of personal responsibility. It is necessary to discover how to integrate this personal morality into the new social reality by a semantic transposition of the virtue of responsibility from that of an the individual to that of the committee or of solidarity. This is not a sociological or political science problem; it is one of eco-ethics.

*Information and Communication
as Objective Modifications of Values*

The major of the contemporary practical syllogism is not a statement of a desired end, but the confirmation of technological power as a gigantic means which can serve for or against humanity. That the human spirit must accept the evident reality of this power as the situation of its actions means that the technological complex now is our environment. When this had been solely nature, prior to moral acts one needed only common information and good sense--for example, about which mushrooms are poisonous and which are edible, or about the power of water, fire, wind, etc. Now that our modern environment is no longer solely one of nature but also of technical interaction, however, we must obtain at least enough information to be able to make sense of it, e.g., some basic knowledge of electricity, bio-chemistry, bio-technology and atomic physics. As sciences in their own domain these are not easy, but education in science should not be directed only towards the preparation of future specialists. Everyone needs at least basic scientific information regarding such basic aspects of our environment, for just as the study of classics is necessary for culture, the study of technology and scientific information is necessary for modern civilization. Similarly, just as some information and interpretation of the nation's history is a duty and hence a social virtue of the cultivated citizen, today an amateur's ordinary knowledge of technology also is a duty and thus a social virtue.

To climb a tree or swim in water are sports with a touch of gymnastics; though not specifically ethical they enable one to aid a drowning person or one who wants to pick fruit: strength and gymnastic capabilities serve the ethical by making it active. This approximates an ethical virtue or at least can be transformed into ethical virtue. In a parallel manner in a technological society driving a car, steering a boat and managing a computer might be called gymnomechanics for they enable one to help many people. In effect, learning at least one machine technology in the modern world has become an ethical virtue.

Information supposes communication which in specific domains entails the abbreviation of terminology and thus the use of jargon. This results in mutual alienation between specialists in different public domains. Naturally specialists must use scientific and technological abbreviations not mastered by the general public. For interdisciplinary exchange of exact information some control of jargon is a professional virtue.

Further, for linguistic information in a technological world a new intellectual virtue is required of every citizen, namely, the acquisition of an appropriate language. Modern technology has so advanced the possibility of international travel and correspondence that as a technological unit today's society is characterized by mobility and communication; it constitutes a vast meeting place for the whole world, either by chance or by necessity. Because to communicate effectively with others one needs to know at least one foreign language, the atmosphere of the contemporary technological unity is entirely bilingual. This does not imply a disregard of the capacity to read texts in the esoteric language of the elite of one's society, but the need to speak effectively in today's mobile world means that learning a foreign language is a virtue for international friendship.

Tolerance: An Objective Modification
of the Traditional Virtue

Having become a technopolis, the megalopolis is now one of the most important bases of international transportation and great cities have become meeting places for people of all nationalities. Their meeting is not only temporary, as with tourism, but also permanent because the megalopolis is able to provide job opportunities for foreigners due to the new primacy of sign over language and of universal technology over historical specificity. This means that the person in the technopolis as a factor in the technological effort can obtain citizenship in the megalopolis. For this only an ability for mechanical work is required; it does not include one's religious or cultural outlook.

Tolerance as generosity of thought now becomes the first condition of such coexistence. Whereas the classical virtue of tolerance meant patience with another person who caused embarrassment, in our technological society tolerance implies the generosity to allow for the validity of other ideas or religious systems. In a technological age public professional interaction requires neutrality of thought for effective collaboration and political coexistence. As an administrative attitude neutrality differs from tolerance which is an ethical virtue; but neutrality in the professional sphere is implied and included within the ethical virtue of tolerance. Note that this objective modification of the virtue of tolerance, from patience in regard to other persons' defective acts to permission of different types of activity, is an objective modification of virtue in our technological society.

Progressively modern technology so expands the impact of machine efficiency that daily appliances can be run by remote control. When a citizen of Tokyo can telephone a person in Paris without difficulty they become technological neighbors. This technological relationship, however, is entirely different from classical relations in which neighbors are spatially close to one another, speak face-to-face, are mutually visible and limited in number. In modern technological structures one interacts with an unlimited number of persons while all remain mutually invisible. Due to distance one does not see directly the situation of one's indetermined and unknown interlocutors, and under cover of the technological apparatus one can forget shame and embarrassment. At midnight by telephone one can more easily engage an unknown person in a distant city than knock at the door of one's neighbor. Willingness to commit massive homicide by a bomb is made possible by the technological means which enable one to ignore those whom one attacks. One would have to imagine the suffering of unknown, undetermined and distant people in order to evoke the direct sympathy involved in a face-to-face meeting. To render moral our actions in technological structures it is necessary to cultivate the imagination through aesthetic activity in art, the learning of which becomes a propedeutic for eco-ethics in a technological civilization: aesthetics has become a necessary discipline for morality.

In any case, the content of the virtue of love of neighbor has been modified effectively through contemporary technological structures which free one's outlook on love of neighbor from the limited surroundings of one's residence, opening it to the vast horizon of humanity, now and in coming generations. This, too, is an objective modification of virtue.

The Invention of New Virtues

First, in a technological context any delay through defects or errors in the operation of a machine becomes important inasmuch as such work requires punctuality. In the past this was not numbered among the virtues, but regarded as the sign of a narrow spirit, whereas generosity which did not attend to minor matters was a sign of the greatness of the person. While generosity remains one of the most important virtues, in the present technological society punctuality has become a new virtue.

Second, as the technological horizon is also international, alongside national loyalty one must be international and world brotherhood has replaced feudal loyalties.

Third, the need to limit population makes control of birth and Malthusianism necessary, and there are many new means for this. Sexual relations without generation are counseled so universally in married life that in this perspective the principle goal of sexual relations could become, not the birth of an infant, but sexual pleasure. As this would raise a question regarding restriction of sexual relations to marriage, an eco-ethics must discuss the problem of sexuality. Scriptures of the traditional religions concerned with the well-being of humanity which have viewed marriage as engendering many children begin to be out of harmony with ethical opinion confronting the present crisis of humanity. Such eco-ethical problems must be thought through for the future of humanity.

Finally, technology has transformed men into bio-mechanisms for whom death becomes ever less necessary. Must one always extend one's life despite the misgivings of one's conscience in view of degenerating health? Can one not say that there is reason to die as well as to live? Thus, euthanasia becomes a topic for contemporary ethics.

The research atmosphere for such an eco-ethics must be interdisciplinary. Eco-ethics itself, however, is not a collective study, but must be constructed and systematized by each person thinking philosophically. It is, nevertheless, a discipline for humanity in its technological context.

Broadening the Horizons of Moral Thought

We have cited the *Lun-yu* text of Confucius on the dynamic of the notion of virtue and used the word "responsibility." But that is a modernized interpretation of the ancient Chinese text, for the word "responsibility" originated in the modern European tradition. This suggests the need to broaden one's historical and philosophical horizon in order to think, not at a provincial level, but at the level of humanism.

In the orient where society traditionally does not sufficiently appreciate the individual and overestimates inter-personal relations the outlook of traditional virtue differs from the West. In Confucius's ethical system charity and responsibility are the most important virtues. The Chinese word to which we apply the term "responsibility," Y, signifies idiogramatically the situation in which I take on my shoulders the lamb for sacrifice. That is to say, I must be responsible vertically to God and horizontally to members of my society. Y expresses responsibility as correspondence between two things, as for example between a signification and its word.

This broadened reflection on the virtue of responsibility teaches us that innovations in virtue within a philosophic tradition is not new within the extended context of human culture. For the innovation in moral virtue required for spiritual progress a comparative study of philosophy is very important. It becomes a phase of eco-ethics as the human environment broadens into a generalized technological world and life in society comes to depend upon world information. This change of human environment demands international communication between different civilizations and thus knowledge of the ethics of other civilizations, not only in order to listen to others, but to be integrated with them.

Finally, ethical innovation is not limited to the realm of virtue, but extends also to the ontology of human acts. Without the concepts of person and personality one cannot speak in a sufficiently philosophical manner of freedom or responsibility. In this sense Christianity has endowed humanity with a great ethical innovation. In the East where the Christian tradition is not truly rooted, the concept of responsibility still has not affected the notion of the person. At the end of the 17th century Wang Yang Min taught the notion *Rientse*, which meant conscience as the subject of knowledge (*Gewissen*); this perhaps is close to the notion of person. But in the East, as the ontological notion of person has not been distinguished from the historical notion of personality, the ontological notion of the dignity of the individual has remained confused with personal honor as an historical concern.

University of Tokyo
Tokyo, Japan

CHAPTER XVI

ON NATURE, VALUES AND IDEOLOGY

MANUEL DY

This paper concerns the rupture between man or humankind and nature, and eventually between man and fellowman, brought about by modernization and industrialization. The complexity of the problem does not suggest clear-cut instant solutions, but it does demand a clarification at a theoretical level of the meaning of nature, value, and ideology. Hopefully, once the tree is identified, the forest can be traversed.

The problem is focused specifically upon oriental societies where the traditional values face a transformation or even disintegration. Elsewhere I singled out some of these values (integration and cohesion, natural and organic, communitarian self-realization, and family), and pointed out that their encounter with Western rationalism has resulted in something pathological--in Habermas's term, "ideological."[1] What then can nature, value, ideology mean for orientals today?

NATURE

We speak of nature in many diverse ways: as the non-human which surrounds and permeates man, as the "natural" in contrast to the artificial, as the "nature" of such and such a thing, or "human nature." The meaning varies in the intentionality of the subject or even of the culture. Nature means something different for the farmer who tills, plants, waits and harvests; for the city dweller who seeks a respite from the work, noise and the pollution of city-life; and for the scientist probing into a phenomenon such as AIDS. As one cannot talk of nature independently of its relationship with man, it is more proper to speak of the relationship between man and nature.

Maurice Merleau-Ponty likens this relationship to that between the lived-body and the environment.[2] Utilizing Gestalt psychology, he sees man and nature as forming a dialectical relationship of figure and background; the field, however, is never fixed. Like the lived-body and the environment, a tenuous equilibrium exists between man and nature: nature is sometimes benevolent, but at other times overwhelms man.[3] Edmund Husserl describes three stages of the attitudes of man towards nature.[4]

1. The first attitude is *mythico-religious*. At the level of the life-world, nature is ambiguous. It is overwhelming, threatening and engulfing, inescapable or ineluctable; but it is also sustaining, surrounding, pervading and supporting. Nature is "both that to which man belongs and that which constantly

jeopardizes man's plans and even his very life."[5] Here man's orientation is practical in the sense of maintaining an equilibrium with this ambiguous mysterious force. Social institutions are mediations or lines of communication between man and nature. They are the pathways of the concrete life of a particular society and therefore cannot be universalized.

The traditional oriental religions may well fit into the above description of Husserl. Confucianism, Taoism and Hinduism always have conceived man as part of nature. Nature is that totality in which man finds a space, a home wherein he is born, grows and rests. Yet it is also beyond man's control; it is that with which man must harmonize himself. Taoism, for instance, describes tranquility as the original state of man before feelings are aroused, and equilibrium as the end after the aroused feelings. Confucianism at times identifies *T'ien* or Heaven not only as the physical sky, but also as nature in its totality. Mencius speaks of "nature" as "that endowed by Heaven." As the totality overwhelming and sustaining man, nature is then sacred and inviolable.

2. The second or *theoretical* attitude is a transformation of the mythico-religious attitude. Nature is now conceived objectively as the intentional correlate of science, as ideal objectivities, it is a field of objects-in-themselves to be revealed through *episteme* or theory (versus *doxa* or opinion).[6] For the theoretical attitude nature is no longer sustaining, overwhelming and ineluctable, but *physical* (versus metaphysical). "Physical nature is experienced as a reflection *of*, or an approximation *to*, or a striving *toward*, or a degeneration *from*, the dimension of that which ineluctably sustains and overwhelms man."[7] Here, physical nature becomes the mediator between man and the metaphysical--now the sustaining, overwhelming and ineluctable. Social institutions mediate no longer between man and nature, but between man and the metaphysical. Thus, nature becomes the sedimentation of man's freedom, while, unlike the mythico-religious attitude, this theoretical attitude can be universalized.

I am not sure if a corresponding attitude exists in oriental philosophies. However, I suspect that the attempts of Neo-Confucianists like Chu Hsi and Wang Yang-ming to seek principles in things or in the mind, or the Hindu concept of *dharma*, may be similar to the theoretical attitude described by Husserl.

3. The third or *technological* attitude attempts to master rather than to objectify nature, to grasp its inner workings so as to control and utilize it for man's ends. "Science and technology become the means of establishing man's dominion over nature."[8] Nature now loses its definitive relationship to the sustaining, overwhelming, and ineluctable, and becomes the field

of the development and exercise of technology. The metaphysical is now a hollow idol. Nature no longer being the sustaining, overwhelming, and ineluctable, nor the mediator between man and the metaphysical, man is delivered to anguish, alienation, nihilism. "Today, technology is the dimension of the sustaining, overwhelming, and ineluctable,"[9] and nature appears no longer as sacred but brute and subject to being apprehended and tamed by man.

From these different attitudes towards nature, we can distinguish the following meanings of nature:

First, nature is the totality of man's situatedness, that into which he is born. What is inborn can be said to be "natural." What is not man's freedom to choose is given to him; it is a gift, and therefore sacred.

Second, nature is physical nature for, insofar as man is subjectivity, nature is the object or the non-subject.

Third, as the object of man's inquiry, nature is the essence of the thing objectified by man. Human nature in this sense is distinct from the sub-human because as self-becoming man's essence escapes conceptualization. (In Sartre's dictum, his existence precedes his essence.)

Fourth, nature is the non-human, the anti-thesis of man that is yet to be subjected to man's technologizing. Nature is the primitive to be tamed and harnessed for the goals of human civilization.

VALUES

Underlying one's attitudes toward nature is the reality of values or, more precisely, one's act of valuation. Values are to be distinguished first of all from goods, or things that carry a value ("carriers" or "bearers" of value). Values are *qualities* which transcend the goods that bear them. These qualities, however, are not perceivable by the senses or able to be grasped in psychic states. Instead, they are "intended" by the spiritual acts of feeling, those acts of loving and hating, or preferring and placing after.[10] It is the heart that sees values; these are not thought but felt. They are immediately distinguished from an horizon of value. Our feelings are our spontaneous response to the world, and more immediate than thinking.

Are values subjective or objective? Max Scheler holds to the objectivity of values, but without discounting their *relation* to man. Values are objective insofar as they are qualities independent of man's situation, feeling-states and striving. Justice as justice will remain a value, regardless of the changes of man's history and of whether man values it or not. When man disregards a value, it is not the value that is destroyed but man himself. Values are not subjective for Scheler insofar as their quality as value does not depend on man. Just as the color green is green and will always be green and not black even if the green blackboard is now painted black, so justice will be a value regardless of whether a man is just or not. If subjective" is to mean "related to man," however, then clearly values are subjective in the sense of being objects of man's intentional feelings.

Whence do values come? It was not difficult for pre-modern philosophy to conceive values as derivative of being, for the cosmos or God was the center of philosophical attention. But the focus of modern and present-day thinkers upon man has placed values at the forefront rather than as derivations of being or God. Perhaps then the answer to the question of the origin of values can be found in man's actuation. Even prior to the answer, the question makes sense only when placed in the context of man's interest in himself: Why does man do what he does? Hence, the more pressing question has become not "Why is there Being rather than nothing," but "Why do we do what we do?"

The key to the connection between action and value is the phenomenon of privation. Values generate an ought-to-be and an ought-to-do, but unless my being is wanting I am not moved to act, to will beyond my privation. Through privation and in privation something like value first appears.[11]

Value, however, is not a property of privation, but rather an *horizon* in which something valuable appears to me as such. As origin of specific values it is never immediately given, but mediated in concrete values.[12] Values are not abstract, but inherent in a situation, in the life world of man, against a background of value. Privation entails distinguishing values from this background, which mediates itself continually in man's willing and wishing, in that which is valuable. This is one reason why we often confuse values with norms and goods.

Do values change? It would be more accurate to say that they do not, but that man's perception or value-ception (to use Scheler's terminology) does. In the life-world, the ability and act of distinguishing in privation is a kind of *understanding* of values, which enables man to act responsibly. To gain understanding, however, requires a reflective analysis of the situation, an inquiry into the rationality of the acceptance of particular values, a rigorous science.[13]

Though necessary, understanding is not a sufficient condition for change. Praxis is a *common* activity in the life-world, and hence the understanding necessary to effect change is a *shared* understanding.[14] "Value-change" requires the mediation of culture and its "rationality of action" or ideology.

IDEOLOGY

Paul Ricoeur contends that basically the term "ideology" should not have the pejorative Marxist sense of a distortion of reality under the influence of covert class interests.[15] What follows is a summary of positive and negative meanings of ideology based upon Ricoeur's attempt to develop a phenomenology of ideology.

1. The first concept of ideology is based on the conditions of *social integration*. Because of the distance that separates the "founding event" and the social memory of that event, any social group needs to give itself an *image*, to "represent" itself, in order to preserve and diffuse the initial conviction of the Founding Fathers. Thus ideology here is an interpretation, a practical hermeneutics, a "meaningful action" in Weber's terms, to serve the integrative function of a society.

From this integrative function of ideology, certain negative meanings may come in:

1.a Ideology may then serve as a *justification*, an argumentative device to prove to the members of the group that they are right to be what they are.

1.b As justification or apology, ideology appears as simplifying and schematic; it becomes a *code*, giving rise to all sorts of isms.

1.c As a code of interpretation, ideology is something out of which we think, rather than something that we think--thus putting us under a *spell*.

1.d With this non-transparency of ideology, it is not so difficult for ideology to become an *inertia* that leads to *intolerance*.

2. The second concept of ideology takes place in the context of *domination*, though not yet in the Marxist sense, when there is a differentiation between the governing entity and the rest of the group. Such an authority raises a claim to legitimacy, and ideology serves as a code of interpretation which secures societal integration by *justifying* the existing system of authority.

Here again negative qualifications may enter into the concept of ideology:

2.a As justification of authority, ideology may claim more than what the citizenry believes. Ideology works as a *justification* of a political *over-value*.

2.b With ideology serving as a justification of a political over-value, ideology can easily become a distortion.

3. The third concept of ideology is the Marxist concept of

ideology; ideology as a function of domination by a ruling *class* in a situation of conflict. Ideology for the young Marx is *distortion* as reversal, and works as an inverted image of reality. Religion is the paradigm of this reversal because "it puts everything upside down and formulates in heavenly terms what is primarily earthly."[16] When the paradigm is extended to the realm of ideas, idealism as

> the doctrine according to which ideas precede and generate things . . . becomes the model of ideology. Then the concept of ideology gets its purely negative connotation to the extent that it describes a general device, thanks to which the process of real life is obscured and replaced by what human beings say, imagine, conceive. Ideology becomes the name given to this mistaken substitution of image for reality.[17]

Since this sense of ideology is generated by real life itself, only a revolution of its material basis can put an end to this illusion. For Marx, no critique of ideas can by itself destroy the illusion; this can be done only by praxis.

This third concept of ideology when placed with the previous two concepts narrows down the general function of ideology as integrating and justifying. The Marxist concept defines ideology in terms of a specific content--religion--and not in terms of its function.[18] If we separate the ideological function from the ideological content the same thing can happen to science and technology, to any ethical system, and even to Marxism itself, as when it is used, for instance, to justify the Party's claim to be the avante-garde of the working class.[19]

The foregoing phenomenology of ideology illustrates a basic thesis for Ricoeur, namely, "that ideology is an unavoidable phenomenon of social existence, since social reality has always been systematically constituted, social relations themselves experiencing their interpretation in pictures and presentations."[20]

TOWARDS A CRITIQUE OF IDEOLOGY

What has the above explicitation of nature, values, and ideology brought us? Simply stated, it is this: that man and nature cannot be divorced--just as man can never be without his body; that man's relationship with nature is *value*-ridden; that this valuation is mediated in the shared understanding of culture; and that culture needs to symbolize, represent, and justify itself in ideology.

Perhaps, what may be added to this relationship of man with nature is the fact that the movement of man's interaction with nature always involves the aspects of labor, language, and power. Under these aspects, ideologies can be seen in their negative qualifications as "*deviations* from the genuine course of things," while still keeping in mind the need of any social group for an ideology, because a society without ideology would be a society without a general project.[21] As deviations, ideologies must be criticized.

The critique of ideology is explained well by Jurgen Habermas who grounds it in his notion of three basic human *interests*--the technical, the practical, and the emancipatory.[22]

The *technical* interest refers to man's drive for instrumental action to master and control nature. Instrumental action here is purposive-rational, a means-end rationality whose aim is the exploitation of the world. The empirical-analytical sciences correspond to this interest.

The *practical* interest refers to man's symbolic interaction in a cultural tradition(s), to man's need for interpersonal communication. The "historical-hermeneutic sciences" correspond to this interest. Here, assertions no longer refer to possible mediation and technical exploitation as with technical interests, but to the understanding of sense and signification. Understanding takes place in ordinary-language communication, in the interpretation of traditional texts, and in the internalization of norms which institutionalize social roles.

The *emancipatory* interest criticizes the ideological tendencies of the first two interests. As such the sciences which correspond to this sphere are the critical sciences, philosophy and psychoanalysis. Ideology-critique enters here. The action is one of unmasking the forces of domination, dogmatism, and repression lying behind the reproduction of labor and the institutionally secured forms of general and public communication.

Both technical and practical interests achieve the power of *self-reflection*. Emancipatory interest seeks to break the barriers to open communication by social groups and persons, raising their self-consciousness "to the point where it attains the level of *critique* and frees itself from all ideological delusions."[23] The technical interest of self-preservation cannot be segregated from the cultural conditions of human life, for society must first interpret what it considers as life. But hermeneutic understanding is not enough. Symbolic interpretations must likewise be submitted for evaluation to the ideas of the good life, "to the criterion of what a society intends for itself as *the good life*."[24] This entails open communication, for the notion of the ideal is not a fixed essence, pure convention or unconditioned; it depends on symbolic interaction and material exchange with nature.[25]

Both technical and practical interests can have ideological

tendencies "to submit reality to dreams," to develop an escapist isolationism which is virtually schizophrenic, an inverted image, and "a systematic domination,"[26] because labor, language, and power constitute a triad which cannot be separated from each other.

For Habermas, the dominant ideology of our time is the ideology of science and technology. Technology, as the "scientifically rationalized control of objectified processes,"[27] has indeed satisfied the material needs of society, but it has also given rise to what Gabriel Marcel calls "technocracy." In highly technologically advanced countries, the person is reduced to an efficient mechanical tool, if not to a number or stage of production. Relationships of man and fellowman cease to be interpersonal and become functional: one is identified and objectified by what he functions for. Instead of bringing human fulfillment, work becomes monotonous and depersonalizes. Means become ends in themselves, for the industrial system must become and remain functional and be further enhanced. This subjects the individual person to the enormous apparatus of production and distribution. The sub-system of instrumental action has now become a system itself, entering and dominating the sphere of communicative action. This repression of the person can disappear from the consciousness of the populace by a kind of legitimation of the domination--the "constantly increasing production of nature which keeps individuals . . . living in increasing comfort."[28] In this way the domination of nature by technology can lead to the domination of man by man.

The ideological tendency in the practical sphere can take various forms. It can be the result of the domination of technology in all spheres of culture where the state legitimizes itself on the basis of its management of material reproduction, resorting to a diffused mass loyalty by keeping the citizens oriented to career, leisure, and consumption. It can also take the form of neo-colonialism with the dominant culture maintaining its influence on a former colony on the basis of its own technical (economic) interest. Ultra-nationalism can also be ideological in the attempt of a social group to defend itself from any outside influence on its traditional culture. Within a nation, ideology may function to bridge the disparity between the authority and the citizenry, or between the intellectual elite and the masses.

The need for a critique of ideology cannot be understated, for the vital link of labor and language with power opens the possibility of violence in forms that are explicit (murder, war), and implicit (manipulative persuasion, flattery, blackmail, monology of information and discussion, apathy). "Distortion is always traced back to the repressive action of an authority, i.e., to violence."²⁹

Culture plays a decisive role in the critique of ideology, for culture includes every human expression, every product of humanity. The authentic role of culture is to be, not passive or evasive, but "an instrument of radical autonomous analysis in respect to any attempt of coercion and instrumentalization . . . to place man in a condition to exercise his own possibilities, to discover and develop the possibilities of the world."³⁰ This entails "examining the concrete situation on the basis of universal theoretical criteria of 'value' so as to establish what is positive or negative for humanity."³¹ The critique of ideology is more than interpretation of tradition from an historical standpoint. It is also a critique of the values of one's culture in the light of what can make mankind more human, more free and autonomous in the horizon of universalizable values. In this sense, the critique of ideology in terms of emancipatory interests is of the order of anticipation, of hope, and of eschatology.³²

Where then would a critique of ideology bring us: return to primitive nature, return to traditional culture? Perhaps a synthesis is possible, namely, institutions which mediate man and technology, and which render nature more humanized and man more "naturalized" or at home with his world. Ideology in its original sense of integration may then become a utopia, and man co-creator with the One.

Ataneo de Manila University
Manila, Philippines

NOTES

1. Manuel B. Dy, Jr., "Rationalism and Oriental Value Systems," in Raul J. Bonoan, S.J., ed., *Higher Education for National Reconstruction* (Manila: National, 1987), pp. 129-145.

2. Maurice Merleau-Ponty, *Phenomenology of Perception* (London: Routledge and Kegan Paul, 1962), pp. 299-345.

3. Francis F. Seeburger, "The Conversion of Nature and Technology," in Anna-Teresa Tymieniecka, ed., *The Crisis of Culture* (Boston: D. Riedel Publishing Co., 1976), pp. 281-282.

4. Edmund Husserl, *The Crisis of European Sciences and Transcendental Phenomenology*, trans. by David Cars (Evanston: Northwestern University Press, 1970), pp. 283 ff., and expounded by Francis F. Seeburger, *op. cit.*, pp. 282 ff.

5. Francis F. Seeburger, *op. cit.*, p. 283.

6. *Ibid.*, p. 283.

7. *Ibid.*, p. 285.

8. *Ibid.*, p. 287.
9. *Ibid.*, p. 288.
10. Cf. Max Scheler, *Formalism in Ethics and Non-Formal Ethics of Values* (Evanston: Northwestern University Press, 19-73).
11. Henning L. Meyn, "Values and the Life-World in the Problem of *Crisis*" in Anna-Teresa Tymieniecka, ed., *The Crisis of Culture*, p. 140.
12. *Ibid.*
13. *Ibid.*, p. 139ff.
14. *Ibid.*, p. 146.
15. Paul Ricoeur, "Can There Be A Scientific Concept of Ideology?" in Joseph Bien, ed., *Phenomenology and the Social Sciences, A Dialogue* (The Hague: Martinus Nijhoff, 1978), pp. 44-52. Also, Paul Ricoeur, "Ideology and Ideology Critique," in Bernard Waldenfels, *et al. Phenomenology and Marxism* (London: Routledge & Kegan Paul, 1984), pp. 134ff.
16. Paul Ricoeur, "Can There Be A Scientific Concept of Ideology?" p. 50.
17. *Ibid.*, p. 50.
18. Paul Ricoeur, "Ideology and Ideology Critique," p. 140.
19. *Ibid.*, p. 141. Also, "Can There Be A Scientific Concept of Ideology?" pp. 51-52.
20. Paul Ricoeur, "Ideology and Ideology Critique," p. 141.
21. *Ibid.*, p. 151.
22. Jurgen Habermas, *Knowledge and Human Interests* (Boston: Beacon Press, 1971).
23. Thomas McCarthy, *The Critical Theory of Jurgen Habermas* (Cambridge: The MIT Press, 1978), p. 88.
24. Jurgen Habermas, *op. cit.*, p. 313.
25. Thomas McCarthy, *op. cit.*, pp. 90-91.
26. Robert Sweeney, "Values and Ideology," in A.T. Tymieniecka and C.O. Schrag, eds., *Analecta Husserliana* (D. Reidel Publishing Co., 1983), XV, 395-396.
27. Jurgen Habermas, *Towards a Rational Society* (Boston: Beacon Press, 1971), p. 57.
28. *Ibid.*, p. 83.
29. Paul Ricoeur, "Ideology and Ideology Critique," p. 155.
30. Angela Ales Bello, "Culture and Utopia in Phenomenology" in A.T. Tymineiecka, ed., *Crisis of Culture*, p. 330.
31. *Ibid.*, p. 330.
32. Paul Ricoeur, "Ethics and Culture," *Political and Social Essays* (Athens, Ohio: Ohio University Press, 1974), p. 257.

INDEX

A Speech on Heaven 32
A Treatise on Heaven 32
Aaron 195
action 136
Adorno 51
Advaita 87
aesthetics 196, 202, 216
Agni 95
alienation 221
Anaximander 37
Anaximenes 169
andreía 210
anthropologists 206
anthropology 204
application 62
Aquinas 174
areté 209
Aristotle 38, 52, 115, 144, 169-173, 211-212
Aron 197, 200, 202-204, 207, 208
audacity 210
austerity 93
authority 60
autonomy 195
Bacon 41, 121, 176
beautiful 21
being 171
Bello 228
Bergson 138
Berkeley 178
biology 205
Black 50
Bo Le 9
body 136
Bohm 45
Bohr 138
boldness 209
Bolivar 61
bravery 209
Bu Yentu 20
Caputo 69
categorical 200
cause 136
Chan 25
Chang Tsai 3, 6, 7, 161

Chatterjee ix, 50, 53, 85
Chen Kuide ix, 51, 131, 143, 145, 147
Cheng 17
Cheng Hao 3, 161
Cheng Mingdao 161
Cheng Yi 3, 16, 17, 161
Cheng Yichuan 161
Chi Kang (Ji Kang) 160
Ching Kai-shek 166
Christianity 34, 39, 121, 211, 218
Chu Hsi 5, 220
Chuang-tzu 9, 11, 134, 135
Cicero 210
Community 58, 61
concern 64
Condillac 36
Confucius 3, 7, 14, 16, 21, 23-24, 61, 117, 134, 156-158, 160, 163, 165, 210
consequentialism 202, 203
contradiction 147
Copernicus 36, 181
Cratylus 172
culture 33, 88, 132, 145, 206
D'Holbach 36, 178
Da Yuxi Tian Lun Shu 25
Da Zhong Shi 134
Dai Zhen 162, 165
Daoist 13, 14
DeGeorge ix, 143
democracy 195, 196, 198
deontological 204
Descartes 36, 40, 41, 52, 57, 121, 154, 176, 177
descriptive 196
Dewey 138, 195, 197, 204
Didache 211
Diderot 124, 177
Dietrich 178
Diogenes 170
divinity 97
Dong 14
Dong Zhongshu (Tung Chung-Shu) 13, 159

Index

dualism 146
duties 197
Dy x, 219, 227
Earth 87, 95
economics 147, 148, 202
education 196
effect 136
Egypt 34
Eleatics 171
Ellrod 207
emancipatory 225
empiricism 144, 208
Engels 109, 112, 127
enlarging 197
environmental 144
equilibrium 210, 220
Erikson 205
essentialist 204
ethics 197, 204
evil 28
evocation 91
experience 171, 195
Fang ix, 25
Farrelly x, 195
fatalism 115
feudalism 122
Feuerbach 124, 153, 187-190
Fichte 53, 154
fidelity 210
forbearance 23
France 144
Frankena 207
freedom 60, 62, 146, 147, 195, 206
Friend ix, 113
Gadamer 58, 65, 69, 70
Galileo 36
Gandhi 61
Geertz 206, 208
generativity 205
Germany 144
Gestalt 219
Gilson 52
God 35, 119, 133, 136, 143, 152, 153, 165, 222
Goethe 43

good 28, 199
Goudsblom 208
Great Harmony 23, 123
Great Learnings 22
Greece 36, 37, 39, 43, 113, 131-133, 136, 143, 144, 146, 151
Guo Xiang (Kuo Hsiang) 14, 160
Habermas 67, 68, 70, 226, 228
Han 25, 118
Han Yu 25, 160
happiness 204
harmonious 116
harmony 147
Hayden-Roy 53
He Yan 13
Heaven ix, 3, 6, 8, 14, 15, 25, 29-32, 117, 156, 158, 164
Hebrew 132, 133, 136, 143-144
Hegel 52, 122, 126, 127, 154, 184-186, 187, 189
Heidegger 67-68, 138
Heisenburg 138
Helvetius 177
Heraclitus 170
heritage ix, 57
hermeneutics ix, 57
Hinduism 220
Hippocrates 132
history 206
Hobbes 41, 146, 192
Holbach 124, 127
Homer 209
Hominization 44, 48
honesty 23
Hong Xiuquan 123
horizon 64, 66-67
Horkheimer 51
Hsun-tzu (Xun Zi) 6, 7, 9-11
Hua Yan 25
Huang ix, 103
Huang Nan-sheng 103
Huang Zongxi 17
humanism 61, 121

Hume 93, 178, 179
Humean 199
Husserl 219, 220, 227
hypothetical 200-203
idea 136
idealism 146, 172, 186
idealist 154
ideology x, 147, 151, 203, 219, 223, 226
imagination 197
Imamichi 50
immanence 146
Indian ix, 37
indoctrination 200
intellect 64
invocation 91
James 138
Ji Kang 14, 159, 165
Jin 13
Jin Xin 134
Judeo-Christian 145, 195
judgments 196, 199
justice 197
Kang Youwei 123
Kant 41, 43, 50, 53, 122, 127, 154, 155, 180-185, 189, 196, 199, 208
Kepler 36
King 61
knowledge 18, 23, 136
Kohlberg 67, 70, 195, 197, 200-203, 207
Kun 7
Kuo Hsiang (Guo Xiang) 160
Lakshmi 94
La Mettrie 124, 154
language 140
Lanney 99
Lao Zi (Lao-tzu) 8. 117, 134, 157
Laozi 14
law 202
legalists 117
Leibnitz 42, 177, 180
Li Zhen ix, 50, 113
liberalism 203

Lickona 207
Lincoln 61
Liu Yu-xi 6-7, 25-32, 160, 163
Liu Zongyuan 25-32
Locke 65, 177, 180
Logos 114
Lu Chiu-yuan (Lu Xiangshan) 162
Lucretius 41
Lun-yu 210, 217
M'Bedy 51
MacIntyre 208
Mahabarata 59
Man ix, 4, 95, 97, 103, 136, 143, 148
Mann 207
Maoshan 13
market 195
Marx ix, 57, 104, 111, 112, 124, 127, 146-147, 153, 175, 191, 192, 223-224
master ix, 113
materialism 138, 143, 146
McCarthy 228
McLean ix, 50, 57, 207
mechanism 45
megalopsychia 211
Mencius 4, 7, 14, 16, 33, 134, 158, 220
Merleau-Ponty 219, 227
Metaphysics ix
Meyn 228
Middle 152, 153
Mill 211
mind 143
Ming 8, 18, 24, 160, 162
Mo Tzu 3
modern 147
monism 147
morality 193, 196
Munzer 123
mysticism 115
naturalistic 199
Nature x, 32, 86, 97, 104, 114, 116, 123, 131, 143, 148,

232 *Index*

195, 198, 205, 219
Neo-Confucianism 19. 161-162, 220
Neo-Platonism 115, 117
Newton 41, 42, 45
Nietzsche 155
norm 203
novelty 62
object 136, 143
Ockham 174
opinion 136
paradigms ix, 195
Parmenides 171
Passmore 97
phenomenology 201. 202
Piaget 205
Plato 41, 114, 144, 151-152, 172-173, 192
play 93
pluralism 204, 206
politics 147
Popper 147
Porphry 174
practical 225
practice 16
Praxis 222
prescriptive 196, 200, 202
Prigogine 139
privation 222
Prometheus 115
providence 27
prudence 64, 196
psychologists 195, 205
Pythagoras 170
Qin 118
Quian 7
Qing 8, 18, 160
Quiles 51
rationalism 144, 176
Rawls 202, 208
reductionist 201
relativism 200, 206
Ren 9
renaissance 57, 120, 146, 153, 154, 165
respectful 200

responsibility 213
Ricoeur 67, 69, 70, 223, 224, 228
rights 197
Roman 39
Rousseau 93
Ruan Chi (Ruan Ji) 160, 165
Ruan Ji 14, 165
sacred 221
sagacity 64
Saivism 94
Samkhya 86
Sang 116
Sankara 89
Scheler 228
Schelling 43, 53, 154
Schindler 207
Schmitz ix, 33, 52
Scholastic 179
Schopenhauer 155
science 145-148, 195
Seeburger 227
self-awareness 165
Shaw 132
Shun 117
Sima Qian (Ssu-ma Ch'ien) 13
slave ix, 113
Snow 44
social 148
socialism 147
Socrates 115, 152, 172, 209, 211
Sokolowski 52
Song 8, 16, 24, 160, 162
sophia 151
soul 136
Spinoza 146, 177
spirit 136, 138, 146
Ssu-ma (Sima Auian) 13
Ssu-ma Ch'ien 3
Stevens's 99
Stoicism 117
subject 136, 143, 147, 163
Subjectivity ix, 146, 149, 150, 164
Sui 160

Sullivan 203
Sun Yat-sen (Sun Zhongshan) 16, 123
Surya 95
Sweeney 228
syllogism 212
Tagore 95
Tan Sitong 123
Tang ix, 8, 13, 50, 51, 160
Tao Hongjing 13
Taoism 11, 160, 163, 220
tapeinophrosyne 211
Taylor 204, 208
techné 47
technology 45, 195, 196, 198, 215, 220
Teilhard 53
teleological 196, 197, 204
The Golden Mean 22
theology 120
theory 136, 220
Theresa 61
Thomas 52
Tian Dui 25
Tian Lun 25
Tian ming 25
Tian Shuo 25
Tian Yi 25
Tian-Di 134, 135
Tian-ming 158
Time 58
Tolerance 215
Toynbee 132
Tradition 58, 60
transcendence 146, 147
Tung Chung-shu 3-4, 7, 8, 159, 161
Tzu Ch'an 156
unity 90
universalization 200, 202
utilitarian 202
value 198-199, 200, 219, 222
Values x, 198, 222
Vatsyayan's 97
virtue 204, 209
Wang Bi (Wang Pi) 14, 159

Wang Ch'ung 3
Wang Chuanshan 165
Wang Fuzhi 15, 16, 18, 21
Wang Guowei 19, 20
Wang Pi 159
Wang Yang Min 218
Wang Yangming 15, 17, 19
Way of Heaven 134
Wei 13
Wen Yan Zhuan 11
Whitehead 137, 138
Will of Heaven 25
Xi Ci Zhuan 11
Xian Wen 134
Xiang Zhuan 10
Xie Zhen 21
Xun Zi 13-14, 16, 117, 158-159 163
Yan Tingzhi 20
Yan Yuan 162, 165
Yang Chu 157
Yang Chuanshan 162
Yang Sheng 157
Yang Zhu (Yang chu) 157, 158
Ye Jiaying 19
Yi Zhuan 8-11, 134
Yuan 160
Yuan Dao 25
Yuan Ren 25
Yuan Ren Lun 25
Zhang ix, 3, 161
Zhang Binglin 123
Zhang Dai-nian 167
Zhang Shi-ying 149
Zhang Zai (Chang Tsai) 14, 161
Zhao Guangwu 103
Zhong Rong 20
Zhou Dunyi 14
Zhou Yi 10
Zhu ix, 17, 169
Zhu Desheng 169
Zhu Xi 14, 16, 161
Zhuan 5
Zhuan Xu 5

Zhuang Zi (Chuang Tzu) 13.
  14. 117
zhuguanxing 150
zhutixing 150
Zi Cha 156
Zi Chan 5
Zong Mi 25
Zongyuan ix

THE COUNCIL FOR RESEARCH IN VALUES AND PHILOSOPHY (RVP)

Purpose

Today there is urgent need to attend to the nature and dignity of the person, to the quality of human life, to the purpose and goal of the physical transformation of our environment, and to the relation of all this to the development of social and political life. This, in turn, requires philosophic clarification of the basis upon which freedom is exercised, that is, of the values which provide stability and guidance to one's decisions.

Such studies must be able to reach deeply into the cultures of one's nation--and often of other parts of the world from which they derive--in order to uncover the roots of the dignity of persons and of the societies built upon their relations one with another. They must be able to identify the conceptual forms in terms of which modern industrial and technological developments are structured and how these impact human self-understanding. Above all, they must be able to bring these elements together in the creative understanding essential for setting our goals and determining our modes of our interaction. In the present complex circumstances this is a condition for growing together with trust and justice, honest dedication and mutual concern.

The Council for Studies in Values and Philosophy is a group of scholars who share the above concerns and are interested in the application thereto of existing capabilities in the field of philosophy and other disciplines. Its work is to identify areas in which study is needed, the intellectual resources which can be brought to bear thereupon, and the financial resources required. In bringing these together its goal is scientific discovery and publication which contributes to the promotion of human life in our times.

In sum, our times present both the need and the opportunity for deeper and ever more progressive understanding of the person and of the foundations of social life. The development of such understanding is the goal of the Council for Research in Values and Philosophy (RVP).

Projects

A set of related research efforts are currently in process, some developed initially by the RVP and others now being carried forward by it either solely or conjointly.

1. *Foundations of Moral Education and Character Development.* A study in values and education which unites philosophers, psychologists and scholars in education in the elaboration of ways of enriching the moral content of education and character development.

2. *Cultural Heritage and Contemporary Life: Philosophical Foundations for Social Life.* Sets of focused and mutually coordinated continuing seminars in university centers, each preparing a volume as part of an integrated philosophic search for self-understanding differentiated by continent. This work in the First, Second and Third Worlds focuses upon evolving a more adequate understanding of the person in society and looks to the cultural heritage of each for the resources to respond to its own specific contemporary issues.

3. *Seminars on Culture and Contemporary Issues.* This series of 10 week seminars is being coordinated by the RVP in Washington.

4. *Joint-Colloquia* with institutes of philosophy of the national Academies of Science, philosophy departments or societies in Eastern Europe and China concerning the person in contemporary society.

5. *The Mediation of Values to Social Life.* The development of a four volume study on the mediation of values to social life is a corporate effort of philosophers throughout the world.

The personnel for these projects consists of established scholars willing to contribute their time and research as part of their professional commitment to life in our society. The Council directly sponsors some projects and seeks support for projects sponsored by other organizations. For the resources to implement this work the Council, as a non-profit organization incorporated in the District of Colombia, looks to various private foundations, public programs, and enterprises.

Publications on Cultural Heritage and Contemporary Life

   Series I.   Culture and Values
   Series II. Africa
   Series III. Asia
   Series IV. Europe and North America
   Series V.   Latin America
   Series VI. Foundations of Moral Education

PROJECT ON CULTURAL VALUES CHARACTER DEVELOPMENT AND SOCIAL LIFE IN THE XXIst CENTURY

A. Cultural Heritage & Contemporary Life

Series:
 I *Culture & Values*
  I.1 Research on Culture & Values
  I.2 Methodology & the Study of Values
  I.3 Reading Philosophy for XXIst Century
  I.4 Relations Between Cultures
  I.5 Urbanization and Values
  I.6 Person and Society

 II *Africa*
  II.1 Person and Community

 III *Asia*
  III.1 Man & Nature

 IV *Europe & N. America*

 V *Latin America*
  V.1 Social Context of Values
  V.2 Culture, Human Rights & Peace

B. Foundational Research on Moral Education and Character Development

Series VI *Foundations of Moral Education*
 VI.1 Philosophical Foundations
 VI.2 Psychological Foundations
 VI.3 Educational Foundations
 VI.4 Social Context of Values: Lat. Am.
 VI.5 Chinese Foundations
 VI.6 Love & Morality: Lat. Am.

C. Educational Methods and Materials

THE COUNCIL FOR RESEARCH IN VALUES AND PHILOSOPHY

S. *Aveniri*, Israel
P. *Balasubramaniam*, India
P. *Bodunrin*, Nigeria
V. *Cauchy*, Canada
M. *Chatterjee*, India
R. *De George*, USA
M. *Dy*, Philippines
I.T. *Frolov*, USSR
H.G. *Gadamer*, BDR
A. *Gallo*, Guatemala
K. *Gyekye*, Ghana
P. *Henrici*, Italy
J. *Hoyos Vellez*, Colombia
T. *Imamichi*, Japan
A. *Irala Burgos*, Paraguay
J. *Kellerman*, Hungary
M. *Kente*, Tanzania
R. *Knowles*, USA
J. *Ladrière*, Belgium
P. *Laleye*, Senegal
H.D. *Lewis*, UK

S. *Lokuang*, Taipei, China
A. *Lopez Quintas*, Spain
M. *Markovic*, Yugoslavia
H. *Nasr*, USA/Iran
Ngwey Ngond'a Ndenge, Zaire
J. *Nyasani*, Kenya
C. *Pan*, Singapore
Paulus Gregorios, India
O. *Pegoraro*, Brazil
C. *Ramirez*, Costa Rica
P. *Ricoeur*, France
M. *Sastrapatedja*, Indonesia
J. *Scannone*, Argentina
K. *Schmitz*, Canada
V. *Shen*, Taipei, China
W. *Strozewski*, Poland
Tang Yi-jie, Peking, China
J. *Teran-Dutari*, Ecuador
G. *Tlaba*, Lesotho
Wang Miao-yang, Shng., China
N. *Zevallos*, Peru
(Invited)

George F. McLean, Secretary

THE COUNCIL FOR RESEARCH IN VALUES AND PHILOSOPHY
CULTURAL HERITAGE AND CONTEMPORARY LIFE

Series I. Culture and Values

Vol. I.1 *Research on Culture and Values: Intersection of Universities, Churches and Nations*, George F. McLean

Vol. I.2 *The Knowledge of Values: A Methodological Introduction*, A. Lopez Quintas

Vol. I.3 *Reading Philosophy for the XXIst Century*
George F. McLean

Volumes in preparation will treat inter-cultural harmony, urbanization and values, and the humanization of social structures.

Series II. Africa

Series III. Asia

Vol. III.1 *Man and Nature: The Chinese Tradition and the Future*, Tang Yi-jie, Li Zhen

Vol. III.2 *Chinese Foundations for Moral Education and Character Development*, Tran van Doan

Series IV. Europe and North America

Series V. Latin America

Vol. V.1 *The Social Context and Values: Perspectives of the Americas*, O. Pegoraro

Vol. V.2 *Culture, Human Rights and Peace in Central America*
Raul Molina, Timothy Ready

Series VI. Foundations of Moral Education

Vol. VI.1 *Philosophical Foundations for Moral Education and Character Development: Act and Agent*, G. McLean

Vol. VI.2 *Psychological Foundations for Moral Education and Character Development: An Integrated Theory of Moral Development*, R. Knowles

Vol. VI.3 A volume by professors of education

Vol. VI.4 *The Social Context and Values: Perspectives of the Americas*, O. Pegoraro

Vol. VI.5 *Chinese Foundations for Moral Education and Character Development*, V. Shen and Tran van Doan

The series is co-published by: The University Press of America (UPA), 4720 Boston Way, Lanham, MD 20706, Tel. 301/459-3366; The Council for Research in Values and Philosophy, Washington, D.C. 20064, Tel. 202/635-5636.

To order: U.S. and Canada: UPA, as above

U.K. and Europe: Eurospan, Ltd., 3 Henrietta St., London WC2E 8LU.

All other locations: Feffer and Simons, Inc., 1114 Avenue of the America's, New York, NY 10036.